T0305180

South Africa and the World Economy

Rochester Studies in African History and the Diaspora

Toyin Falola, Series Editor
The Jacob and Frances Sanger Mossiker Chair in the
Humanities and University Distinguished Teaching Professor
University of Texas at Austin

(ISSN: 1092-5228)

A complete list of titles in the Rochester Studies in African History and the
Diaspora series may be found on our website, www.urpress.com.

South Africa and the World Economy

Remaking Race, State, and Region

William G. Martin

UNIVERSITY OF ROCHESTER PRESS

First published 2013

University of Rochester Press
668 Mt. Hope Avenue, Rochester, NY 14620, USA
www.urpress.com
and Boydell & Brewer Limited
PO Box 9, Woodbridge, Suffolk IP12 3DF, UK
www.boydellandbrewer.com

ISBN-13: 978-1-58046-431-4
ISSN: 1092-5228

Library of Congress Cataloging-in-Publication Data

Martin, William G., 1952–
    South Africa and the world economy : remaking race, state, and region /
William G. Martin.
        p. cm. — (Rochester studies in African history and the diaspora ; v. 57)
    Includes bibliographical references and index.
    ISBN 978-1-58046-431-4 (hardcover : alk. paper) 1. South Africa—Foreign
economic relations. 2. South Africa—Economic policy. 3. South Africa—
Economic conditions. 4. South Africa—Race relations—Economic aspects.
5. Regional economic disparities. I. Title. II. Series: Rochester studies in
African history and the diaspora ; v. 57.
    HF1613.4.M37 2013
    337.68—dc23   2012050849

A catalogue record for this title is available from the British Library.

This publication is printed on acid-free paper.
Printed in the United States of America.

Parts of chapter 2 were previously published in the following:

"The Making of an Industrial South Africa: Trade and Tariffs in the Interwar
Period," *International Journal of African Historical Studies* 23, no. 2 (1990): 59–85. ©
The Trustees of Boston University. Reproduced with permission.

"Region Formation under Crisis Conditions: South vs. Southern Africa in the Interwar Period." *Journal of Southern African Studies* 16, no. 1 (March 1990): 112–38.
Reproduced with permission from Taylor & Francis Group, www.tandfonline.com.

To MB

Contents

Illustrations

Acknowledgments

I have been favored with far too many acts of assistance, over the far too long a time span encompassed by work on this text, to acknowledge with any real degree of justice. Hardly a single line could have been written without the support of librarians and archivists in New York, Champaign (IL), Johannesburg, Pretoria, and Cape Town. My first forays to learn something about South and southern Africa at first hand, undertaken during the apartheid era, were facilitated by the hospitality of the University of the Witwatersrand's African Studies Institute, and Ian Phimister's encouragement was particularly appreciated. In the early 1990s assistance from friends at the University of the Western Cape, particularly at the Center for Southern African Studies, was invaluable. UWC's History Department hosted me in 2003, a visit made possible by a Fulbright award, and I learned much from fellow staff and students there, then and since.

As for the ideas and conceptions that frame this study, they have, as usual, collective origins. The crucible was the remarkable graduate and research program constructed by Terence K. Hopkins and Immanuel Wallerstein at the State University of New York at Binghamton, including the collaborative Research Working Groups associated with the Fernand Braudel Center. Drawn back into the United States and crossing disciplinary boundaries, I found guides in this community of scholars and activists for the pursuit of a world-historical understanding of present-day upheavals and struggles. Giovanni Arrighi's contribution in this atmosphere proved essential, and without his encouragement and intervention at key points this study would never have been brought to fruition. The friendship and often bracing criticism of Merle Bowen, Jim Cason, Torry Dickinson, Zenebeworke Tadesse, and, especially, Michael West have been invaluable and deeply appreciated. Mark Beittel's constant support and insistent advice that this text be finished, from the beginning of this project until the day of its delivery to the press, frames a long and faithful friendship. These and other friends in the United States, Europe, and Africa provided, often under considerably difficult conditions, the sustenance to return time and again to an unwieldy endeavor.

Others sustained and propelled this effort as well by inspiration and example. Among these were many students, activists, and incarcerated persons in the United States and Africa who have consistently pressed me to move beyond the limits of my location, miseducation, and lived experiences.

The inspiration by example—even if contact was brief and not directly related to the arguments contained here—of scholar-activists like Aquino de Bragança, Ruth First, Ben Magubane, David Webster, and Harold Wolpe was greater than they could have known.

Among the many lessons I have learned in the process of this work, one stands out: while academic research and writing all too often appear to be isolated and lonely tasks, a community of friends and family makes the work possible. I owe this group, most notably my parents, more than can be expressed in mere words.

Introduction

Rethinking State, Race, and Region

Redeemers and Renaissances

Mandela as a heavenly saint and Rwanda as hell: these were the images that the Western media and policymakers used to frame Africa as the twentieth century came to a close.[1] It was a stark pairing, setting South Africa's nascent democracy and racial reconciliation against depictions of collapsing states, AIDS, war, and genocide. Implicit in this pairing was the hope that a powerful postapartheid South Africa would lead the continent in addressing the challenges of democratization, globalization, and conflict resolution. An African renaissance, led by new leaders like Mandela, was widely heralded as Africa's best and perhaps last hope.

While this caricature emanated from North America and Europe, the expectation of a new era was widespread across Africa as well. Radical democratic struggles in the 1980s and 1990s had toppled decades-old autocratic regimes and developmental policies. The promise of these trends seemed to be confirmed when Mandela was freed and led the African National Congress to a landslide election victory in 1994. Across the continent expectations of a more prosperous, democratic, and peaceful era advanced as long-standing authoritarian regimes continued to fall, one after another, in the face of popular uprisings.

By the turn of the new century far more sobering realities asserted themselves. For while the new South African government's adherence to strict monetary and fiscal policies had led to lower budget deficits and lower inflation, these were accompanied by increasing levels of unemployment, disappointing levels of foreign investment, white flight from the country, increasing poverty, and a level of inequality among the highest in the world. Similar patterns reverberated farther north, where the overthrow of Cold War-era dictators, the holding of multiparty elections, and the application of neoliberal state policies had shrunk the state and often lowered inflation, but failed to stem rising poverty, unemployment, and, increasingly, political violence within and across state borders—all factors that accelerated the spread of the AIDS pandemic.

The simultaneous appearance of these phenomena across southern and continental Africa suggests not simply shared, national fates, but regional and continental processes at work. This was starkly illustrated with the fall of Mobutu's Zaire, for far from securing peace and a national political dialogue, Mobutu's departure from Kinshasa in 1997 led to Africa's first multinational, postcolonial war, engaging the forces of Angola, the Democratic Republic of the Congo, Namibia, Rwanda, Uganda, and Zimbabwe. This was certainly not the expected result of the end of the Cold War, African dictatorships, and apartheid.

These events provoked reluctant South African intervention. Mandela's government (1994–99) had warily, and embarrassingly, ventured forth into regional and continental affairs—publicly failing to prevent Ken Saro-Wiwa's execution in Nigeria in 1995 and bungling badly a military intervention in Lesotho in 1998. Meanwhile foreign investors, the Western media, and the United States and European governments all began to express concern over whether their exceptional South Africa, rather than curing Africa, would catch what they saw as pervasive African diseases. European and North American politicians were particularly aghast at the possible spread beyond Zimbabwe of the seizure of white farms. Collapsing currencies, shrinking markets, and growing protest all across Africa against single-party governments and the structural adjustment programs of the IMF and the World Bank all served to dim the glow that surrounded Mandela's early presidency. If Mandela had in 1994 been portrayed as the man to save Africa, by the turn of the century his successor, President Thabo Mbeki (1999–2008), was being derided in the West as an increasingly erratic African autocrat. President Jacob Zuma (2009–) has fared even worse: given his personal peccadilloes, it has proven all too easy for the Western media to portray him as yet another corrupt, if jovial, tribal African.

Mbeki's response to such depictions was far more forceful than Mandela's: South Africa's considerable power—increasingly evident in the expansion of South African commercial and financial interests across the region and the continent—would be deployed to rebut the Afro-pessimism and racially tinged stereotypes emanating from Europe and North America. It would also, and not just coincidentally, serve the interests of South African political and economic elites by expanding South African power northward. This endeavor had foundations: no other African state had anywhere near the combined industrial, financial, military, and political power of South Africa; no other state possessed the degree of continental and international legitimacy.

South Africa's ambitions and interventions accelerated as Thabo Mbeki came to dominate the reins of state power.[2] Mbeki's program took intellectual shape in his calls for an "African Renaissance,"[3] which paralleled the precepts of neoliberal economic policies and neorealist international relations;[4] it also drew on and resonated with the worldwide wave of Afrocentric, cultural black nationalism of the late 1980s and early 1990s.[5] The aim was clearly to counter both Northern racism and African despotism, a formulation that

easily irritated African and European leaders alike—although for quite different reasons. While rich residents of the "Global North" resented and rebuffed
Mbeki's references to the enduring legacy of colonial racism, African leaders
were equally nervous at the assertion of South African power. South Africa's
dominant position was evident in the new interstate formations promoted and
dominated by South Africa: the New Partnership for Africa's Development
(NEPAD) in 2001, the African Union (AU) in 2002, and the Pan-African
Parliament in 2004. Under these auspices African unity, democratic governance, free markets, and cooperative peacekeeping were to provide the foundations for resolving regional and continental conflicts—with South Africa
explicitly leading the way.

At the root of all these actions by South African, European, or North
American states and leaders stood a single factor: South Africa's pivotal
position in the region, continental Africa, and the world. South Africa's
"pivotal" status derives not only from its sheer economic resources, as
measured by comparative industrial or income statistics, but rather from
its nodal position in regulating relationships between the rich Global
North and poorer Africa. In the postapartheid period these relationships
expanded as the South African state reasserted itself regionally, continentally, and internationally, while South African firms rapidly expanded
across the region and the continent. What is extraordinary, however, is
that scholars have rarely probed how this powerful and pivotal position
was attained and sustained, much less what it portends for South Africa's
future in "the age of globalization."

This issue is tackled here with a straightforward thesis: South Africa's
remarkable national economic strength, regional position, and world standing have been forged through a series of radical struggles to shape uneven
and highly racialized relationships across the region *and* between Africa and
the rich North. Under white nationalist rule, particularly in the *pre*apartheid period, the South African state vigorously reforged relationships with
the Global North and South. In the apartheid and postapartheid periods,
by contrast, the state has sought a far more accommodationist and far less
advantageous relationship with the North, while returns from the region
have steadily declined. These historical transitions are especially important
today as developmental opportunities once gain blossom amid the global
economic crisis and the reordering of North-South relations, driven in large
part by the disruptive resurgence of African-Asian ties.

Racing States: Paradoxes and Misguided Paradigms

This thesis and historical approach stand in stark contrast to either the
national accounts of the past, which isolated the internal dynamics of

segregation and apartheid, or the fashionably global, ahistorical, and nonracial accounts of the present. The story of South Africa is, from the perspective advanced here, to be found instead in the history of "racing states" in a double sense: (1) states and dominant classes competing to advance in the formally sovereign but interdependent interstate system, and (2) states, movements, and classes struggling within and reshaping the extensive racial hierarchies and inequalities that structure the interstate system and underwrite accumulation across the modern world economy.

We have few concepts much less theories to approach these transnational relationships and racial hierarchies. Given the violence that structural categories easily impose on their intended subjects, this is not necessarily a bad situation. Yet it is impossible to make sense of social and political relationships over time without attending to enduring racial and world-economic relationships. Their salience is openly marked by the analytical power embodied in the shifting historical terms of "white/black/brown," "First/Third World," "West/East," and, today, "Global North/Global South." All these terms reflect, at different moments and for different movements, lived experiences and struggles across the world.

In this text, concerned as I am to move across the last century, world inequalities are indicated by the unstable terms of "core," "semiperipheral," or "peripheral"—and one must remember these are not fixed boxes into which to dump data, but relationally formed conceptions. The much more recent, and even more homogenizing, term "Global South" similarly indicates the attempt to mobilize peoples by their common opposition to the rich, white North. Racial categories are even more charged and flexible. The term "black" in particular radically shifts meaning as one moves at any one moment, for example, across the 300 miles separating Johannesburg and Maputo, or across the very different individual and communal boundaries of a South African township in 1965, 1985, or today. This complexity is heightened here given the wide spatial and temporal span of this work. Despite these caveats, unless otherwise noted "white" refers to persons of European descent and privilege; "African" refers to indigenous persons subject to colonialism and apartheid; and "black" refers, for South Africa, to all those who were subject to colonial and continuing racial oppression, including officially classified "Coloureds" and "Asians."

As these terminological warnings suggest, there is no straightforward correlation between race and state power that has generated South Africa's position in the world economy. Indeed, the construction, management, and creative destruction of transnational economic relationships have always entailed contradictory racial processes—as will be traced here through unearthing the successive refashioning of racial alliances and institutions over a long century. South Africa's rise from a colonial outpost producing raw materials for Europe to an industrializing state encompassed, it will be argued here, a white settler state's active struggle not only against Africans but also against fellow settlers in the region and the very colonial powers that had granted independent state status to South Africa in 1910. Apartheid is subsequently constructed as a response to the achievements of this effort and the crisis it engendered, only to collapse upon itself as a new neoliberal and neoracist world economy was ushered in during the tumultuous closing decades of the twentieth century. And the future of South and southern Africa is predicted to be even more volatile as the US-led postwar economic and racial order collapses, and new global relations and identities are redrawn as the center of the world economy shifts from North to East.

Past accounts of South and southern Africa have rarely analyzed these shifting transnational relationships, while present analyses usually celebrate racial reconciliation and a historical rupture with the end of apartheid and the onset of globalization. The absence of a systematic account of the long-term power of the South African state in relation to other states and the world economy is especially puzzling. It is not for a lack of scholarly attention and publication. As a trip to the shelves of any major North American, European, or South African library or Internet search would reveal, South Africa has long been the predominant focus for both scholars and policy analysts of the continent.

The explanation lies instead elsewhere, in two fundamental assumptions that deflect attention from racialized regional and world relationships. The first is readily evident in recent literature that explicitly asserts that we have entered a new era of "globalization," where national boundaries, identities, and economies have collapsed—leaving South Africa and Africa to face the novel problems of a postcolonial, post–Cold War age. A second and reinforcing claim is to be found in the common argument that the end of apartheid has opened up a new epoch in which a deracialized and democratic South Africa is now able to join, at last, the wider world community.

Both these claims deserve serious consideration. Both in different ways seek to place South Africa within a global context. Yet both seriously mislead us about South and southern Africa's past and future possibilities. Their primary limitation is easily pinpointed: the unquestioned acceptance of a deracialized world economy and, especially, the continuing construction of national histories derived from models of more "advanced" European and North American states. Even conceptions of "globalization" fall prey to these errors, by arguing that the postapartheid period is a unique rupture from isolated past *national* patterns.

The critical literatures on political power, economic development, and the state provide a clear example of the difficulties imposed by these nationalist conceptions and methodologies. This has been an area of much recent work, given the rise of free market policies on the one hand and the overthrow of long-standing dictatorships on the other. Indeed, in the early

1990s, African states, including South Africa, were often cast as part of a "third wave" of democratization, a global transition toward democracy and development felicitously marching across Latin America, southern Europe, eastern Europe, and then Africa and the Middle East.[6]

As the 1990s proceeded the promise of democratic prosperity was steadily replaced by accelerating inequality and political unrest in both the East and the South, with African states being targeted as the center of a coming period of worldwide anarchy and chaos—most notably in Robert Kaplan's influential 1994 article on the "coming anarchy."[7] Northern academics subsequently developed new categories for African states, describing them in turn as "fragmented," "collapsed," "imploded," or simply "failed" states.[8] These were states unable to provide the most basic security, education, health, or infrastructural services, and where "social and ethnic groups feel neglected and alienated," leading to a situation where "organization, participation, security, and allocation fall into the hands of those who will fight for it—warlords and gang leaders, often using the ethnic principle as source of identity and control in the absence of anything else."[9] Into this ideal type have been fitted Somalia, the Democratic Republic of the Congo, Sierra Leone, Ethiopia, Liberia, and Rwanda, to mention but a few. It was thus hardly surprising that the Mandela government, emerging at this very moment, sought to place South Africa outside Western policymakers' Afro-pessimism, emphasizing South Africa's affiliation not to Africa, but to Europe and North America. South African exceptionalism could at last, it seemed, be turned to an advantage.

To do so required countering policymakers' and scholars' long-standing assumptions regarding African states and politics more generally, most notably the effect of "traditional" African ethnic and tribal divisions. The core belief is easily stated, namely that "the distinctive institutional hallmark of African regimes is neopatrimonialism" whereby "the interaction between the 'big man' and his extended retinue *defines* African politics, from the highest reaches of the presidential palace to the humblest village assembly."[10] It follows that "violence in Africa is a function of leaders trying to stay in power in systems where institutions are weak. Because the struggle for power takes place in a context where the resources most easily at hand to be mobilized are ethnic ones, conflict is often ethnic conflict."[11] Dysfunctional states and violent conflict are invariably traced back to distinctive African values and social systems. Faced with these dominant views from the North, early post-apartheid governments' attempts to escape from these categories were quite understandable.

What might have made practical sense, however, undermined any ability to make sense of South Africa's past or future developmental possibilities. As Magubane and Mafeje pointed out forty years ago, lurking beneath the surface of such conceptions is an invented racial ideology of an ossified and isolated "traditional," most commonly "tribal," Africa.[12] This notion has produced a body of scholarship over several decades that has, as Olukoshi observed, "focused exclusively on the internal sources of the African crisis; the role of external factors was completely downplayed or totally discounted."[13] As African scholars have charted, over the course of the last several decades a very different, transnational process has been under way: basic state functions and sources of legitimacy in the fields of health, education, refugee relief, and security have been relocated to international financial institutions in Washington, official aid agencies, and nongovernmental service providers, most notably NGOs and newly privatized service providers.[14] This suggests that the institutional capacities, legitimacy, and stability of African states have not been so much fragmented from within as collapsed from without.

Under these pressures long-held boundaries between "internal" and "external" units of analysis also have collapsed, undermining in the process the related assumptions of national state sovereignty and national economic development. State power is increasingly constructed through relationships among agencies and institutions above and below the level of the national state. To push these observations forward suggests a stark, alternative approach: state formation, rather than the national process that has been so heavily defined by the history of the Western state, is a *historical* and *world-relational* process. In other words, state development and state *under*development are as linked as economic development and underdevelopment.

This is not a phenomenon of the recent "globalization" era, as can be seen in different ways in recent studies of African states. Field and archival research has demonstrated, for example, that the policies and institutional construction of autocratic states have deep roots in the colonial period. This has held even for radical states, such as Mozambique, that sought to make the sharpest break with colonial practices and institutions.[15] Basil Davidson made the more general case quite early on arguing that the root cause of today's crises is an imposed, Western state form, which needs to be replaced with more equitable, indigenous forms of political rule.[16]

Mamdani's widely discussed volume *Citizen and Subject* pushed these claims forward by arguing the broader case that indirect rule under colonialism formed and entrenched a bifurcated, racial state that granted civil rights to Europeans only, while natives were ruled as subjects through state-constructed "customary" or "ethnic" authorities. With independence "there was little change in the nature of power," leaving despotic rulers and citizens in urban areas, while unreformed ethnic authorities ruled in rural areas; in short: "the bifurcated state that was created with colonialism was deracialized, but it was not democratized."[17] Ethnic divisions are thus, inevitably, rooted in the colonial order, as Mamdani's analysis of Rwanda exemplifies.[18] One of the advantages of this formulation is that South Africa, far from being unique, becomes a model for Africa, from the early introduction of indirect rule to the apartheid's state's construction of white South African citizens and native subjects in rural Bantustans. As Mamdani suggests, "apartheid, usually considered unique to South Africa, is actually the generic form of the colonial state in Africa."[19]

Mamdani's insistence on "Africa as a unit of analysis" and the autonomy of the postcolonial state, however, limits the usefulness of his work for my purposes here.[20] For while his premises allow him to attack European models of state formation, the assumption of postindependence deracialization and state autonomy works against analyzing the postindependence and racialized relationship between African and European state formation. Thus it is all too easy to slip back into the language of "external" and "internal" factors, and of separate and isolated models of state development. There is not much guidance here, for example, for those addressing the transcontinental operation of sovereignty and state power, from the days of direct colonial rule to today's "globalization." What does it mean, to put it in Mamdani's terms, to be a "citizen" of an impoverished state when the state and its population are "subjects" of a postcolonial interstate system and wider world economy? How do nationally bound distinctions of citizen/subject assist us to understand the "external factors" implicated in the impoverishment of most African states and, by contrast, South Africa's distinguished record of industrialization and regional power over other African states? Or more pointedly for our purpose: how do we account for the transforming salience of race in postapartheid South Africa, southern Africa, and indeed our "globalized" world?

Here Mamdani's essential innovation by comparison to academic Africanists' arguments—an insistence on the endurance of colonial racial and political relationships—can be usefully developed.[21] For as in discussions of "coloniality" in postindependence Latin America, the cross-national aspects of racial and political power endemic to the colonial order might well be traced throughout the nineteenth, twentieth, *and* twenty-first centuries.[22] At the heart of the matter is the definition and exercise of resources, power, and rights across racial, state, and continental boundaries. To approach state formation as embedded in world relationships and a global hierarchy of racialized states fundamentally challenges the assertion that with independence African states were sovereign, nationalized, and deracialized. Processes of regional and global racial alliances and regimes subsequently become open historical questions.

This is especially pertinent for the study of the most explicitly racialized state, South Africa. Regional and international relationships have rarely been considered important to the construction of segregation and the apartheid state, whether in the classic writings of procapitalist liberals or anticapitalist radicals.[23] Across this range of views the central actors were invariably the apartheid state and national classes. In the postapartheid period race is effaced due to majority rule, the collapse of rigid racial categories and identities, and the ongoing construction of the "rainbow" nation. *Racial* apartheid, as many radical scholars put it, has been replaced by *class* apartheid.[24]

If the colonial and apartheid state are seen as part of a racialized interstate system and capitalist world economy, however, then a very different conception and history of African states might be approached. This possibility has been posed in past literatures on the development of underdevelopment[25] and on regional and international support for apartheid[26] as well as in the literature on "settler" states in Africa[27] and, more recently, on "creole" and "settler" states in Latin America.[28] Yet neither continental African scholars nor Northern scholars pursued such conceptions: African states, including the South African state, have remained isolated cases.

The aim here is to push beyond these past national paradigms and open up new approaches to world-historical state formation, the role of the interstate system in relation to capitalist accumulation, and the ever-changing ideologies and global processes of racism. This demands a methodology that rejects the purported exceptionalism and formal comparison of South Africa to other states and seeks instead to embed South Africa within regional and global processes of capitalist development and racial formation. This approach represents a response to a challenge posed by world-historical methodologists a generation ago: to develop an understanding of state formation as a relational process. As Hopkins trenchantly observed in 1979, "Strong states, in relation to others, develop in core *areas*; weak states, in relation to others, develop or rather are developed in peripheral areas"; significantly, he quickly adds: "It is important to have in mind that "'peripheral'" does not mean marginal in the sense of dispensable: without peripheries, no cores; without both, no capitalist development."[29] Rarely, however, do we see these "processes of state-formation and deformation" used to illustrate how state power and institutions are formed as part of a global political and economic system.[30]

Even more rarely studied are contingent and codeterminant processes of racial alliance and formation among states, particularly outside core areas of the world economy. Studies of states as *racial* states are exceedingly rare, and remain bounded by national racial formations—and European ones at that—as exemplified by David Theo Goldberg's singular *Racial State*.[31] Studies of racial formation that relate state formation and deformation across continental boundaries are almost entirely absent. Growing attention to colonial and imperial relationships across the Atlantic have begun to explore this theme, yet have remained primarily focused on cultural domination and interimperial similarities and alliance.[32] Howard Winant's *World Is a Ghetto* stands out by contrast as a remarkable attempt to trace racial formation worldwide.[33] Yet the limits of what can be achieved in a single monograph are indicated by the subtitle: *Race and Democracy since World War II*. As even favorable reviewers have noted, the cases are few and both temporally and geographically limited.[34] Particularly critical for our present purposes, racial formation as a transnational process remains underdeveloped, a limitation best exemplified by the short chapter that examines South Africa as a national case. Relating racial formation to both state construction and world-economic developments remains a very open challenge.

Formation and Deformation: The South African State

Approaching state power as an interstate and racialized process is especially critical for the exploration of South Africa's distinctive position in the interstate system and world economy: South Africa is far more powerful than other African states, far more industrially advanced, and wields far more power regionally and continentally. No other African state stands in this position, not even the larger, oil-rich and more heavily populated Nigeria. Typical of neither rich core states nor very poor peripheral states, South Africa is more commonly classified as a "middle-income" state or, more appropriately, if awkwardly, a "semiperipheral" state.[35] When and how South Africa achieved its "middle" position remains unclear. It appears so exceptional, largely due to apartheid it would seem, that it has rarely if ever been termed a "newly industrializing" country much less an "emerging market" state. Equally uncertain is how this position might operate to shape, limit, or advance South Africa's developmental relationships over time with stronger core states and weaker African states.

Yet South Africa was not always "semiperipheral." Throughout the seventeenth, eighteenth, and nineteenth centuries, South Africa's position in the capitalist world mirrored much of Asia, Africa, and Latin America: a consumer of manufactured imports from Northern core and high-wage areas of the world economy, and an exporter of primary products based on cheap and coerced indigenous labor. Up to at least World War II, an escape from poorly remunerated and low technology work remained an unachievable goal for the vast majority of the peoples and states of the planet, as it remains so today. South Africa's movement from primary production to ever higher-wage, industrial, and technologically advanced production thus stands out as a singular achievement.

For both liberal and radical students of South Africa, this transformation remains a natural step on the course of national economic development, and one that took place during the post–World War II apartheid years. As Merle Lipton, the most explicit defender of the liberal argument that apartheid hindered big business, put it in the mid-1980s, "During the last few decades, the SA economy has grown rapidly and changed, shifting from dependence upon mining and agriculture . . . to greater dependence on manufacturing and services."[36] While radical scholars claimed apartheid served the interests of capital, their periodization reproduced a similarly linear and national narrative, arguing that monopoly capital consolidated its base in mining during the 1950s and then led an advancing industrial economy during the boom years of the 1960s and early 1970s.[37]

The focus on apartheid is understandable. But long-term data fail to support models of a natural progression to an industrial stage of economic growth ushered in by the 1948 apartheid election. Here basic evidence intrudes, for South Africa by World War II had already decisively shifted away from agrarian and mineral forms of production and toward higher-wage industrial production. By 1945 the contribution of private manufacturing to gross domestic product was twice that of mining,[38] while manufacturing provided more jobs than mining for both white and black workers.[39] As the war came to a close, state officials congratulated themselves on a record of unbounded success. Indeed, as one government report put it in 1945, the country "is clearly not just entering the industrial stage. On the contrary, the industrial development of the country is already well advanced."[40] Complacency and self-congratulation were shaken as a wave of strikes and nationalist demonstrations erupted in the early postwar years, a common phenomenon all across the world economy.[41] These challenges, and the apartheid election outcome they led to in 1948, were rooted, however, in the very *success* of the state's highly racialized economic policies during the interwar period.

What these brief observations suggest is that any analysis of South Africa's break from primary production and underdevelopment must begin by looking not to the last half of the twentieth century, but to the first half, uncovering how South Africa moved away from being an agrarian-mineral producer and toward being an industrial power. The key interwar period was, of course, marked by considerable social and economic disruption all across the world economy, and economic nationalism was widely implemented as a response to international economic crisis and competition. Yet with few exceptions such efforts failed, particularly outside core areas of the world economy.[42] South Africa was a rare success story: the country was one of the very few outside Europe and North America to advance economically during the interwar period, and certainly the only African one. Yet one searches the literature on South Africa almost in vain for an explanation of this breakthrough. Quite telling, it is most often attributed to residual and unique "external" factors. For most scholars the key factor is easily pinpointed: the dramatic rise of the international price of gold in the wake of the Great Crash.[43] As an old liberal adage coined by noted economic historian C. W. de Kiewiet put it, "South Africa has advanced politically by disasters and economically by windfalls."[44]

Reducing economic advance to surprising shifts in "external" factors only begs the question, particularly if these factors have clear patterns and explanations themselves—as in the long-term, world-economic cycles of both gold production and prices.[45] And as so many commodity boom cycles have illustrated, high mineral prices do not necessarily lead to industrialization or wealth; windfall profits have far more often been consumed by colonial powers, local plantation owners, settler farmers, state bureaucrats, or mine owners themselves. Certainly the historical evidence for Africa and Latin America in the nineteenth, twentieth, and even the twenty-first centuries indicates that no direct road leads from commodity booms to advanced, high-wage production processes. The early twentieth century commodity boom has confirmed this judgment, leading to an extensive literature on oil and minerals as a developmental "resource curse."[46]

If the preapartheid period is misconstrued, claims and accounts regarding South Africa in the apartheid era are even more conflicted. It was a new era: globally a new world order emerged under US hegemony, marked by a long worldwide economic boom, new international political and financial institutions, a new international division of labor carried forward by multinational corporations, and the full flowering of the legitimating ideology of liberalism as expressed in decolonization, national development planning, and the promise of civil rights. For African states the fruits of decolonization and modernization theory quickly proved elusive. South Africa again appeared to be an exception to such trends, booming as foreign capital flowed in and industrialization advanced. As one South African scholar claimed, in the middle to late 1960s South Africa was "among the fastest growing industrial economies in the capitalist world at this time, ahead of those in Western Europe and North America."[47]

Under these conditions the tendency to apply concepts and models derived from richer economies accelerated, and the study of South Africa became increasingly delinked from the rest of Africa. While liberals decried state intervention, they clearly saw modernization as well under way, and directly applied models derived from the study of Europe and North America.[48] Radical and neo-Marxist scholars offered alternative accounts drawn from theoretical debates over the nature and future of advanced capitalist societies. Such efforts ranged from analyses of the autonomy of the state and relations among different "fractions" (international, national, sectoral) of capital,[49] through theories of a "new petty bourgeoisie" and the white working class,[50] to the supposed articulation of modes of production between urban centers of capitalist wage work and shrinking "pre-capitalist" zones in the countryside.[51]

What such studies did not achieve is any substantive understanding of South Africa's position in the regional or global economy: the shared assumptions of a bounded national economy, nation-state, and national racial determinants held firm. As resistance against apartheid accelerated in the 1980s and regional conflicts deepened, new work did tackle uneven regional economic and military relationships, most notably between South Africa and its "frontline" states, and the role of foreign and especially US support for the South African regime.[52] New scholarship in these areas was matched by accounts of the role of state firms such as the energy supplier Eskom and South African conglomerates such as Anglo American in generating the apartheid boom.[53] What these studies did not anticipate was the economic crisis that erupted in the mid-1970s and deepened in the 1980s, and which made the state and business groups so susceptible to popular resistance.

This was, as is now well known, a global process marking the end of the postwar Anglo American–led global economic and political system. By the early 1980s increasing international dependence and debt had driven most African states to accept structural adjustment programs, devalued currencies, deregulated markets, and deindustrialization. Gone were the days of liberal development planning. The decline of US hegemony, the collapse of the Soviet Union, and the beginning in the mid-1970s of a long period of global stagnation, would lead to the imposition of neoliberal policies throughout the global economy. South Africa at first seemed to be immune to these conditions. When the United States was forced to break the link between the dollar and gold, which had kept the price of gold fixed at US$35 per ounce from 1934 to 1968, the gold price rose to over US$600 in 1980. As in the interwar period fifty years earlier, South Africa seemed to reap an unexpected, external windfall from unruly commodity markets and currencies.

By the mid-1980s, however, it was impossible for South Africa's rulers to ignore falling rates of capital investment, accelerating unemployment and inflation, declining demand and output, rising capital outflows, and the necessity to devalue the rand (R). Interwoven as these developments were with burgeoning resistance to apartheid, the country's economic crisis was easily attributed to unique and contingent national factors. Thus while the best studies of South Africa's "organic crisis" included external economic factors and events, they stressed national determinants—using concepts such as "racial Fordism" drawn from the far more advanced states of Europe and North America.[54]

With the coming of majority rule in the late 1980s and early 1990s it became increasingly difficult to project economic growth in the footsteps of rich Northern countries. The falling international gold price, halved from its momentary peak in 1980, was but one of many harsh revelations of South Africa's financial, technological, and trade dependence on global markets. Both liberal and radical analyses of modernizing national economies became less and less useful for understanding the country's economic plight in the face of hostile world-economic conditions. As regional and international relations grew in importance, the self-assurance of scholarly analyses sharply declined, while recourse to claims of a historical rupture or "external," "exogenous" explanations once again increased. The language of "globalization," with its assertion of a new epoch severed from the past, became especially attractive.

Events following the first democratic elections in 1994 quickly demonstrated realities that fit no existing paradigm, and within two years the new ANC government abandoned any pretense of national economic planning, and wholeheartedly endorsed neoliberal policies of privatization, deregulation, and open capital and trade flows. Breaking with its own past traditions as expressed in the Freedom Charter of 1955—which had called for the nationalization of industry and the mines and the redistribution of land—President Mandela and Deputy President Mbeki openly embraced free market ideologies, international financial institutions, and the leading role of local and international capital. This constituted both an admission and acceptance of the country's deep integration into the world economy, and its dependent position in international commodity, financial, and investment markets. South Africans were sharply awakened to their marginal status within the world economy, startling new neoliberal policies, and deepening inequality and poverty within the country. This was not the outcome expected by either those who had commanded the heights of the apartheid economy and state or those who had struggled against it. Certainly scholars had not predicted it, or provided a paradigm to understand it. And when global economic crises erupted, as they would in the new century, South Africa would prove to be particularly vulnerable to the chill winds emanating from the North.

These world-economic realities indict not only past paradigms; they call for a wholesale reassessment of South Africa's developmental pathways and its future possibilities. We are not well equipped to do this. Not a single book treating twentieth-century South Africa from a dependency, dependent-development, or world-economic perspective existed on the eve of majority rule in 1994. The coming of the end of apartheid, accompanied as it was by the world media's celebrations of a nonracial South Africa, prefigured a new era of growth and peace. Among the most optimistic and early were projections that South Africa would follow the path of the mature, newly industrializing countries in East Asia (e.g., South Korea, Taiwan, Singapore, Hong Kong).[55] More sobering and accurate analyses emerged by the turn of the century, charting the harsh realities of the world economy and the costs at home of the state's new neoliberal policies.[56]

Attempts to grapple with these anomalies inevitably involve exploring what had long been studiously ignored: South Africa's tenuous position within a radically changing world economy. Equally surprising was the unexpected intrusion of regional relationships, from the xenophobia and violent attacks directed at migrants from neighboring African states, through the revived expansion of South African firms across the region and continent, to the South African state's promotion of new regional and continental institutions. For many South Africans it was a puzzling, brave new world. Majority rule had been attained, only to meet increasing indifference, indeed dismissal and increasing demands, on the part of Northern states, multinational firms and investors, and international financial intuitions. Meanwhile the region and the rest of the continent became depicted by South Africa's media and politicians as a threat to the nation's public safety, jobs, and prosperity. White farmers, businessmen, and foreign investors all warned of the danger of contagion from neighboring African states, most notably from Zimbabwe, where land invasions were rampant. Meanwhile the media and politicians constructed tales of criminal foreigners, fostering a literally deadly xenophobia among South Africans. Such fear and loathing should not have been unexpected, given the continuing realities of who possesses land, wealth, and racial privilege across South and southern Africa. Yet its brutal appearance, set against the claims of a rainbow nation and racial reconciliation, was all the more shocking and inexplicable.

The Plotline: From NIC to NUC

This book is a response to these historical puzzles and the anguished search for alternatives to the world the past has bequeathed to us. It is driven by a narrow imperative: to comprehend how the fate of the peoples of South and southern Africa has been shaped by a highly unequal and racialized region and world economy. There are lessons here I hope both for those interested in southern Africa and for those concerned with the larger world economy. For students of southern Africa, this text tackles in depth South Africa's contradictory relationship with the region and world economy; for students of the world economy, this work illuminates how race matters on a global as well as on a local scale.

We start from the anomalies opened up above. Plotting South Africa for the first time within regional and world-economic relationships allows one to frame a research agenda. For to chart South Africa's position over time, by even the simplest economic measure of its distance from neighboring and core states, generates surprising results. For example, if one takes data on long-term gross national income per capita and compares South Africa to both core European and North American states on the one hand, and to similar middle-income or semiperipheral states on the other, the results are startling. Figure I.1 illustrates South Africa's distance from core country averages since 1929 by plotting its national income per capita as a percentage of the average of four core countries (the United Kingdom, the United States, France, and Germany). As South Africa closes the gap with core countries, its line rises.[57]

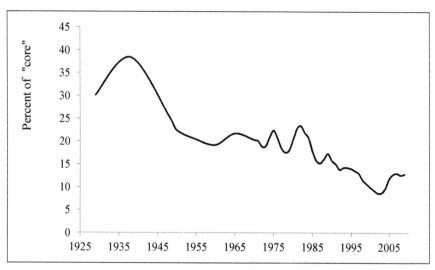

Figure I.1. South Africa's national income per capita, shown as a percentage of that of core states. Key Core = France, Germany, UK, US; for 1948–71: GDP/capita; for 1972–2008: GNI/capita. United Nations, *Statistical Yearbook*; World Bank, *World Tables* and *World Development Indicators*.

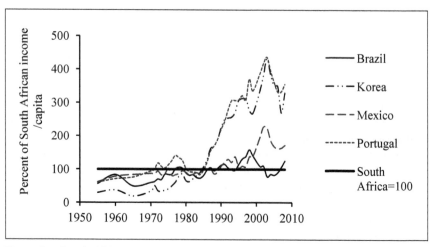

Figure I.2. South Africa versus other semiperipheral states: gross national income per capita. World Bank, *World Tables*, *World Development Report*, and *World Development Indicators*.

As the figure indicates, the period of the celebrated apartheid boom witnessed no closing of the gap between South Africa and core countries; within the international division of labor South Africa maintained, but did not advance, its position. South Africa's decline after the mid-1970s global crisis is also starkly evident.

Figure I.2 illustrates the trajectory of similarly situated states by measuring other states' national income per capita as a percentage of South Africa's: other states rise and fall in relation to South Africa's fixed (indexed to 100) position.

As can be seen from figure I.2, prior to the apartheid boom years South Africa stood well above countries such as Mexico, Brazil, South Korea, and even Portugal—only to be relentlessly overtaken in the last thirty years. The most recent commodity boom, which we might have expected to significantly improve the prospects of a mineral exporter like South Africa in the global hierarchy of wealth and power, has only marginally narrowed the gap between South Africa and other "semiperipheral" states.

These are, of course, only crude indicators of inequality that tell us little of income, standards of living, and measures of well-being across racial lines, or the processes that produced such outcomes. They do identify, however, what needs explanation by roughly charting South Africa's approximate standing in world hierarchies of production, industrial technology, and financial power over time. As such they provide stark evidence of the country's steady downward drift in the post–World War II era and, especially, the postapartheid period. In short: if in the interwar period South Africa was a "newly industrializing country," by the late 1980s it was more properly seen as a "newly underdeveloping country." If South Africa's interwar advance calls for explanation, contrary to received wisdom, so too does the impoverished economy inherited from the apartheid period and its further downward slide since.

From these simple trend lines flow questions: How did South Africa, so deeply integrated into the world economy as a primary producer by the late nineteenth century, manage to break the chains of this role and advance toward industrial status in the interwar period? How did it become a nuclear-armed, regional power in the apartheid period? Have shifts in the international division of labor and world hegemony, from the rise and fall of British and now US hegemony to the deindustrialization of core zones and the industrialization of peripheral areas, strengthened or weakened the country's economic opportunities and policies—including the fortunes of South African as well as foreign multinational firms? What effect has the state's racial makeup, from its beginnings as an independent white settler state in 1910 *and* as a black-ruled republic after 1994, had in advancing or checking relationships with other states in the region and the world at large? And more urgently and surely more speculatively: how might the rise of Asia and the decline of the European North change global processes of capital accumulation and racial formation, particularly for the peoples, businesses, and states of South and southern Africa?

A New Agenda: South Africa in World-Historical Perspective

My attempt to answer these questions falls into three parts. The first task is a concrete one: to examine in detail the world-economic and world-political relationships and struggles that led to the industrial powerhouse that emerged in the first half of the twentieth century. I address this task in the first three chapters, which examine the post–World War I crisis, the post-1924 government's radical reshaping of relationships with core areas and colonial territories, and the reconstruction of the state and state enterprises.

Tracking the emergence of apartheid amid the construction of the postwar US world order forms a second task, which I recount in chapters 4 and 5. As after World War I, the early post–World War II years were a time of worldwide unrest and political disorder, which in South Africa led to the overthrow of British-aligned political parties, the adoption of apartheid, and adaptation to the unexpected features of the liberal, free enterprise US-dominated world order. The cost of compromise for South Africa, in contrast to other semiperipheral states, was the turning back of interwar economic nationalism and foreclosing of further advance in the world economy.

The long-term costs became evident in the 1970s, when protests worldwide led to the end of the liberal world order over a long period of creative destruction. Chapters 6 and 7 trace this third part of the story, from the collapse of liberal developmentalism and an economically-integrated southern African region, through the late apartheid state's adoption of neoliberal and neoracist policies to protect racial and class inequalities, to the postapartheid state's and South African firms' bids for continental power. Complicating all projections is the entrance of two new factors: the resurgence of local and global social movements and the displacement of the North as Asia emerges as the center of the world economy. Taken together, these factors offer a startling range of future possibilities that, in the wake of the historical costs and present disintegration of Western liberalisms, can only be welcomed.

1

World Crisis, Racial Crisis

The twentieth century began with Great Britain's imperial armies being humbled at the hands of Afrikaner republican guerrilla forces. From the British side the war was ostensibly in defense of citizenship rights for white British citizens living in the Afrikaner-ruled South African Republic. Yet the real cause of what would prove to be Britain's greatest colonial war was evident worldwide: a battle over the glittering wealth and power that emanated from the Transvaal's massive gold mines. It took Britain years longer than expected to win the war, at a cost of several million pounds, 22,000 troops dead (out of 250,000 fielded), and a severe blow to its global power. Afrikaners and Africans lost far more in lives and livelihood. Peace came with the signing of a treaty in 1902, which laid out the path toward the creation in 1910 of the modern state of South Africa. This merger of British colonial territories and Afrikaner republics was an agreement among white men; Asians, Africans, and women were excluded from negotiations, offices of the state, and the electorate.

The road to an independent settler state had been a long one. The southern tip of Africa had long been occupied and fought over by successive European powers. In the late fifteenth century, the Portuguese had explored and established settlements in the region; in the mid-eighteenth century, the Dutch had brought settlers and slaves to the Cape area; and in the early nineteenth century, the British had wrested control of Cape Town from the Dutch and brought in yet another, larger wave of European settlers and missionaries. It was only in the last third of the nineteenth century, however, that African resistance was overcome and a formal colonial order established across the whole region. This last push was driven by two factors: a global depression that propelled a scramble for colonial markets, and the European discovery of stunningly rich diamond and gold deposits. South Africa's mines quickly proved to be among the most extensive and profitable enterprises in the British Empire. Mining technology and machinery were imported from Europe and North America, European financial houses scrambled to provide millions of pounds of portfolio investment, railroads snaked their way into the interior from multiple coastal ports, local food-stuff production by both white and black farmers for the new mining centers accelerated, and labor flowed toward the mines from across the far reaches of Europe, Australasia, and southern Africa. By the opening decades of the twentieth century, mineral exploitation tied together colonial officials and settlers in one great endeavor, stretching from labor recruitment stations in distant African villages and Asian cities, through the brutal mining com-pounds and richly paneled boardrooms belonging to Johannesburg's great mining houses, to the City of London. This was globalization with a ven-geance, sustained by the ideology of free trade and naked imperial power.

As a site for primary production, southern Africa shared the characteris-tics of much of Africa, Asia, and Latin America. Racial, social, and political relationships were shaped by the imperatives of export production, a sub-ordinate colonial status in relation to Europe, and the racial and gender classifications and hierarchies of the day. Where southern and South Africa's colonial history differed from most of Africa's and Asia's experience was in one key aspect: successive waves of the incorporation of the region into the world economy under Dutch and British hegemony had left behind signifi-cant settler populations.

Colonial power and white settlers were a volatile mix everywhere, as France, Britain, and Spain had learned during the course of eighteenth- and early-nineteenth-century Creole revolts and revolutions in the Americas. The Anglo-Boer War of 1899–1902, fought not against indig-enous kingdoms but Afrikaner settlers, was thus hardly exceptional given the stakes involved. Yet the outcome of the war served both Britain and, it would seem, the white settlers well. As Magubane has shown in his analy-sis of the deliberations of British and South African statesmen between 1870 and 1910, the formation of the Union of South Africa was part of an explicit strategy to preserve empire by enfolding white settler states within a racialized imperial framework.[1] The problem facing Great Britain was how to govern through white settlers, who could not be treated as colonial subjects, and who irascibly demanded political power in their own right. Britain and its white settlers might need each other as brothers and sis-ters in a common racial domination over indigenous populations, yet they could equally detest each other's claim to the reward that came from this racial, colonial order.

In the colonial world of the early twentieth century, Britain's solution to this conundrum was found by promoting the formation of "dominion" states, defined along racial lines and wedded by history, culture, patriarchy, and bilateral economic relationships to the mother country. Welding these interests together was a global racial consciousness. As Magubane observes, "Advocates of British imperialism made much ado about the Anglo-Saxons as a separate, innately superior people. In the white settler colonies it was made quite clear that as they were constituted into dominions they would be part of a white, Anglo-Saxon 'Greater Britain'; other white races would be absorbed within the existing entities while so-called 'nonwhite' races would be rigorously excluded from any equal participation in citizenship."[2] South Africa fit snugly within this constellation; not surprisingly, the greatest cultural proponent of patriarchy and imperial white rule, Rudyard Kipling, spent his winter holidays there.

South African settlers faced a significant problem, however: South Africa was neither white enough nor British enough by comparison to the other candidates for dominion status. Australia, New Zealand, and Canada all had overwhelming white populations following the near extermination of indigenous peoples. As Lord Milner, the British strategist behind the unification of Afrikaner republics and British colonies, put it at the time, South Africa with its low proportion of white and especially British descendants, "is and will long remain the weakest link in the Imperial chain, and she will be the last of the Dominions to enter an Imperial Union."[3] In terms of the racial hierarchy that marked and legitimized the colonial system, South Africa thus occupied an unstable position.

The bid by South African settlers to become part of the wealthy club of white states was beset with obstacles. As the economic histories of the Americas illustrate, settler power and the exploitation of local labor and mineral resources did not necessarily generate high wages and great wealth: it would take a struggle to advance fully into the gentlemen's club. And unlike Canada, Australia, or New Zealand, South Africa possessed a far smaller proportion of high-wage white workers and the industries that might sustain them. The great difficulty facing South Africa's first white prime ministers was thus not unlike that still present as the twentieth century ended: how to avoid being treated like the rest of Africa as a captive market for overseas manufacturers and a source of low-wage labor and cheap raw materials and foodstuffs.

South Africa certainly played this peripheral role for Europe in the early twentieth century, fulfilling the fondest hopes of British statesmen, financiers, and their most prominent local allies, local mining magnates. Even with solidly Afrikaner governments, the South African state after 1910 assiduously followed the dictates of mine owners and the imperial and world-economic networks on which mining had been founded. Rising world demand for the products of white commercial agriculture seemed to further confirm the wisdom of tying the future of white South Africa to the ceaseless exploitation of the country's natural resources. What was not foreseen was that the very success of quickly reestablishing the mines under British control and tying agriculture to an expanding world market would, in a very brief time, produce an economic and racial crisis for the white community.

At the time of the formation of the Union in 1910, a commitment to both the capitalist world market and a collective white supremacy seemed a reasonable gambit. As the Anglo-Boer War came to an end, prosperity surfaced once again across the world economy, displacing the uncertainties and fears engendered by the global stagnation that had marked the last quarter of the nineteenth century. Industrial production in leading core states leaped upward, as did export-oriented primary production across the periphery of the world economy. This phenomenon took place, moreover, on terms that promised rising returns to peripheral producers. Raw material prices, which fell during the last three decades of the nineteenth century, rose in the new century.[4] When combined with the widening of the peripheral zone due to late-nineteenth-century colonial conquests, the result was an outpouring of commodities. Tea flowed from new plantations in India and Ceylon, palm oil and cocoa from West Africa, and rubber and rice from Africa and Asia.[5]

South Africa's contribution was gold, underpinning Britain's worldwide trading and financial network. Gold did not, however, follow the usual boom-and-bust cycle of other commodities. The value of gold had long been inversely related to global cycles, rising in periods of global economic crisis and falling in periods of global prosperity. Rising real gold prices in the global depression of the late nineteenth century stimulated exploration worldwide, and it was precisely in this period when Europeans came to rapidly exploit gold deposits in the Witwatersrand area. The Anglo-Boer War severely disrupted gold mining and devastated commercial agricultural production in the interior. In the wake of the war British colonial officials worked overtime to revive gold production and resettle and restock Afrikaner farmers in the former republics, forging a "maize and gold" alliance between white farmers and mining magnates.[6] By 1910, with a newly elected Afrikaner government pursuing reconciliation with local mining houses and with Great Britain internationally, South Africa's place in the expanding world economy was put on a new and solid footing.

The complacency of South Africa's new rulers at this solution was rudely shaken by overlapping social and economic reversals at the end of World War I. Gold mines, assumed to be the foundation stones of future prosperity, became unprofitable and started to close. After enjoying years of high prices and increasing output, settler farmers saw market forces move rapidly against them. Nascent industrialists, after enjoying a boom during World War I, were reducing output, closing factory gates, and dismissing black and white workers alike. Incipient class and racial struggles soon erupted into open conflict. The epicenter of these was located in the crucial mining industry, with large strikes by African miners in 1920 and white miners in 1922. When armed white workers appeared in the streets in the course of the 1922 Rand Revolt, the ruling South African Party government responded with machine guns and aerial bombardment.

These events led directly to the election in 1924 of the "Pact" government, an alliance between Afrikaner nationalists and elements of the white labor movement—an outcome deeply troubling to both British imperial interests and the mining houses. The political struggles that led to the Pact's victory and the subsequent reorganization of political and racial alliances have been extensively charted and generally focus on two issues: the extent to which the Pact marked a radical change in the capitalist character of the state,[7] and the degree to which the Pact government's policies reflected the influence of, and benefited, the white working class.[8]

What the debates around these two issues ignore are the fundamental and intractable contradictions among different segments of the white community, and white producers' often quite different and mutually-exclusive relationships with black communities. These tensions would be sharply revealed in the early postwar crisis and would prove crucial to changing the power of the state and the course of the country's position in the world economy.

Gold Mining and the World Economy

Gold was not simply a valuable commodity: it underwrote the gold standard that supported Britain's place in the world and British hopes for the revival of the free trade system. By comparison with other nineteenth-century gold discoveries, the South African deposits were massive but low-grade, requiring increasingly vast expenditures of labor and capital to make a profit—which in turn fostered the development of interconnected, internationalized, and powerful mining firms. In histories of capital accumulation in Europe and the United States that chart the movement from finance capital at the turn of the century to monopoly capital under US hegemony, South African mining firms are often collectively described as "international monopoly" capital—as opposed to local, "national" capital.[9]

This conception captures distinctive features of South Africa's mining houses, including the international origins of the financing of the mining industry, the mine owners' close and institutionalized alliance in the Chamber of Mines, and, most important of all, the mining companies' shared monopsonistic labor-recruiting agencies. Yet despite apparent correspondences of size and imperial ambitions, South African mining firms hardly replicated the pattern of "monopoly capital" in core areas as conceived by, for example, Baran and Sweezy in their foundational work on the US economy.[10] South African mining companies shared few if any of the defining characteristics of "monopoly" or even oligopolistic firms as they emerged in core areas: mine owners lacked the ability to set prices for their product, depended heavily on distant capital markets rather than self-financing for recurring capital needs, and did not possess a corporatively organized and self-perpetuating management.

That the mining houses were the creation of and dependent on international financial markets is indisputable. Yet, as Kubicek's research shows, the mining magnates were hardly direct extensions of either powerful overseas capital or imperial political interests.[11] Indeed, the British South African entrepreneurs who founded and ran the mining houses came from diverse ethnic and geographical backgrounds, and were deeply committed to their future in southern Africa. Yet if execution and control were locally based, it was equally apparent that these very large operations relied on core areas for the high-wage capital goods, skilled white labor, and technology, especially the engineering skills that made deep-level mining possible. All these resources came from abroad, primarily from Great Britain but also from the rising new powers of the United States and Germany.

Mining firms' divergence from core corporate models was further accentuated by their very product. During the nineteenth century the price of gold was fixed as the universal monetary equivalent under the gold–British pound standard. This meant an assured price for gold producers, but one whose real value rose or fell relative to prices for other commodities. Thus the value of gold and the profitability of the mines rose in periods of price deflation and economic depression, as happened in the last quarter of the nineteenth century—triggering a worldwide spurt of exploration during which the Witwatersrand fields were developed. Conversely, in periods of price inflation gold's value vis-à-vis other commodities fell. This was a very different pattern than the one marked by the high prices and profits of "monopoly" capital in core zones, which were generated by innovative technology and production processes under the control of oligopolistic enterprises.

Gold producers were thus embedded in a curious position in the international division of labor. Heavily dependent on core areas for portfolio investment funds, technology, capital goods, and markets, mining was not a self-reliant "national" enterprise. By comparison to "monopoly" or "finance" capital of the day, South African mining firms had little control over costs for their commodity inputs or markets for their product. The mines' management and operational structures were, moreover, firmly rooted in South Africa and not in core states. Mining capital was certainly not an outpost of imperialist or multinational capital controlled and directed from London, New York, Paris, or Berlin. In short: while overshadowing other mining or plantation operations in the colonial world, South Africa's mining houses typified in key respects the condition of commodity producers operating under the dependent and competitive conditions of production along the lower rung of the global division of labor. And this vulnerable, dependent position would eventually unleash devastating forces beyond the control of either the mining houses or the government.

Mining and the Long Durée: The Economics of Decline

Pressures against the continued profitability of the mines steadily mounted as they revived in the wake of the Anglo-Boer War. The pressures emanated, moreover, from sources far beyond the control of mining magnates. Despite increased flows of investment capital from core to peripheral areas of the world economy in this period, equity capital investment in South African gold mines actually declined. The value of gold shares, for example, was almost halved between 1902 and the early 1920s.[12]

Investors' lack of confidence in the mines reflected not just the political uncertainties of the period, but also the increasing difficulties of making the mines profitable. Simply stated, the forces of the world economy had moved against the mines: mining firms became caught between the flat, internationally fixed price for their product and the inexorably rising costs of inputs on the world market, particularly after 1910. Whether indexed by the cost of imports or the local consumer price index, the value of gold was in free fall after 1910, dropping by half in the next decade.[13] From the establishment of the Union onward, working costs per ton of milled ore rose inexorably. Mining companies could do little about the steady rise in the cost of stores and the fixed price of gold, both of which were directly traceable to long-term, global price cycles far beyond South African mining magnates' influence. By World War I both mining company spokesmen and public officials were predicting the closure of low-grade mines and the demise of mining as the driving force of economic growth in the region.

There was one factor cost mining magnates could reduce in the struggle to maintain profitability: labor. The Randlords, as the mining capitalists were popularly called, had long been preoccupied with the problem of assuring an adequate supply of labor at a sufficiently modest level of remuneration. While mine owners were the dominant economic and social power in the region, they nevertheless had to contend with a competing array of local, racially privileged employers such as white farmers, as well as resistance by those targeted to feed the mines' appetite for labor. And the appetite was insatiable: in 1890, just four years after opening, the mines employed some 14,000 men. By 1897 88,000 were toiling in the mines, and by 1910 more than 200,000 were employed.[14] Mobilizing this army of labor was all the more remarkable given the sparse, dry interior's distance from supply areas overseas, local or regional labor sources, ports, and water and power resources.

Under these conditions the marshaling of labor became a highly globalized and racialized endeavor. Skilled miners and supervisory personnel were recruited largely from the United Kingdom, especially the mining centers of Cornwall, Lancashire, and Scotland. They formed, as Hyslop has documented for this period, an imperial white working class united by a common ideology of White Labourism.[15] South Africa was thus a privileged outpost for this worldwide white working class. In order to attract skilled white men to the Rand, with its much publicized high cost of living, wage rates were pegged well above levels obtaining in Europe even after multiple railways reached the Rand and began to lower costs. In 1914 skilled artisan wages in Johannesburg were reported to be over three times the prevailing British rates and double those in France.[16] White miners in South Africa regularly earned double the current wages paid in the United States, Canada, Australia, and Britain. Shift bosses' wages per shift on the Witwatersrand were 26 shillings (s.) compared, for example, to the 11s. paid shift bosses in Sydney.[17] These wage rates allowed skilled white workers to maintain a standard of living equal to or greater than highly skilled white workers in other world regions, which enabled them to employ African domestic servants.[18]

Offsetting the high cost of white labor was the low wage bill for an army of African laborers who worked under white supervision, outnumbered the white labor force by roughly eight to one, and whose wages were *one-ninth* of white workers' wages.[19] In common parlance it was the "ultra-cheapness" of African workers, who lacked the scarce skills of most white miners, that made possible the latter's rate of pay. This differential was enhanced by the social and gender construction of attracting and reproducing this labor force. On the one hand, living costs for white artisans in this distant outpost were considerably higher than in other locales. On the other hand, the costs of unskilled labor were lower than in core countries due to the existence of rural homesteads of male, migrant African workers, which covered the daily and generational costs of feeding and caring for the young, old, and most women. Employers thus set wages to cover only the daily needs of a migrant worker and only for part of his lifetime. While white miners and their urban households thus constituted a "classic" working class, highly dependent over their lifetimes on wage labor for their survival, African miners and their households were "part-lifetime" proletarians: they mixed cash wages from part-lifetime waged work with nonwaged returns from agricultural labor, particularly female labor, in the countryside as well as from exchanges with extensive kin and community networks.

Underwriting this racial and gender hierarchy was not just repression and ideology, but vast racial and gender differences in the household and social networks that supported and reproduced labor. Employers were well aware of this. In areas contiguous to the mines and along the coast, white farmers militantly defended their control over African populations whom they had dispossessed in the decades prior to the development of the mining industry. The demands of white settlers, plantation companies, and concessionary companies in the Rhodesias, Nyasaland, and the Portuguese colonies of Angola and Mozambique also served to block or raise the cost of recruiting labor from nearby colonial territories.[20] Finally, and most importantly, in those areas of the region marked by the relative availability of land, there were few inducements for Africans to cross consistently into the wage labor market; African farmers could sell surpluses on the developing internal market to meet cash needs or withdraw into less commodified production and consumption.

The Chamber of Mines was organized in 1899 primarily to overcome these obstacles by presenting a united front toward African labor and competing employers. After years of competitive bidding for African labor, the formation of the Chamber heralded the prospect of a new era of monopolistic labor recruitment. Yet even the creation of a centralized recruiting agency, the equalization of wage rates across mines, and the backing of British officials and the South African state did not guarantee immediate success. As an extensive study of the mining houses' drive to secure African labor has documented, "The mines achieved centralized control of recruiting only with great difficulty and prolonged effort."[21]

The struggle to obtain adequate labor supplies was matched by the mining companies' determination to contain wage levels, aims that were bedeviled by competition among white employers and colonial and settler political authorities. Equally important were the sources of African workers' marketplace bargaining power. African miners derived their power vis-à-vis capital not from the scarcity of their skills, like white artisans, but from their ability to distance themselves from the wage labor market. This, in turn, rested on the existence of alternative social and productive structures in the countryside. During the early years of incorporation of these areas into colonial and world markets, and especially in areas far from the heartland of settler and colonial power, it was still possible for African households to reject wage labor and rely on agricultural production. Even as incorporation was intensified, alternatives to part-lifetime employment in the mines arose in commodity production for the market, tenant farming, or employment in urban-industrial areas. Although the fact is rarely noticed, *African* miners' wages in the first decade of the mines' operations were significantly higher by comparison to later periods on the Rand and also to unskilled wage levels in other peripheral and even some core areas of the world economy.

The mines in their early years also paid higher wages by comparison to many other local employers. Taking the region as a whole, African wage rates increased as one moved toward the Rand, while white wages similarly increased as one moved northward from the coast to the Rand. Planters in Nyasaland to the far north, for example, paid but one-twentieth the African wage rate prevailing on the Rand. As settler and colonial power was extended throughout the region and pressures on Africans to enter commodity production increased, the Randlords were emboldened to lower their bid for male African labor, a process that accelerated after the formation of the recruiting agencies of the Chamber of Mines. During and after the Anglo-Boer War, wage rates were reduced to 30s (thirty shifts) from a prewar standard of 50s. This took place in the face of an intense clamor for cheap African labor on the part of all white employers. Mine owners and other employers were united in arguing that high wages would not elicit larger labor supplies. After estimating an improbably exact labor shortfall of 307,528 African workers, the South African Native Affairs Commission of 1903–5 came to the conclusion that "the supply available from local sources is capable of being increased and the Commission has given considerable attention as to how this is to done. Any recommendation as to higher wages is quite out of place."[22]

The strength of African bargaining power soon became evident when the chamber lowered wages at the turn of the century: a drastic shortage of African labor soon ensued. Using their British imperial connections, mine owners responded by turning to the largest global source of mobile, racially subordinate workers: Chinese labor. Beginning in 1904, the first of 62,000 Chinese arrived in South Africa to work for wages well below African wage rates. This was, however, a temporary expedient. Fierce white resistance to Chinese labor succeeded in forcing the repatriation of almost all Chinese laborers by the time of the founding of the Union of South Africa in 1910; as a result, the mines had to revert to the prewar standard of pay. Wage data for white workers are not available in any detail over this early period, but the best estimates are that by contrast they rose between 1889 and 1911.[23]

Mining companies persevered, however, seeking to extend the range of their recruiting operations and at the same time to deepen the dependence of African cultivators on migrant wage labor by reducing alternative sources of income and access to land—a story well told in many accounts.[24] Shortages of African labor continued as did low wages. Both nominal and real African wages were in fact reduced between 1911 and 1921, with real wages falling from an index figure (1936 = 100) of 111 in 1911 to 77 in 1921.[25] The astonishing success of this policy became apparent in the long term: African miners' wages would remain flat from the formation of the Union until the mid-1970s.

The tactics applied in relation to white labor were threefold, reflecting very different racial, social, and gendered household networks. First, mining firms sought to undercut white artisans' hold on a central location in the technical division of labor through altering the labor process. Technical innovations, particularly those concerning drilling, led to deskilling through job fragmentation. Second, mining owners localized the supply of skilled white workers, drawing particularly on newcomers who would be willing to accept locations in the newly emerging technical division of labor. In this aim mining firms were assisted by the ongoing commercialization of agriculture, which displaced many Afrikaner farmers from the land and provided a new pool of white labor. Between 1902 and 1920 the percentage of white miners born in South Africa rose from 18 percent of the white labor force to above 50 percent.[26] As part of this process, the number of white miners with families on the Rand dramatically increased from 12 percent to more than 40 percent between 1897 and 1912.[27] Finally, mining firms matched these two moves with a third: reducing the proportion of white miners in the total labor force.

As mining firms pressed forward with these efforts, they triggered a running battle with skilled and unionized white workers, with white miners striking in 1902, 1907, 1913, 1914, and 1922. Mine owners, at least in the opening salvos, welcomed the opportunity to subjugate decisively the unruly white labor force. As the strike wave developed, polarization between labor on one side and the state and capital on the other grew: both the 1913 and the 1922 strikes were general strikes that threatened the broader social order. After an initial period of indecision, most evident in response to the 1913 strike, the state came down heavily on the side of mine owners, ending in 1922 with the state's brutal suppression of the Rand Revolt. As after previous victories in 1907 and 1914, the mining companies immediately cut white workers' wages.[28] The ratio of African to white labor also increased from 8.2 to 1 in 1921 to over 11 to 1 the following year.[29]

The political costs were, however, large. For while naked coercion had long been unleashed against African strikers (as in response to the 1914 and 1920 strikes), its use against white workers threatened to undermine the common racial alliance among employers and white citizens. This alliance, commanded by the mining houses and the state, served to legitimize the state, the dominance of mining firms, and post-Union governments. What had thus begun as an economic struggle in the mining industry evolved into a general crisis of the legitimacy of private accumulation and state power. At the next general election Afrikaner and British workers alike deserted the ruling South African Party, sweeping into power the "Pact" alliance between the National Party and the Labour Party.

Almost all accounts attribute this outcome to national economic and political struggles between white workers, mining companies, and the state. The analysis of the declining fortunes of mining in South Africa indicate, however, processes reaching far beyond the state and the wage labor market to regional and world-economic processes. Mining firms' launching of an offensive against labor represented not simply the pursuit of greater profits, but a desperate response to changing circumstances in the worldwide capital, labor, and commodity relationships within which mining was embedded. That this response initiated the localization of white labor only rebounded upon capital: as imported bachelors were replaced by local white miners, an even more militant and enfranchised male white labor force was forged. For mine owners and their allies, it was a cruel outcome: they had been undermined by the very international forces that had propelled their success. Compressed on the local scene were now all the effects of hostile cycles and trends of the world economy at large. Amplifying the crisis within mining, moreover, were similar trends in other key sectors.

The Fortunes of Agriculture: Contradictions of Success

For understandable reasons the mining sector has dominated discussions of the political and economic crises of the early 1920s. Manufacturing was a very, very small enterprise by comparison. Agriculture, however, was altogether different, as indicated by the distribution of the economically active population: in 1921 agriculture engaged 63 percent of the workforce, to mining's 10 percent, and manufacturing's 6 percent.[30] During the first two decades of the twentieth century, agriculture, in sharp contrast to mining, suffered hardly at all from contraction and decline. Indeed, the expanding world economy offered new and profitable opportunities for accumulation—which would eventually, however, intersect and accentuate the sociopolitical conflicts developing in mining.

Intensive commercial farming has always been a tenuous enterprise in South Africa, marked as the country is by areas ill-suited to intensive cultivation and often subject to outbreaks of disease and drought. While the years after the Anglo-Boer War had their share of natural disasters, they were primarily notable for the deepening of agriculture's integration in the world economy and the transformation of class relations in the countryside. Prices and output steadily accelerated from 1905 onward for almost all major crops, particularly the big three: sugar, maize, and wool.[31]

Rising prices for maize, sugar, and wool were matched by increases in the volume of production. Like mining, commercial agriculture was securely locked into the world economy through price and marketing mechanisms. Given South Africa's free trade policy and excellent railway system, world market prices dictated competitive conditions for local agricultural producers. Exports of these three commodities steadily rose during opening decades of the century, as indicated in figure 1.1.

The most valuable agricultural good, wool, was produced almost entirely for export. Even the cultivation of maize, the next most valuable crop and one with a large and expanding internal market, became increasingly tied to foreign markets and thus export oriented. While at the turn of the century little if any maize was exported, by the early to mid-1920s up to a third of the crop was destined for overseas markets.[32] As Tim Keegan has argued in explaining the increase in agricultural production after 1907, "The crucial

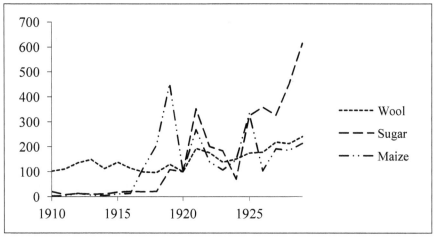

Figure 1.1. Wool, sugar, and maize export volumes, 1911–29 (wool = 10,000 lbs.; maize and sugar = 1,000 lbs.). South Africa, *Handbook of Agricultural Statistics*, tables 100, 110, 113.

new variable was the opening up of export markets for maize, which enabled farmers to grow unlimited quantities in the sure knowledge that the internal price would be maintained at a profitable level."[33]

What aggregate figures on prices and production volumes do not record is the uneven dispersion and social characteristics of the commercialization process. Over the course of the late nineteenth century and in the decades following the Anglo-Boer War, the transformation of South African agriculture was marked by two related movements. First, the farms of white landlords, both resident- and absentee-owned, were oriented away from rentier uses and toward commercial crop production. Second, cultivation by Africans—which took place under many forms of production from rent-paying tenancy and sharecropping on white farms, to production by independent producers on their own land—was increasingly excluded from the market. A continuing class struggle in the countryside carried these transitions forward, with white farmers being backed by the power of the state.

In areas long since incorporated into the world economy, such as the coastal regions of the Cape and Natal, these processes had been under way from at least the mid-nineteenth century as the production of wool, wheat, and sugar accelerated. The effects of the Anglo-Boer War, a rise in world commodity prices, and the political centralization brought about by formation of the Union in 1910 all served to quicken the pace of the transformation. Nowhere was this more pronounced than in the country's interior, where the marketing of heavy agricultural commodities was assured only after the arrival of railways to feed the gold mines.

As commercialization of agriculture in the interior proceeded, it became evident that not all of the multiple forms of African and settler, household-based agricultural production would survive. While settlers dominated the countryside politically, it was by no means apparent during the nineteenth century which if any of the various settler farming systems would dominate the supply of agricultural produce for local and world markets. African cultivators proved quite early on that they could supply local needs if given access to markets.[34] Besides the direct ownership of land by Africans (often obtained by purchases after the period of conquest), African cultivators rented land from absentee landlords, the Crown, and most particularly from resident white landlords with far too much land and far too little capital to farm their holdings effectively. Access to absentee-owned land was especially marked in the Transvaal and Natal; Trapido estimates that, as of 1900, almost 20 percent of the land in the Transvaal was claimed by absentee owners or land companies.[35]

As wealthier white farmers sought to seize the market opportunities offered them in the early twentieth century, and particularly after the post–Anglo Boer War depression lifted around 1907, they intensified their assault on African competitors while attempting to shelter their own sources of labor from other employers. The 1913 Natives Land Act, which sought to outlaw sharecropping and African ownership in all but 13 percent of the land area of the Union, signified the severity of the attack on African competitors. Rather than providing goods to local and export markets, as occurred elsewhere in peripheral areas of the world economy in this period, African households increasingly became the source of cheap coerced labor for settler farmers.

Crossing Crises: Accumulation Paths and Political Revolts

The successful commercialization of settler farming contrasted sharply with the mining sector's declining fortunes. Ironically, the very success of settler farming would produce a major transformation of racial and class positions, which in turn propelled the political crisis that broke out after World War I. Above all, the commercialization of agriculture meant the forcible expulsion of many farmers from the land. As this process accelerated, with settler farmers expanding cereal production and fencing in pastoral lands, white commercial farmers increased their efforts to eliminate competitors. African farmers increasingly found themselves confronted with a forced choice: either move to reserve areas steadily impoverished by overcrowding or accept labor tenant positions with reduced access to land for their own stock and cereal production. Since tenant relationships meant an increasing diversion of African household members' labor time from their own agricultural operations to those of a commercializing settler farmer, this transition signaled a wholesale transformation of class relations in the countryside.

The options were quite different for white farmers with less land and fewer resources, many of whom relied on African sharecroppers for income or were even tenants (*bywoners*) themselves. Like their African counterparts, they too locked up land and labor resources that rapidly commercializing farmers desired. Unlike African cultivators, however, they were hardly a source of cheap manual labor. To commercializing farmers, poor white farmers were thus doubly redundant, and their expulsion from the countryside proceeded apace, providing urban areas with a steady stream of "poor whites," in the parlance of the day. Originally used to designate displaced Afrikaner farmers, the term expanded to cover poor urban whites as well. As numerous commissions and inquiries charted, this stratum grew sharply in the first two decades of the twentieth century. By the early 1920s, estimates placed upward of 120,000 persons in this category.[36]

From this group came the white labor reserve that allowed mine owners to internalize their supply of supervisory labor and undermine the power of artisan miners. Newly proletarianized Afrikaners did not, however, constitute the quiescent and malleable labor force that mine owners desired. While many were employed by mining firms as strikebreakers in 1907, by 1913 many were supporting strike action. And in the 1914 general strike, lower-skilled miners were more heavily in favor of sympathy strikes than their fellow artisans. By the time of the 1922 Rand Revolt, the largest part of the body of the rebellion was composed of Afrikaners. The insecurity of semiskilled and unskilled white workers, subject as they were to competition from African workers in the labor market, made them a far more volatile economic and political force than either mine owners or Afrikaner elites had ever expected.

As the number of poor whites grew, the dominant economic and political class increasingly feared the social and political implications of such a large body of discontented and yet enfranchised whites. On the one hand, the social barriers between poor whites and blacks, deemed so essential to the ideology and stability of white supremacy, were dissolving under the impact of ever closer contact between the races both in the workplace and in multiracial urban slums. Overt breakdowns of white superiority, as evidenced by whites begging food from Africans or even by whites working for Africans, were viewed with horror by government officials. On the other hand, poor whites by their very existence threatened the racial hierarchies that legitimized the state and the white man's place in the labor force. The role of unemployed whites in the rebellions of 1914 and 1922 was a fearful portent for politicians and businessmen alike. As Prime Minister Jan Smuts declared, "The poor whites, people without any calling or education . . . who owing to the various disasters in this country and social conditions have gravitated to the towns," were, in 1922, decisive in "setting things towards revolution."[37]

The possibility of the two streams of black and white resistance uniting was the most feared prospect of all for employers and the state. While there was little evidence at the time to indicate substantive multiracial unity, the growing militancy and sophistication of African strikes in 1913, and especially in 1920, made the potential convergence of parallel streams of labor unruliness a truly frightening specter. If the 1922 Rand Revolt has been enshrined as *the* pivotal strike of the century due to its direct electoral effects, the rising tide of strikes by unskilled African workers that peaked in 1920 was at least as significant in social-structural terms.

And the 1920 strike by African workers was not a spontaneous, one-shot affair: it was preceded by a major strike in 1913, a mining stores boycott in 1918, and signs of incipient unrest across the whole period. When the strike broke out, it rapidly spread to include 71,000 workers at twenty-one mines. Strikers demanded better wages, lower prices in mine concession stores, and an end to the color bar.[38] The forces propelling African resistance, while sharing some aspects in common with those behind the struggles by white workers and poor whites, were based on the quite different structural location of the African labor force. Thus, while African workers felt, as did whites, the effects of price inflation during the war, their integral ties to rural areas set them apart from the conditions affecting the white section of the labor force based in urban areas. In this regard, the concurrent pressures on African agriculture enumerated above proved crucial, for as rural incomes fell, reliance on migrant and urban wages increased. Swelling African unrest in the midst of already unstable relations between capital and white labor left no area of capital-labor relations stable and assured.

Faced with this unstable cauldron of African and white militancy, the state was most concerned with challenges posed by white unemployment and unrest. The government's open alliance with mining capital and Great Britain in the years prior to 1924 undercut, however, the possibility of resolving the problems of urban whites. Indeed, mining's own long-term difficulties called for state policies and actions at the cost of employed and unemployed whites. As mining firms pressed forward with measures to minimize the cost of white labor, it also became quite clear that the mines would not in the future offer an avenue of employment for the swelling ranks of the white unemployed. Early attempts to use unskilled white miners, such as mine manager Cresswell's 1903 experiment at the Village Reef Mine, fell by the wayside.[39] Afrikaner struggles for state assistance did, after the Anglo-Boer War, lead to the expansion of public relief programs, labor bureaus, training and educational schemes, and public relief works. These were hardly able, however, to stem the increasing flow of poor whites to urban areas. And although the employment of whites in the government sector escalated, this was no final solution to the problem. How, asked successive commissions and public officials, could this dangerous social stratum be neutralized? If the mines could or would not use a larger proportion of whites, that left only agriculture and industry as potential employers of white labor. There was, however, no turning back the tide of commercialization in the agricultural sector, which was the primary source of the problem. Various schemes to resettle whites on the land were attempted, but they came to naught.

One possible solution was to find employment for poor whites in manufacturing, which had long maintained a low ratio of African to white employees. While the ratio of Africans to whites in mining hovered around 8:1,[40] in manufacturing the ratio fluctuated from 1.5:1 to 2.1:1.[41] There was little prospect, however, for a significant expansion of white employment in this sector since it, like mining and agriculture, was left open to the forces of competition on the world market. Indeed, the government's policies toward both sectors only served to exacerbate the problem. Financial aid to wealthier farmers and legislation such as the 1913 Natives Land Act accelerated the transformation of agriculture, while the lack of support to industry constrained employment prospects in manufacturing.

The Post–World War I Crisis

The worldwide depression following World War I explosively combined these global economic and local political processes that had been building since the turn of the century. The gold mines' long decline accelerated, with dire predictions abounding about the end of the industry. By 1919 factor-cost inflation had led to the closure of three mines, while twenty-one mines were working at a loss or at a profit of less than two shillings per ton.[42] A rise in the price of gold in 1919 (due to the divergence between sterling and the dollar area balance of payments) briefly alleviated factor-cost inflation. Known as the "gold premium," this brief spike began in July 1919 but then fell sharply after 1921 and practically disappeared by early 1925.

Agriculture experienced an equally sharp reversal as long-term increases in producer prices were suddenly reversed in the postwar period, as indicated by figure 1.2.

As the *Farmers Weekly* of March 2, 1921, put it, the white South African farmer "regards the future with dismay, and turns hither and thither in search of a plank that will bridge him over the gulf of ruin which appears in his path." And the source of the problem was starkly evident: "Unfortunately, the fortunes of the farmer of this country, as regards his staple products, are absolutely dependent upon the consuming capacity of the open markets of the world." Even the smaller industrial sector had its contribution to make to the general economic crisis, as gross output, employment levels, and wages all fell sharply in the early 1920s.[43] The government workforce

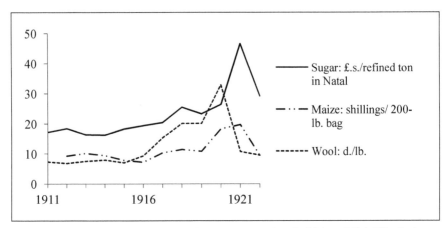

Figure 1.2. Agricultural producer prices, 1911–22. South Africa, *Official Yearbook,* *1929–30,* 427; South Africa, *Handbook of Agricultural Statistics,* 183.

added its bit too, with retrenchment occurring most notably in the railway administration.

When an employers' offensive to cut costs was launched, especially in the mining sector, a long-simmering economic and social crisis turned into a political conflagration. Not only were white workers disaffected with the state, but so too were white farmers; both groups were taken aback by the state's naked, armed alliance with the Randlords. The convergence of local and global trends was especially evident in farming areas that had grown in the shadow of the expansion of the mines. The maize districts of the eastern and western Transvaal had expanded commercial production to feed the mining compounds, and as maize production accelerated, production for export also grew. The sharp fall in world market prices after World War I led mine owners to bypass local producers and import even cheaper Argentinean maize. In the face of the mines' profitability crisis, the government shunned attempts to preserve local markets for white farmers and assist their exports, while singing the praises of free enterprise and free markets.[44] Leading farmers and their organizations were not deceived, and they became increasingly disaffected from both mine owners and the state. By the time of the 1924 election, desertions from the ranks of the Afrikaner-led, but promining, South African Party were widespread across the veld.

Convergence: A Crisis of Racial, Peripheral Development

South Africa's government was hardly alone in facing extreme difficulties after the world war: this was a worldwide period of unrest and rebellion.

Economic uncertainty, strikes, and the overthrow of governing coalitions were rampant from the core to the periphery, from Europe to Africa to Latin America and Asia. For those along the periphery of the world economy, economic life would continue to spiral downward for the rest of the 1920s; overproduction and falling prices continued unabated throughout the decade.[45]

For peoples under direct and unrelenting colonial rule, life became harsher throughout the interwar years, as returns from coerced, small-scale commodity production faltered. European-owned plantations, concession companies, and settler farmers faced the same bleak forces, but could rely at least on their privileged relationship with the colonial state and, accordingly, on state protection and assistance in colonial labor and commodity markets. The future was, however, hardly assured where conflict between African and settler producers existed. For while the exercise of colonial power might secure cheap labor and proprietary markets for Kenyan settlers, for example, it was equally capable of recognizing in neighboring Uganda that small-scale African cultivators, as opposed to settler farmers, were more capable of meeting the demand for export products.

As these examples suggest, the racialization of political power integral to colonialism was to prove as critical as racially segmented labor and commodity markets. For the formation of the Union of South Africa in 1910 had created a state ruled by its male settler citizens, precluding direct colonial controls by Great Britain—a factor exacerbated for Britain by the presence of poor, and non-British, white settlers. Yet settler state power did not provide any ready answers for postwar problems, integrated as South Africa's difficulties were with both world-economic processes and increasingly antagonistic relations among white employers and workers. As charted above, white farmers, mine owners, and workers often had mutually exclusive economic interests and divergent modes of relating to the African population. The traditional scholarly focus on either "external," international factors or "subsistence" forms of production versus "modern capitalist" ones serves us poorly. For such approaches greatly obscure the racialized and world-economic forces at work. As has been argued here, white-owned farms, mines, and commercial operations were all deeply integrated into the capitalist world economy and depended on their owners' status as white citizens to assure their privileged place and power.

As global boom turned to bust after World War I, however, the racial and class alliances that had sustained the first governments of the new South Africa fell apart. Of the main sectors of the economy, gold mining exhibited the most serious and continuous decline, eliciting the most sustained public debate from the turn of the century forward. The integration of agriculture into the world market, while permitting a deep commercialization in the expansionary years after 1907, also meant a new susceptibility to global market forces. This was rapidly exposed in the early 1920s as commercial farmers were plunged into an economic abyss. Even manufacturing, which had blossomed during World War I, found itself entrenched in difficulties with the new openness of South Africa's economy following the end of the war. In very different ways, each of these three sets of producers found the forces of the postwar world economy threatening their survival.

At the same time, the long-term transformations of the country's labor force and class structure that accompanied the diverse and antagonistic forms of the commodification of land and labor generated increasingly unruly forces. These would in turn challenge the legitimacy of both mining capital and the state itself—as was all too apparent in the massive African workers' strike of 1920 and then the appearance of self-proclaimed "Soviets" in the streets of Johannesburg during the 1922 Rand Revolt. Set against long-term trends, the events of the early 1920s indicate a far more serious conjuncture than can be captured by the terms of a national "legitimation" or even "accumulation" crisis; pitched at the level of a nation-state, such conceptualizations direct attention away from the globally embedded character of the challenge that faced South Africa. At issue was not only declining profitability, or even the dissolution of the social basis of the local white state, but the sustainability of the economic and political regime that had been forged on integration with the capitalist world economy and the British colonial and racial order.

This process demonstrates as well the theoretical poverty of linear conceptions of the relentless capitalist commodification of land and labor, conceptions that have been recently revived to explain neoliberal globalization. Concepts of primitive accumulation for radical political economists, or of commodification for those working more in the Weberian tradition, might be used to describe the commodification of land and labor in South and southern Africa in both the early interwar period and the early twenty-first century. Yet as the tracing above of the varied and tightly configured labor and production processes associated with deep-level mining and the multiple complexes of settler and African farming illustrates, such linear representations of capitalist progress fail to capture the spatial formation of mutually exclusive class and production complexes that produced the postwar crisis.

As peripheral areas of the world economy plunged into crisis, South Africa's fate took on an all too common cast. The challenge to dominant classes, and particularly those holding the reins of the state, was to secure the means to reestablish the legitimacy of a capitalist economic and political order. Confronted with the impossibility of reversing world trends through efforts at the national level, this task proved beyond the capacity of non-core states and their dominant classes. As a result, political convulsions would reverberate across the periphery of the world economy throughout the interwar period. This made the subsequent outcome in South Africa, the forging of a stable political order and prosperity for dominant and supportive classes, all the more striking. Underpinning this outcome was a new government's direct confrontation with the reality that the country's role as a mineral and agricultural producer among the world of nations offered little in the way of either stability or prosperity for white South Africans. From this confrontation would emerge state policies directed not so much toward restructuring South Africa's internal racial order, but the country's economic and racialized relationships with colonizing core states *and* surrounding colonies and African peoples.

2

South Africa First!

"South Africa First!" was the rallying cry of the National Party in 1924, aimed squarely at the Smuts government's alliance with the Randlords and Great Britain. As the post–World War I crisis erupted, key segments of the white community found common cause in protesting against the sacrifice of their interests in favor of those of the mining magnates and their political allies. The future of South Africa, Prime Ministers Louis Botha and Jan Smuts had long maintained, was married to gold and Great Britain. The National Party proposed an alternative: the country's wealth would be localized through manufacturing and agricultural production for the home market.

This appeal was not unusual: independent states outside Europe had long sought to privilege local, national interests in order to advance within the international division of labor and wealth, particularly in periods of global economic and political crisis. The 1920s offered just such conditions across Africa, Asia, and Latin America.[1] Yet only a very few states succeeded in these attempts in the interwar period. South Africa was one of these. Even before the global crash of 1929, the state had already reconfigured relationships with core countries to produce a remarkable leap forward to the production of consumer and machine goods based on an integrated steel sector. Net industrial output grew by 63 percent during the five years before 1929, a trend that continued, at a slower pace, in the five years after 1929.[2] As this program was put in place in opposition to core states, unforeseen conflicts emerged with neighboring states and producers, leading the South African state to reconfigure labor, capital, and market relationships across the region as well. From an almost flat peripheral plain emerged, for the first time, a highly uneven and integrated region with semiperipheral South Africa rising at its center.

How this transformation came about remains a lacuna in the history of southern Africa. State policy from 1910 forward had been firmly based on the principle that the future of the country's white population rested on gold and the British colonial system. Post–World War I upheavals called this

principle into question, challenging long-standing beliefs in British hegemony, the free trade system, and South Africa's place in the world economy.
The pivotal development was a confrontation over the policies and practices
that had sustained mining and agricultural exports at the expense of industrial and agricultural production for the home market. Policy discussions
initially focused on the British colonial trade policies that had underwritten
the country's path of accumulation for almost a century. Changing these
policies could potentially reconfigure the center-hinterland relationships
that bound South Africa with core areas of the world economy. What was
so surprising is that changes in relations with Europe and North America
would so substantially alter South Africa's relationships with neighboring
colonial territories, white settlers, and African communities.

Free Trade and the Colonial Order

Throughout the nineteenth century the development of the lucrative markets of southern Africa had been intimately tied to British control over trade
and tariffs. The initial period of British rule at the Cape witnessed the application of mercantilist policies;[3] however, by 1850 the triumph of British
hegemony led to the successive application of free trade policies throughout
the world economy. While some areas of white settlement such as Canada
moved toward protectionism at the expense of Great Britain as early as 1846,
the Cape, still a small colony and militarily dependent on Britain, adopted
a free trade commercial policy. Not even the granting of local Responsible
Government status in 1872 shook the Cape's belief in free trade.

The construction by white settlers of new political territories in Natal
(annexed by Great Britain in 1843) and the Afrikaner republics of the
Transvaal and Orange Free State (which gained independence in 1852 and
1854, respectively) led to increasing tensions over the direction of trade
and the substantial revenues derived from customs and transport tariffs. A
second set of conflicts erupted as urban and mining centers in the interior
were developed, and different territories began to struggle over access to
markets for local products sheltered from distant overseas competition by
factors such as weight or perishability (e.g., meat, maize, dairy products,
wine and spirits, carts and wagons).

Natal, seeking to capture trade with the interior, consistently established
lower duties than the Cape. The Transvaal, for its part, signed a treaty of
friendship and commerce with Portugal in 1869 and proclaimed import
duties significantly higher than those effective in either Natal or the Cape.
All these actions threatened the Cape Colony's struggle to remain the dominant political power in southern Africa. As control over transport lines
and trade to the interior increasingly passed out of its hands, the Cape

unsuccessfully attempted in the late 1880s and 1890s to create a common customs union. With the advent of gold mining in 1886, the Transvaal was provided with the means to dramatically free itself from demands emanating from the British Cape.

Following the defeat of the Afrikaner republics in the Anglo-Boer War (1899–1902), Britain was finally able to impose its colonial authority throughout the area. The result was a customs union that included the Cape, Natal, the former Afrikaner republics, Southern Rhodesia, British Bechuanaland, and the Basutoland Protectorate; Swaziland and Northwestern Rhodesia joined in 1904 and 1905, respectively. The basic principle of this union was the creation of free trade among the signatories, which would allow the free flow of goods and labor to and from centers of low-wage, primary production across southern Africa. Such a principle did not apply, however, to foreign countries outside the region, reflecting the demise of free trade as older industries in Britain were increasingly pressed by younger, industrial competitors located in rising core powers. The United States in particular had already surpassed Britain as a supplier for many of the advanced goods required by the mining and agricultural communities of southern Africa.[4] Following the movement for imperial preference in Britain, Lord Milner accordingly forced upon the Customs Convention of 1903 the acceptance of *preferential* duties for British products across the board.

Regional interests quickly pressed for the revision of the agreement. Each of the major political partners to the agreement made demands reflecting their different locations within southern Africa's markets. Southern Rhodesian officials, corresponding to their country's lack of industry and distance from the coast, wanted cheap imports and thus lower duties. Officials representing the Cape Colony and Natal sought higher revenues, duties on goods that would compete with their own products, and imperial preference. Representatives of the Transvaal, situated in the heartland of economic activity in the region, demanded cheap imports for mining production, while at the same time favoring duties on goods from *both* other South African colonies and overseas areas. The final result was mixed: revision of the agreement in 1906 saw preference on goods from the United Kingdom extended, while duties were generally raised for revenue purposes. Nascent manufacturers had little if any role in these discussions; as the 1908 Customs and Industries Commission noted, "Apart from mining and agriculture the industries at present in operation in this country are few in number."[5]

Subsequent intercolonial meetings settled none of these disputes within or between the colonies. Indeed, they revealed instead, in the words of the last intercolonial meeting in 1908, the "practical impossibility under existing conditions to reconcile the financial requirements and economic policies of the various South African governments."[6] With the creation of the Union of South Africa in 1910, the adjustment of existing colonial duties and agreements (including a Portuguese East Africa–Transvaal treaty) fell squarely on the parliament of the new Union, which would have to decide whether to adhere to the economic policies established under direct British rule or to chart a different course.

Smoke and Mirrors: Early Union Government Policy

One of its first acts of the new Union government was to appoint a Commission into the Conditions of Trade and Industries under the chairmanship of T. M. Cullinan. The commission's first policy recommendation read: "The Commission considers that it is in the best interests of the country as a whole that adequate protection should be given to agricultural and industrial undertakings."[7] Such statements did not mean assistance to manufacturing as many have asserted, since "industry" in the terminology of the day included primary-product "industries."[8] South Africa's manufacturing future was, in the view of the commission, hemmed in by the insuperable handicaps of a small, widely dispersed home market, world market competition, a high cost of living, and a high (white) wage structure. As for protection, the commission noted that it had "in many instances, been asked to recommend prohibitive rates of duty, but its aim is not to coddle but to assist. . . . Prohibition or excessive protection would lead to inefficiency and eventual decay, as the healthy stimulus of competition would be absent."[9] The Union's new tariff would remain an instrument for generating revenue, and not a tool for altering the free flow of manufactured goods into the country and the accelerated export of primary products and raw materials.

Nascent manufacturers, who had expected support, were dismayed. While the new government's quick creation of a Department of Commerce and Industries had hinted at support for manufacturers, the commission's report and the change of the department's name to the Department of Mines and Industries revealed the government's real intent. Rising in defense of an industrial future for South Africa was William J. Laite, the primary champion for manufacturers throughout the first half of the twentieth century. Drawing on observations from an extensive tour of Canada, the United States, and Australia, Laite launched a full-scale attack on the commission in his book *The Union Tariff and Its Relation to Industrial and Agricultural Development.* His opening sentences led the charge: "With the publication of the Majority and Minority Reports of the Industries Commission early last year, the industrial community realized the utter futility of expecting a proper appreciation of its needs at the hands of men whose position, training and interests necessarily influence their judgment when dealing with economic problems."[10]

Laite then proceeded to demonstrate that the commission's policy both ignored the lessons of successful manufacturing countries' tariffs and the necessity, as local manufacturers argued, for a permanent tariff board with broad investigatory and regulatory powers. Industrialists similarly argued the need for a separate ministry to handle commerce and industry. Such appeals fell on deaf ears.

The outbreak of World War I forced the government's hand as the links between South African producers and their overseas suppliers were broken. South Africa's entry into the war on the side of the Allies worsened the situation by committing the government to supply goods to the war effort. Under these conditions the government in October 1916 appointed, following an initiative of the Councils of the Scientific and Technical Societies of South Africa, an honorary Industries Advisory Board. Yet notably absent from the board's terms of reference was any mention of customs and trade policies. In November 1918 the board finally received a mandate to investigate the tariff question, although the government made it quite clear to the committee in private communications that it would not consider any revision of the tariff.[11]

The final report of the board in April 1920 confirmed the government's stance. While the board proposed a three-column "scientific" tariff, only a few, relatively small increases in tariff duties were recommended in the "Industries" column.[12] Indeed, the future for manufacturing was made even dimmer as the third schedule for commodities to be used in manufacturing *lowered* import rates for many products capable of being produced in South Africa (e.g., chemicals, papers, cloth). As for "infant industries," the full board in its report recommended no protection at all: "It does not appear to be fair or reasonable that a community generally should be penalized in order to assist in establishing these struggling industries."[13]

In 1921 the debate over trade policy quickly shifted to a new Board of Trade and Industries. Designed to be a weak and quiescent adviser to the government, this board was composed of four full members and one secretary, and was overseen by three government officials from the very departments that had the most to lose from any independent initiatives on the part of the board: Mines and Industries, Customs and Excise, and the Railways and Harbours Administration. At its first meeting, Acting Prime Minister F. S. Malan told members to avoid "the general question of industry as a whole," and to be "reasonable" and "practical" regarding protection.[14] They were, furthermore, neither to schedule public inquiries without ministerial approval nor to regard themselves "as holding a roving commission."[15]

Manufacturers were quite dissatisfied by a board so limited in its powers.[16] Even members of the board fought against the restrictions on their activity. They first presented their own broad interpretation of their terms of reference;[17] they then threatened to resign in order to prepare the way for a reconstituted board.[18] In 1923 they were finally given a few statutory powers regarding the collection of evidence.[19] By this time local producers were pleading for support as the protection afforded by wartime conditions had faded away. Yet once again the government declined to provide any significant measures of assistance. When a subcommittee of the Advisory Board of Industry and Science recommended duties up to 40 percent on boot and shoe imports—one of South Africa's premier industries at the time, which was on the verge of complete collapse[20]—the government responded with a very limited import permit system. Fifteen years after the establishment of the Union, there was thus little prospect of the state directly promoting industrial activities. For manufacturers, who saw their counterparts in the other white Dominions securing the fruits of protection, this was intolerable.

The Pact in Power: South Africa versus the North

On June 30, 1924, the coalition of the National Party and the Labour Party assumed the reins of government. Among the very first actions of the new government was a wholesale reassessment of the Union's long-standing customs and tariff policy. Toward this end, it reconstituted the Board of Trade and Industries, greatly enhanced its powers, and instructed its new members to completely recast the Union's customs tariff. The break with the past was evident in the board's personnel, who had few links with the dominant economic powers of the day. Of the four—A. J. Bruwer, M. H. de Kock, F. J. Fahey, and H. E. S. Fremantle—only Fremantle had ties with previous boards and he would serve less than a year. Chairing the board was Bruwer, who, like his fellow board member de Kock, had studied and received his PhD not in Britain, or even Holland, but in the United States; Bruwer's pro-protectionist dissertation had just been published in South Africa.[21]

Defenders of past policies, particularly those attached to mining and the import-export trade, were not pleased. In the words of the "Lion of Commerce," J. W. Jagger, the board was "with one exception, young and enthusiastic economists equipped with University degrees but no business experience."[22] Proponents of protection, such as the editors of the *South African Printer and Stationer*, attacked Jagger in turn: "The right hon. gentleman has long been a pillar of strength among the dwindling band of whole-hogger stalwarts who would, if they could, tie South Africa to Free Trade and free labour as the sacred ark of sound economic theory."[23]

The board's first report in December 1924 restated many of the arguments in Bruwer's dissertation. Whereas previous boards had assumed the inviolability of imperial preference, the new board vigorously attacked its colonial origins: "In spite of the fact that South Africa was definitely against preference, the scheme [British Milner's preference proposals] was carried through."[24] Statistical data were advanced to show that the Union treasury was robbed "for the benefit of British manufacturers" and to the detriment of South Africa's industrial development.[25] The board's 1925 report on revising the tariff meshed these arguments with the government's declared policy of protection.[26] A two-schedule system of maximum and minimum rates was to be constructed, with imperial preference reduced to a quid pro quo basis. A third schedule would allow the free importation of goods necessary for industrial production. The board's recommendations thus deviated from past practice in three significant ways: the tariff became a negotiating instrument for all countries, infant industry protection was encouraged, and tariff assistance to any specific industry was to be "partly conditional" on the degree to which "civilized" (meaning "white" in the terms of the day) labor was employed.

Discussions of the board's report and the subsequent Tariff Act of 1925 have primarily focused on which "fraction" of capital or white labor controlled state actions, advanced the protectionist agenda, and benefited from it.[27] Yet there is little evidence in the archives or public record to support such an instrumental reading: state action was to prove far more autonomous and decisive. What was at stake was, as the chairman of the Board of Trade and Industries put it, "whether South Africa should become an industrial State or remain wedded for good to the purely extractive industries."[28] This was a policy that looked forward to the creation of an industrial sector, not one that was produced by powerful industrial interests.

One group clearly feared the worst from the Pact government: mining capital. Mining companies had openly sided with the South African Party during the election. As a *South African Mining and Engineering Journal* editorial put it in May 1924, "The attitude of the Nationalists and their allies of the Pact is . . . in the nature of a campaign of vendetta against the [mining] industry, and is carried on from day to day and from year to year with a venom."[29] What mine owners feared was increased taxation, alteration of labor supply arrangements, and a frightening away of foreign capital investment in the mines.[30] The announcement of a new Board of Trade and Industries and a firm policy of protection indicated, however, that the new government had grander plans.

As soon as the Board was reconstituted, the Chamber of Mines approached it with representations that echoed its earlier claims: "All other occupations, practically speaking, are subsidiary to agriculture or mining, and . . . the manufacturing industries already established must depend for many years for a market on the population engaged in them." The benefits of free trade were celebrated while denunciations were launched against "the adverse effect of a policy of protection on the two great primary industries of South Africa, Agriculture and Mining."[31] Protection could only hamper both "by increasing the cost of all machinery, implements and stores generally used in production; and indirectly by increasing the cost of labour consequent on the increased cost of living."[32] South Africa's future and salvation was to be found, the chamber and its allies argued, only in the theory and practice of free trade. The chamber refused to countenance any adjustments in the tariff.[33]

Members of the new board were hardly willing to be preached to in such a manner. Indeed, their attitude was one of barely cloaked hostility to the Chamber of Mines. In private communications with the minister of Mines and Industries, the board defended its treatment of the chamber and summarized the chamber's 1924 and 1925 submissions as a British imperial attack on the new government: "The Chamber's Statement of Evidence proceeded on very general and academic lines, and was in effect a treatise on the evils of Protection. It contained copious quotations from the writings of Marshall, the English Economist, and these were especially relied upon to indicate that industrial protection must indubitably lead to political corruption and the undermining of the State."[34] Such a statement was carefully crafted: in two short sentences it appealed to the widespread distrust of the mining magnates and Great Britain while depicting mine owners as attacking the new government as inept and corrupt.

The natural allies of the Chamber of Mines, the Chambers of Commerce, did not fare much better. Local chambers across the country were themselves split over the policy of protection, having fought bitter battles at past annual meetings of the Association of South African Chambers of Commerce (ASSOCOM), most notably in 1916–17. In general, the dominant Cape chambers along the coast promoted a policy of free trade and preference for Britain, representing as they did the big import-export houses with ties to London, while chambers in the interior, without such links and more closely tied to the domestic market and nascent manufacturers, were more sympathetic to the policy of protection. When the Executive Committee of the Southern Section, for example, sought to express its alarm at the rumors of the demise of imperial preference in March 1925, the Northern Section vetoed its proposed telegram of protest to the government.[35] Discussion within ASSOCOM over the government's new policy of protection was similarly divided, with different chambers across the country espousing conflicting positions. ASSOCOM's October 1924 annual congress could reach only a mild compromise with consequently little impact on the government's deliberations.[36]

If commerce and mining had little influence, to what extent can protection be seen as a victory for manufacturers, farmers, or white labor? Of the three candidates usually offered as the progenitors or beneficiaries of the new policy, white labor had the least direct and continuing influence. Its bargaining power was still in tatters from its defeat in the Rand Revolt of 1922. The Labour Party, moreover, remained very much the junior partner in the Pact coalition, and was to be eliminated as a significant influence after its poor showing in the 1929 elections. The National Party was, nevertheless, well aware that its tenure in office depended on continued electoral support from the white section of the working class, including both skilled workers and a broad stratum of predominantly Afrikaner "poor whites" and unskilled workers. The government's designs in this area indicated, however, that it sought to secure both white worker support and industrial peace between labor, capital, and the state—a very different program than support for labor's struggle against capital. The means to this end were quite clear: control market and workplace struggles as far as possible by incorporating white labor into government-controlled institutions, and expand employment opportunities through industrial development. At issue was not the overthrow of mining or agriculture by a "white workers' state," as some have asserted, but rather the stimulation of capitalist development (and employment for whites) based on industrial production for the home market.

The course of the passage of the 1925 Tariff Act demonstrated these aims and balances. As the Board of Trade and Industries met to consider tariff revisions, the Department of Labour forwarded to it labor's demands as composed by a "Conference of the Representatives of Organized Labour" held in Cape Town in August 1924. Among this meeting's resolutions— most of which called for the replacement of black labor by white labor in all fields of work—were those demanding that labor "be adequately represented on the Board of Trade and Industries" and that the board "be instructed to immediately investigate labor conditions obtaining in South African industries in consultation with the Ministry of Labour."[37] Protection for South African industries was also promoted, but "in no case should this be granted where employees in such industry do not include a fair ratio of civilized [white] persons."[38] Financial assistance to South African industries was also recommended, but only on the basis of "a ration [*sic*] of civilized to Native labour commensurate with the nature and circumstances of each industry."[39] Protective duties were specifically singled out for the printing trade and motor vehicle body-building industry.

The sweeping revisions of the conditions of production as proposed in these and allied resolutions far surpassed anything envisioned by the National Party. No mass displacement of black workers by white workers, or even racial ratios, would be imposed on private manufacturing. As for the board, it did make labor conditions a very vague criterion for tariff assistance. Recommendations for the motor vehicle body-building industry were also put forward along the lines that would benefit white workers.[40] Such actions, however, hardly met the major demands of white labor, and did not significantly affect either employers' policies or the application of protection in the interwar period. As others have demonstrated, the benefits for white labor from the tariff and related actions by the Pact government were minimal.[41]

The main beneficiaries of the adoption of a policy of protection were of course South Africa's manufacturers, whose efforts had been galvanized by the election of the Pact government. The pages of their journal, *Industrial South Africa (ISA)*, bristled with ideological justifications for protection and the practical program by which industrial development could be achieved. It quickly hailed the election of the new government, expressing full confidence in the new minister of Mines and Industries, F. W. Beyers.[42] Against the citations of Adam Smith and Alfred Marshall by the Chamber of Mines, the editors of *Industrial South Africa* countered with articles relying on the arguments of Friedrich List in favor of protection. Industrial development under the sheltering shroud of protection in Britain, the United States, and Germany was cited as further proof of the benefits of protection.[43] Repeated as well was the decade-long refrain of South Africa's lack of protection in comparison to the other white Dominions.

These efforts by manufacturers openly played to public opinion by pairing together the implicit economic nationalism of protection with the need to break with the invented tradition of South Africa as a primary producer under the British-led system of free trade. Manufacturers trumpeted government slogans in their favor, particularly Prime Minister J. B. M. Hertzog's statement that "to develop their [manufacturers'] industries would be in consonance with the motto: 'South Africa First.'"[44] Hertzog's opening remarks at the Eighth Annual Convention of the South African Federated Chamber of Industries (1925) were greeted with loud and sustained applause.

Prime Minister Hertzog's remarks at the convention, as well as the composition of the Board of Trade and Industries, should have indicated, however, that government policy was evolving along lines not wholly in consonance with manufacturers' desires. So swift were the board's deliberations that little direct input from manufacturers took place prior to the publication of the board's Report No. 56, which outlined the new tariff program. Laite, writing to the minister of Mines and Industries in his capacity as the general secretary of the South African Federated Chambers of Industry (SAFCI), expressed his concern at these developments by urging the government to immediately meet with manufacturers. Attached to the letter were minutes of a SAFCI tariff committee meeting that documented the serious difficulties of access to the board on the part of manufacturers.[45]

Agricultural interests had even less direct access and influence. Both mining and manufacturing interests had portrayed themselves as the natural allies of white farmers. In this endeavor manufacturing had been more successful, achieving support for protection from the South African Agricultural Union (SAAU) at its 1921 congress. By 1922 the President of the SAAU was writing to the chairman of the Board of Trade and Industries of the SAAU's "full confidence" in the Chamber of Industries, and that the "Agricultural Union has accepted the principle that industries must be fostered in South

Africa."[46] Yet opposing voices subsequently rose up from within the various agricultural unions that made up the SAAU, forcing the executive committee of the SAAU in 1923 to remind farmers of the 1921 resolution passed at the Cape Town congress by which it agreed "to cooperate with the Chamber of Industries in attempting to foster the growth of manufacturing industries in South Africa."[47]

There was to be no joint campaign by agriculture and manufacturing. As the *Farmers Weekly* editorialized, "There have, so far as we know, been no combined representations by the Chamber of Industries and the South African Agricultural Union, and we sincerely trust there never will be such combination."[48] Such divisions reflected those within the agricultural community as a whole: while some farmers were almost wholly dependent on the export market, others could and indeed would benefit from closure of the internal market and expansion of food processing industries.

The tariff bill was passed as quickly as it was formulated; an act of some 103 pages, it took only eight days to proceed from first to third reading. South Africa's relationship with its dominant trading partner, Great Britain, was immediately affected. Enactment of the most-favored nation principle resulted in a sharp fall in the next year of £250,000 in rebates for British goods entering the country.[49] This change was matched by a countervailing rise in rebates provided on South African goods entering Great Britain; by 1929 South Africa was receiving more in rebates than Great Britain.[50] At the same time, South Africa diversified its links to other core areas. Britain's share of South Africa's merchandise imports fell from an average of 55 percent between 1920 and 1924 to 46 percent between 1925 and 1929, and remained at these lower levels up to the eve of World War II.[51] South Africa's merchandise exports followed a similar trend, with Britain's portion falling from a 56 percent share in 1920 and 1924, to 49 percent in 1928, to less than 47 percent in 1938.[52] Meanwhile favorable trade agreements were reached with countries outside the British Empire, the most contentious of which was the German-Union Treaty of Commerce and Navigation approved in 1929. Increasing penetration of the South African market by German and North American manufacturers demonstrated that other core powers would seek out whatever opportunities might appear due to the demise of British imperial preferences.

The new tariff's direct impact in the domestic arena is harder to evaluate. To some, the Pact government had little if any beneficial effect for manufacturers, as in Yudelman's argument that "it is very much a moot point to what extent the Pact tariff-protection measures increased state aid to manufacturing."[53] It is true, as some charge, that contributions to the Union treasury from customs revenue did not increase. This was not, however, the aim of protection, and speaks little to the tariff's effect on domestic markets and production. In a similar fashion none of the direct inputs of agriculture and mining were targeted for higher tariffs; the burdens of protection for producers in these sectors would occur indirectly through increased wage pressures as the cost of living rose for employees. As elsewhere in the Southern Hemisphere, South Africa's infant manufacturing sector was heavily concentrated in light consumer goods such as food and beverages, clothing and textiles, furniture, and paper and stationery products. Protection for these industries proceeded through dumping duties, the raising of tariff walls for imports, and provisions for duty-free entry of raw materials and machinery required for industrial purposes.

The benefits became immediately apparent when manufacturers reversed their early post–World War I decline and experienced accelerated growth. Such expansion proceeded, moreover, through rising intersectoral linkages as manufacturing drew on local raw materials. While World War I had stimulated a reliance on local inputs (as would World War II), a sharp decline ensued after the reopening of the South African market to world competition after the end of the war. The levels attained during World War I were, however, equaled and significantly surpassed even prior to the collapse of world trade after the Great Crash of 1929.[54] Given the degree of industrial growth during the 1930s gold boom and World War II, early post–World War II analysts had no trouble pinpointing the importance of the 1925 tariff. As the Board of Trade and Industries noted in 1945 during an extensive examination of industrial growth, it was commonly accepted that "the assured protective policy declared by Government in 1925 has been very largely responsible for the industrial development since then."[55]

South versus Southern Africa: Regional Formation

As the Pact's new policies were put in place and South Africa's industrialization proceeded apace, unexpected conflicts emerged with surrounding colonial and settler authorities. From these would emerge a new regional formation that would persist long after World War II. Scholars have long argued that southern Africa constituted a region from the late nineteenth century forward based on mining and labor flows.[56] Yet if by "region" we mean not simply flows across a common geographical space, but integrated and uneven development with a minimal division of labor, then a "region" can only be said to have emerged in the interwar period. For it was during this period that struggles between the South African state and surrounding territories would forge for the first time substantive center-hinterland relationships and unequal exchanges *within* southern Africa. Seen in this light, the region of southern Africa emerged not out of colonialism, much less from cooperative alliances across territorial boundaries, but rather from the white South African state's drive to escape the effects of participation in a shared colonial role with its neighbors. The reduction of underdeveloping ties to the North would find its corollary in the advance of South Africa's underdeveloping ties to regional neighbors.

Southern Africa as an Open Peripheral Network

South African policymakers in the early interwar period faced a deeply entrenched pattern of production and trade across southern and central Africa, with multiple forms and sites of export-oriented, primary production. This network suited British hegemony, which rested on controlling the flow of commodities between the independently operated factories, plantations, and farms of core and peripheral areas of the world economy. The widening and deepening of commodity production along the outer boundaries of the world economy also required the regulation of flows of commodities, capital, and labor *within* peripheral zones. Southern and central Africa under British control exemplified this pattern.

As British hegemony declined and interimperialist rivalries broke out in the late nineteenth century, existing core-peripheral relationships became segmented within separate colonial systems. At the same time, acrimonious struggles erupted wherever competing primary producers possessing racial privilege asserted themselves, as in the conflict between settlers and British colonial officials over the growing revenues derived from the control of mining centers in the interior. When the Customs Convention of 1903 was imposed, squabbling quickly broke out among the signatories (the Cape, Natal, the Transvaal, Orange River Colony, Southern Rhodesia, Basutoland, and Bechuanaland).

At the time of the Union of South Africa's creation in 1910, both British and South African authorities expected the British protectorates of Bechuanaland, Basutoland, and Swaziland, as well as Southern and Northern Rhodesia, to join the Union in the near future.[57] A common customs policy, heavily preferential to Britain, would thus operate across most of southern Africa, while bilateral agreements assured continued flows of migrant labor, commodities, and capital with neighboring Portuguese territories. The railway network had also been developed, like the customs union, in order to ensure (1) the movement of goods to sites of low-wage, primary production, (2) the transit of commodities to, from, and through Great Britain, and (3) revenue to pay for colonial and settler administrations.

These patterns and policies reveal the limited applicability of the term "region" to southern Africa at this time. As an area of economic activity, it was marked by a division of labor suited to the production of products typical of a peripheral zone of the world economy. Integration of production processes hardly existed; there were few hierarchical, interindustry linkages.

The specialization of some areas as suppliers of labor indicated this as well, for they provided a low-wage resource for primary producing activities, and not, as was the case for overseas core areas, materials for the production of more advanced consumer or capital goods. The creation of the Union of South Africa did little to alter this open network that drained resources and profits to Europe. As argued above, South African state policy as it developed after 1910 under Prime Ministers Botha and Smuts remained dedicated to imperial preference and export production. Reliance on British tutelage in diplomatic affairs remained almost as complete: the Union was viewed and acted in the international arena as an appendage of Great Britain. No South African department or ministry of foreign affairs existed.

Passage of the 1925 Tariff Act indicated that the set of alliances underpinning open core-peripheral relationships had come to end. At issue was no longer simply a greater share of the profits associated with primary production, or even the flow of capital resources to the region to build larger and more rewarding sites of primary production. For what unexpectedly had to be faced were contradictory developments that arose across southern Africa from the implanting of core-like production activities in the sea of competing peripheral production processes.

On the one hand, the continuation of free trade within the region threatened the attempt by the South African state to further both the consumption and processing of South African natural resources and the expansion of the home market. If the promotion of industrial production was successful, for example, what would prevent South Africa's infant industries from drawing their raw materials (and even labor) from cheaper areas outside the country? If this took place the growth of national income and aggregate consumer demand inside South Africa could be considerably reduced as income accrued to, and was spent by, producers and workers outside the country. On the other hand, producers and consumers in surrounding territories, if bound by the regulations of the new South African tariff law, faced higher commodity prices due to the protectionist tariffs, and thus higher production and living costs, without reaping any of the benefits of South African industrialization. As these implications of South Africa's 1925 Tariff Act became apparent, they triggered a rolling wave of struggles between colonial and settler authorities across southern Africa.

South Africa and Southern Rhodesia: A Parting of the Ways

The most important and contentious conflicts erupted between Southern Rhodesia and South Africa. Rhodesia had been colonized by Great Britain in the early 1890s with the intent of encircling the Afrikaner South African Republic and curtailing the republic's growing economic and political power based on gold mining. The failure of a major gold field to materialize in Southern Rhodesia, and the subsequent promotion of settler agriculture, made Northern and Southern Rhodesia very much the smaller, poorer relations of South Africa by the opening decades of the twentieth century. While Southern Rhodesia had more settlers and a stronger economic base than Northern Rhodesia, both territories were quintessential primary producers.

South Africa by contrast had a much larger and more urbanized settler population, mineral and agricultural sectors, and natural resource endowment. As the land and mining speculation of the late nineteenth century gave way to the hard reality that Southern Rhodesia possessed far fewer natural resources, Southern Rhodesian settlers were forced to confront a destiny linked to that of their southern neighbor. The ties were already significant: South Africa's commercial and transport networks provided access to the sea and to overseas areas, while Rhodesian products such as tobacco and cattle, and particularly those grades unsuitable for overseas export, found ready markets in South Africa's growing urban and mining centers. Southern Rhodesia in turn contained the largest markets, after South Africa, in southern Africa. It was hardly surprising that the Southern Rhodesian Chambers of Commerce were, for example, part of the Association of South African Chambers of Commerce.

As these ties developed it was widely felt that the shared interests of white settlers would lead to a common political unit as was provided for in the founding constitution of the Union. This plan was abandoned for good in the turbulent years immediately following World War I. In 1922 Southern Rhodesians were offered the opportunity of amalgamating with South Africa. Despite a vigorous campaign waged by the South African prime minister, Jan Smuts (who hoped to enlarge his own political base), Rhodesian settlers voted against political unification. White Rhodesians, almost wholly of British extraction, were clearly appalled by both the 1922 Rand Revolt and the strength of Afrikaner nationalism to the south. Rejecting union with South Africa, Great Britain granted Southern Rhodesian whites Responsible Government status in 1923. Imperial affiliations, in this instance, overrode settler allegiances.

One of the effects of Responsible Government status was to endow local settlers with a voice in the regulation of the colony's affairs, including the area of trade and tariff agreements. At first glance there seemed little likelihood of this emerging as an arena of major importance or contestation: in the decades immediately preceding 1924 there had been relatively few disputes of substance between Southern Rhodesian and South African officials beyond the distribution of customs revenues. Political authorities in both areas desired to maintain the lowest possible costs for their primary producers, which dictated tariff schedules constructed with only revenue considerations in mind. Southern Rhodesia's first customs duties in 1899 corresponded closely, for example, to those of the existing customs union between the Cape Colony, the Orange Free State, Natal, Basutoland, and Bechuanaland.[58]

Consolidation of tariff structures was finalized in the 1903 South African Customs Union, an arrangement carried over in the later customs agreements of 1906 and 1910. Subsequent modifications of the South African tariff, most notably in 1914, were matched by new agreements between Southern Rhodesia and South Africa. In all these cases South Africa's tariff stood for Southern Rhodesia, South Africa collected duties on goods destined for Southern Rhodesia, and free trade in the products of the participating parties was guaranteed. A novel arrangement emerged to compensate Southern Rhodesia for any losses or other negative effects of these agreements on the colony's receipts from customs duties, which was the key source of the colony's income—providing a full 56 percent of total revenue in 1916.[59] Losses were in fact sustained because South Africa received duties on industrial raw materials imported from overseas, which were subsequently imported duty-free into Southern Rhodesia as part of the free entry of South African-manufactured goods. In this instance, South Africa agreed to pay £58,000 to Southern Rhodesia and £5,000 to Northern Rhodesia by way of compensation. Needless to say, South African manufacturers were pleased with this arrangement as it kept the door to the North open at a cost borne by the South African state.[60]

Free trade between the two territories facilitated an expanding exchange of products. In the decade after the 1914 agreement, Southern Rhodesia's exports to the Union grew sixfold, while imports from the Union increased by 150 percent.[61] Tobacco and cattle accounted for the bulk of Southern Rhodesia's exports, followed by wheat, butter, hides, and skins. Imports from South Africa were dominated by a wide variety of semiprocessed foodstuffs and consumer goods. Incipient inequalities were clearly at work as settler farmers in Southern Rhodesia increasingly looked to South Africa's large urban and mining markets, while the importance of Southern Rhodesia as an outlet for South Africa's nascent and small-scale manufacturing concerns increased.

Analysis of South Africa's share of total trade over this time period reveals, however, an underlying shift in the importance of the South African market to Southern Rhodesia. While South Africa's share of Southern Rhodesia's total imports remained steady, standing at 22 percent in 1914 and 21 percent a decade later, Britain's share fell from 55 percent to 45 percent over the same period. The Union's share of Southern Rhodesia's merchandise exports over the same span of time rose from less than 5 percent to 14 percent, while Britain's proportion fell sharply from 88 percent to 62 percent.[62] If we exclude gold exports, officially destined for Britain but subsequently reexported, South African and British markets took almost equivalent shares (52 and 49 percent, respectively) by 1924.[63] This was a noticeable shift from the situation in 1914 when South Africa held a 21 percent share and the United Kingdom a 42 percent share of Southern Rhodesia's exports.[64] Southern Rhodesia's producers were clearly becoming more and more dependent on South Africa's urban and mining markets.

It was against this background that negotiations over a new customs agreement took place in October 1924. The agreement reached in 1925 once again stipulated that Southern Rhodesia would adopt South Africa's tariff format, leaving South Africa to collect customs duties on its behalf. The Southern Rhodesian government, despite the divergence between its trade objectives and South Africa's, was forced to accept the radically new tariff nomenclature of South Africa's 1925 Tariff Act and to conform as far as possible to the customs laws, regulations, and interpretations in force in the Union. As a Southern Rhodesian commission retrospectively assessed the 1925 agreement, "The tariff of Southern Rhodesia thus came to be almost identical to that of the Union in form, but to differ materially in content."[65]

Far more serious conflicts arose as the South African government sought to raise protective walls against not just overseas imports but those of surrounding territories. The central items at issue were the cattle and tobacco exports of Southern Rhodesia. In 1924 the Union government pressed Southern Rhodesian officials to accept restrictions on these exports and succeeded: minimum weight limits of 1,050 lbs. for oxen and 750 lbs. for cows were imposed, while the export of lower grades of tobacco (scrap, dust, and stems) was prohibited altogether. Pact ministers trumpeted such results to South African farmers, proclaiming that 750,000 lbs. of tobacco had been excluded by these measures. Weight restrictions on cattle, however, were primarily designed against the smaller cattle of African farmers. Still, as one South African member of parliament put it, he "did not know of a cattle farmer in the Transvaal who would be satisfied with the agreement."[66]

Such restrictions, when placed in light of continued access to Southern Rhodesia on the part of South Africa's growing manufacturing sector, considerably exacerbated the unevenness of the trading relationship between the two territories. In 1924 Southern Rhodesia exported to South Africa 90 percent of the value of its merchandise imports from South Africa; by 1929 this ratio fell to less than 50 percent,[67] with Southern Rhodesia exporting primarily foodstuffs to South Africa and receiving semimanufactured goods in return. Southern Rhodesia exported raw tobacco to South Africa, which returned to Southern Rhodesia, for example, in the form of South African-manufactured cigarettes.

By the late 1920s, Southern Rhodesian officials were increasingly agitated by their inherently unequal relationship with South Africa. In early 1928 the controller of customs recommended that the customs agreement be terminated; the treasurer, in a private memorandum to the prime minister, advised against this, noting that the moment was politically inopportune and that the economic grounds for termination had not been adequately considered.[68] In March 1929 the Southern Rhodesian government finally requested a revision of the 1925 customs agreement, demanding more tariff autonomy, a closure of tariff loopholes presented by the disguised importation of overseas goods from open stocks in the Union, a securing of imperial preference, and the prevention of the automatic extension to Southern Rhodesia of the Union's growing trade treaties with foreign powers. The last two items, and indeed the whole question of revision, was triggered by the South African–German trade treaty of 1929, which challenged Southern Rhodesia's long-standing cultural and economic ties to Great Britain.

Meetings between government officials soon ended in complete deadlock, threatening to rupture the long-standing principle of free trade between the territories and a common external tariff. Southern Rhodesian officials, confident of the righteousness of their position, published an official account of the course of negotiations, to which South Africa's finance minister, N. C. Havenga, replied by way of a public speech; both statements were published widely in South Africa.[69] The long-term implications were starkly put by the governor-general in South Africa, who foresaw that the lack of an agreement would lead British South Africa to break up into "enclaves of protected areas."[70]

The reason for disagreement between the two parties was not hard to discern: far from recognizing Southern Rhodesian complaints, the South Africans used the occasion to press forward their already considerable advantage. In addition to retaining previous limits on lower grades of tobacco and cattle, the South Africans now proposed that tobacco imports be limited to a maximum quota of 2,000,000 lbs. of Virginia leaf and 400,000 lbs. of Turkish leaf. At the same time, South African officials expected to retain the applicability of South Africa's protectionist duties as well as free access for South African producers to the Southern Rhodesian market.

The danger for Southern Rhodesians in taking a strong stand was the threatened loss of access to the South African market. When the Rhodesian Agricultural Union held its annual meeting after the breakup of the conference, an extraordinary deputation of the prime minister, state treasurer, and two agricultural delegates were sent to the meeting to solicit support for a hard bargaining position against the South African demands. They did manage to receive a unanimous resolution in their favor. This occurred, however, only after government officials sketched a future of bright possibilities even if the agreement with South Africa lapsed. Delegates were told of the prospect of establishing tobacco and foodstuff processing factories in Southern Rhodesia, of capturing new markets to the north, and of the rise of anti-imperial sentiments in South Africa.[71]

Reaction on the South African side of the border to the breakdown of negotiations was marked by almost universal dismay on the part of those tied to markets to the north. The failure of negotiations was a surprise, and many business journals editorialized against the government's failure to consult businessmen, farmers, and merchants.[72] Those most immediately affected by the lack of any customs agreement, the commercial community, presented a detailed memorandum to the government backing the demands of Southern Rhodesia.[73] Representatives of manufacturing capital, defending access to a major market, argued that "geographically Rhodesia is part of the Union's natural trading area," while chiding Southern Rhodesians for expecting to develop secondary industries of their own.[74]

South African mining houses, which had vigorously opposed the South African government's turn toward protection, found common cause with the Rhodesian Chamber of Mines and endorsed its resolution calling for reciprocity and free interstate trade.[75] Mining spokesmen raised the specter of Southern Rhodesia attracting capital inflows and industrializing at the expense of South Africa: "If Union manufacturers are heavily taxed at the border, will not capital be transferred from here to carry on factories in Rhodesia? Many of our manufacturers are said to sell sixty percent of their products in Rhodesia, and if a transfer of capital will ensure a continuance of their trade they are not likely to hesitate long."[76]

This was a wildly optimistic assessment of the prospects for foreign investment in Rhodesia. The threatened loss of the Rhodesian market was, however, a very real one; certainly the Rhodesian market could be supplied by overseas producers. And this in turn affected agricultural interests in South Africa as well. As the *Farmers Weekly* pointed out, Union tobacco men might gain the internal market if Rhodesian tobacco was eventually excluded, but they would "feel the rebound from the blow that will fall on the Union's tobacco manufacturing industry." Lack of access to the Southern Rhodesian market was likely, it was further argued, to have "a serious adverse effect upon the Natal sugar trade, as well as upon wine and other agricultural products."[77]

In the end Southern Rhodesian hubris gave way to a recognition of the necessity of maintaining even limited access to the South African market in a period of worldwide decline in the demand and prices for the colony's exports.[78] The agreement reached in 1930 thus demonstrated the strength of the South African government's hand: South African producers retained generous access to the Southern Rhodesian market, while Southern Rhodesian producers were circumscribed from competing in the South African market. Southern Rhodesian exports to South Africa of beef, scrub cattle, and the lower grades of tobacco were prohibited, while the higher grades of tobacco were limited to 2,400,000 lbs. a year. Southern Rhodesian tariff increases on a selected group of South African imports (tobacco, spirits, and motor vehicles) were minimal, and duties were set at rates lower than those levied on British goods. The South African government further agreed to pay duties on South African manufactures exported to Southern Rhodesia; in this manner the market price of South African manufactures was unaffected by tariff rates. Southern Rhodesian officials were incensed when South Africa's finance minister argued that sooner or later this payment would end with Southern Rhodesia's entrance into a political union with South Africa.[79]

No sooner had the ink dried on the 1930 agreement than Southern Rhodesians once again began to decry the inequity of their relationship with South Africa. Yet negotiations for a new agreement in 1935 only confirmed past patterns. As the Rhodesian prime minister argued, "The Union [should] give Rhodesia an unrestricted market for tobacco and cattle, thus re-establishing the principle of free trade between the two Territories."[80] As Phimister's account of this period from the Southern Rhodesian side of the border argues, "The South African response was nasty, brutish and short. Not only was there no question of the market being expanded, but existing concessions were to be withdrawn."[81]

Exacerbating the Southern Rhodesians' sense of mistreatment was a rapid acceleration in the downward spiral of commodity prices after the Great Crash of 1929 and increasing fiscal stringency. In the mid-1930s a decisive break finally occurred, with Southern Rhodesia ending its participation in the customs union and constructing its own tariff schedules. Yet this was not a replication of South Africa's much earlier move toward protection: these efforts were undertaken with the aim of defining the Southern Rhodesian market as a bargaining lever to open overseas markets to Southern Rhodesian primary-product exports. Predictably, Great Britain was given most-preferential treatment. Pressed too far by the South Africans, Southern Rhodesia retreated into the empire.

Northern Rhodesia and the Imperial Embrace

One of the fruits to be reaped through the British connection was privileged access to other colonial markets, a card the Southern Rhodesians expected to play in the north as they moved away from South Africa and cemented their relationship with the British. While Botswana, Lesotho, and Swaziland remained inextricably bound into the South African Customs Union, Northern Rhodesia was a very different case. Far from the borders of South Africa, and lacking the status of Responsible Government given to Southern Rhodesia in 1923, Northern Rhodesia maintained customs and tariff policies that were directly controlled by British colonial authorities and followed closely those of Southern Rhodesia and South Africa.

Such policies lasted until the early 1930s.[82] Even prior to the breakup of the South African–Southern Rhodesian agreement and the Great Crash of 1929, Northern Rhodesian settler farmers had clamored to protect their small but growing local market from being flooded by the products of both Southern Rhodesia and South Africa. Mining of extensive copper deposits in the late 1920s accentuated such arguments, as growing local demand was met by increasing imports of maize and semiprocessed food-stuffs (meats, dairy products, etc.). Squeezed between South Africa and Southern Rhodesia, Northern Rhodesian authorities often found that South Africa offered better terms of entry for Northern Rhodesian goods, and better financial rebates from the collection of import tariffs along the coast. Southern Rhodesia's manipulation of railway tariffs to the disadvantage of Northern Rhodesian farmers only further aggravated discontent with the Southern Rhodesian government. Only direct intervention by the Colonial Office in 1930, for example, overrode Northern Rhodesian settlers' desire to strike a separate deal with independent South Africa at the expense of colonial Southern Rhodesia.[83]

As South Africa inexorably moved toward protection of industry, and Southern Rhodesia toward withdrawal from the customs union, ever more difficult decisions were forced on Northern Rhodesian officials due to the closure of access to the Union's large markets, especially for tobacco. While colonial administrators remained defenders of mining and railway interests, the clamor by settler farmers for protection rose in volume. At issue was not the development of local commerce or manufacturing, but rather the protection of the home market for local foodstuffs, particularly those suited to feeding the workforce of the new copper mines in the north of the territory.

By the mid-1930s such complaints bore fruit as Northern Rhodesian colonial authorities imposed dumping duties and protectionist rates on competing imports from *both* South Africa and Southern Rhodesia. This sheltered the home market for settler farmers—who simultaneously waged a program to exclude African farmers from market production—and allowed the Northern Rhodesian administration to bargain for access to export markets. What Northern Rhodesian officials could not be persuaded to do, however, was to implement protection for manufactured goods; in this arena imperial and mining interests held sway. Northern Rhodesia, far from following the trajectory of either Southern Rhodesia or South Africa, remained captive to the designs of the British Colonial Office.

Mozambique: South African Dependency or Portuguese Colony?

A far more complex situation was revealed in the changing structure of South Africa's relationship with Mozambique. Here South Africa confronted neither a weaker settler power nor British colonial administrators, but rather the political and economic interests of metropolitan Portugal. As one of the least developed countries in Europe, Portugal was able to retain formal control of its African colonies only with British backing. Once the Union of South Africa was established and Smuts emerged as a confidant of the British establishment, British and South African interests began to override the Portuguese-British alliance. Brazen efforts by Smuts to undermine the Portuguese hold over Mozambique, and deepen its dependence on South Africa, were surreptitiously supported by Britain and British firms.[84]

Mozambique was important to South African firms and the South African state in three areas: (1) the provisioning of labor to South Africa's gold and coal mines and sugar plantations, (2) the status of Lourenço Marques (present-day Maputo) as the nearest port by far to the Rand, and (3) the exchange of commodities produced by the two areas. These relationships had been forged over the course of many decades. In 1869 a treaty guaranteeing free trade between the Transvaal Republic and Mozambique was signed. With the discovery of gold, the long-proposed rail link to the eastern coast became, with the assistance of German loans, a reality; Johannesburg and Lourenço Marques were linked in 1894. Agreements regulating the share of rail traffic between the Transvaal and the Cape, Natal, and Mozambique guaranteed at least one-third of the traffic to the line headed to Lourenço Marques.[85]

As the gold mines came into full production, the third pillar of the Mozambique-Transvaal connection, the labor supply to the mines, was constructed. Black Mozambicans, hounded by the local Portuguese administration's forced labor practices and legislation that made men seek waged labor, initially sought employment in South African mines on their own. It is not difficult to see why the mines were so attractive: rates of pay for miners were considerably higher than anywhere in southern Africa, up to five times as much as wage rates prevailing in Mozambique.[86] An agreement between the Transvaal Chamber of Mines and the Mozambican administration in 1896 allowed the Chamber of Mines to establish its own recruiting system in Mozambique while Portuguese authorities maximized revenue associated with a controlled flow of labor.

During the Anglo-Boer War, the British negotiated a modus vivendi regulating relations between the South African colonies and Mozambique. In exchange for labor recruiting rights for the mines, a reversion to prewar rail tariffs and the free entry into South Africa of the products of Mozambique's soil and industry were guaranteed. Political and economic interests in Natal and the Cape were incensed: in return for their support of Britain in the war, they had expected increased shares of the lucrative rail traffic to and from the Rand. Natal had also hoped to secure Mozambican labor for its collieries and sugar estates, while at the same time preventing competition from Mozambican sugar producers in South African markets. In 1909 the Transvaal and Mozambique governments signed a convention that was, in all basic respects, the continuation of the 1901 modus vivendi.

The formation of the Union failed to change these agreements to any significant degree. Indeed, for South African and British officials, closer relations between South Africa and Mozambique were aimed at asserting ever greater domination over the latter. Yet Smuts's persistent pursuit of formal control over Lourenço Marques in the 1910s and especially during and immediately after World War I was unsuccessful despite Portugal's extreme economic and political instability in this period. The scheduled expiration in 1923 of the 1909 convention, however, forced the issue.

Negotiations for the convention's renewal during 1921 proved extremely difficult. Smuts brazenly demanded an independent board to run the poor port facilities of Lourenço Marques and threatened to bypass the city with a new railway line from the Rand through Zululand to the South African coast. Portugal's refusal to countenance any diminution of its sovereignty led to a deadlock and to the lapse of the convention in 1923. Portuguese officials did, however, subsequently agree to continue the labor recruitment agreement provisions of the old convention, viewing South African mining capital as their natural ally.

It was precisely at this moment that Smuts's government fell. The Pact government of 1924 thus confronted a situation where free trade no longer existed between Mozambique and South Africa, where no set percentage of the Rand's railway traffic was assured to Mozambique, and where access to Mozambican labor was nevertheless assured. There were significant advantages to South Africa in having this situation extended, particularly in light of the Pact government's new attitude to foreign trade relations. While labor flows and rail traffic held at prevailing levels in the years immediately after 1923, commodity trade fell on both sides. South African exports to Mozambique, which had averaged £245,000 annually between 1920 and 1924, fell to an average of £192,750 between 1925 and 1929, with notable losses being recorded for animals, maize, tobacco, and cigarettes. Imports from Mozambique fell by a corresponding amount, from a yearly average of £319,000 between 1920 and 1924, to an average of £275,000 between 1925 and 1929.[87] Major declines took place primarily for such agricultural products as fruit, groundnuts, and especially sugar. Attempts to negotiate a new agreement in 1925 and 1926 foundered on the South African demand that protection be upheld and that Mozambican goods be excluded from free access to the South African market. South African manufacturers were especially insistent that free trade not be reestablished, out of a fear that factories might be set up in Mozambique that would utilize its nearby ports and cheap labor.[88] In the end the Portuguese precipitated hard bargaining by announcing in 1927 the termination of the labor agreement.

Unlike its predecessors, the Pact government approached negotiations without any predatory eye over southern Mozambique. Nationalists had little interest in creating a broader British sphere of influence and were unwilling to countenance the close relations with Britain that would have been necessary to enhance their bargaining power with the Portuguese. The Labour Party faction of the Pact government had equal if not stronger reservations about the Mozambican connection. Here the impact of a continuous flow of Mozambican labor to the highly racialized, South African labor market was key. The availability of African labor was seen by a broad segment of the white citizenry as a tool of management to be used against skilled white labor. It was thus hardly surprising to find the newly formed Department of Labour, headed by a leader of the Labour Party, arguing that foreign black labor reduced the incentive of industrialists to train and use "civilized labour," and thus that labor recruiting in Mozambique should be entirely eliminated over a period of four to six years.[89]

Such grandiose proposals had little chance of prevailing as the course of subsequent negotiations demonstrates. Inconclusive negotiations in October 1925 had already, however, seen the Pact government place the principle of protection as a firm obstacle to a reversion to the terms of the 1923 agreement.[90] Discussions between Hertzog and the Portuguese government in Lisbon, while Hertzog was in Europe for the Imperial Conference of October–November 1926, were similarly inconclusive. Further negotiations did, however, lead to a new convention being finalized in Pretoria in September. When the contours of the convention became available, it was clear no simple modification of past agreements had taken place. Labor recruitment was assured but took a new form: a 25 percent reduction in the maximum number of gold miners over the course of the next five years was dictated, only the gold mines were allowed to recruit Mozambican laborers, and the length of contracts was to be strictly regulated. Mining capital's reaction was swift: "in place of safeguarding our supply of labour, the new agreement seriously prejudices the position of the mines."[91] The numbers of Mozambican miners would indeed fall in the next five years from nearly 110,000 to figures well below 80,000, with South African labor making up the shortfall.

Commercial interests pushed for even further restrictions on labor, transport, and trade links with Mozambique. As the president of the Chambers of Commerce argued, "Every native employed from outside South African sources who could be replaced by a South African native means the loss of a certain amount of purchasing power in the Union, and the more the Rand's imports come through Union ports and over South African Railways only, the lower is the incidence of the overhead costs of the South African Railways and Harbours."[92] To such voices were added those of sugar planters in Natal, who were now excluded from recruiting Mozambican labor, and who feared in turn increased competition for the remaining pool of South African black labor, particularly in Zululand, which the mines were targeting. Control over African labor had become increasingly important for sugar planters, as Indian workers deserted the fields for better avenues of employment. When the Chief Native

Commissioner for Natal visited planters' associations in 1928, for example, he was openly assailed over the implications of the 1928 convention.[93]

Protection of South Africa's home market did, however, offer relief to sugar interests. Sugar prices had fallen from £30 a ton in the early 1920s to £21–22 by the middle of the decade. Whereas previous conventions had allowed the free import of Mozambican sugar, the new convention simply guaranteed Mozambique treatment equal to that given other nations. Prior to 1924 this would have assured the free entry of Mozambican sugar. After 1924, however, the newly empowered South African Board of Trade and Industries lumped Mozambican imports with all others, and imposed corresponding dumping duties.[94] In this endeavor South African sugar planters were supported by industrialists.[95] Sugar imports, which had averaged £196,000 per annum between 1920 and 1924, fell to an average of £42,000 between 1925 and 1929.

Other commodity imports from Mozambique fell subject to similar restrictions during the Pact years. Most interesting of all was the case of cement, where the legacy of free trade left South African interests entrenched on both sides of the border. Formed in 1919, the Mozambique Portland Cement Company had an exclusive right to produce cement in Mozambique, and began to supply the Rand as the nearest coastal producer. The firm was, however, South African by birthright, having been registered in the Orange Free State, headquartered in Johannesburg, and owned by a majority of shareholders of South African origin.[96] In the face of a doubling of imports as a percentage of South African production between 1924 and 1926,[97] the Board of Trade and Industries succeeded in having duties raised against cement imports from twelve countries, including Mozambique. Far from supporting the expansion of South African capital in order to serve the South African market, the state constrained such novel operations. As in the case of Southern Rhodesia, the South African state's drive to advance its own industries led to the severing of traditional links between South Africa and its neighbors.

The High Commission Territories: Exceptions?

South Africa's actions vis-à-vis the High Commission Territories of Basutoland, Bechuanaland, and Swaziland during the interwar period contrast sharply with the treatment rendered to the Rhodesias and Mozambique. The reason for this is simple: from the earliest days of the century until the early 1960s South African officials presumed the Territories would eventually be incorporated into the Union. By World War I the Territories' trade, transport, and banking systems were already integrated with South Africa's, and would remain so throughout the interwar period. Imports from or through South Africa consisted largely of clothing, household goods, and agricultural supplies, while commodity exports comprised primary products such as wool (especially from Basutoland), cattle and stock products (especially from Bechuanaland), and mineral products (as in the case of cassiterite tin from Swaziland). Above all these stood the issue of the supply of migrant labor. The Territories offered an alternative, assured source of supply to Mozambique, and workers from these areas spent their wages either in South Africa or within the customs union. The Territories also held forth the promise—if incorporated—of relieving the pressure for the expansion of settler farming or the creation of Native Reserves as called for by the 1913 Natives Land Act. The experience of South West Africa, within the confines of a League of Nations' mandate given to South Africa after World War I, illustrated such possibilities: a rapid immigration of white South African farmers had taken place, with the white population of South West Africa doubling between 1914 and 1925 despite the repatriation of 6,000 Germans.[98]

When J. B. M. Hertzog came to power in 1924 he immediately, and ineptly, pushed Great Britain for the transfer of Swaziland, and if possible Bechuanaland, to the Union. Such efforts failed: British officials were ill disposed to meet the demands of the "anti-imperialist" Hertzog. Yet the British offered few prospects of weaning the Territories away from their long-standing orientation toward South Africa. There was, for example, little consideration given to developing the Territories' infrastructure or natural resources. Nor did the Territories, with their small settler populations and comparatively small agricultural markets, offer much in the way of increased commerce. The integration of the Territories within the South African Customs Union, and their dependence on South Africa's transport system, stalemated the situation.

South African policy toward the Territories during the rest of the interwar period accordingly vacillated between acceptance of them as economic partners and frustration at the inability to immediately bring them under South Africa's direct rule. While labor migration expanded, the exports of the Territories were harried by South African policy. Cattle exports were particularly subject to controls, with the restrictions placed on Southern Rhodesian cattle in 1924 shortly thereafter applied to the Territories as well. As Ettinger has shown in the case of Bechuanaland, such a limitation applied primarily to the lower-weight cattle of African farmers, and did indeed have a significant effect on cattle exports to the Union.[99]

The 1930s: The Effects of the Global Depression and Territorial Responses

By the early 1930s it was evident to all of South Africa's neighbors that the vision of the free flow of factors of production across southern Africa was in serious jeopardy. Indeed, "British South Africa" had steadily dissolved into a series of separate, and increasingly acrimonious, territories. As South Africa became increasingly independent in its actions, so too disappeared the grounds for Portuguese Africa's integration within an allied British–South African sphere of influence. The Great Crash of 1929 accelerated these strains inexorably. Plunging world prices for primary products, the break-down of world trading networks, a desperate scramble for export markets, and rapidly falling state revenues widened the gulf between ever more com-petitive primary producers.[100]

Under these conditions free and open trade within southern Africa was decisively shattered, most notably in the definitive break between the Rhodesias and South Africa over customs and tariff policies. South African hostility to primary product imports was quite apparent long before 1929; there was to be no relief provided by access to South African markets. The result was an urgent emphasis on the solicitation of access to overseas mar-kets, and more narrowly, the British market via preferential arrangements. The coming to power in Portugal of Salazar led to similar conclusions regarding Portuguese Africa. While the British Empire moved from free trade toward protected colonial trade, the *Estado Novo* Portuguese regime sought to carve out a separate economic system for Portugal and its colo-nies.[101] What South Africa's post-1924 policies had initiated, the pressures of the Great Depression accelerated: the southern African market was being inexorably divided into the multiple markets of separate colonial powers.

South African producers, and especially farmers, were not immune to the chilly winds blowing along the periphery of the world economy. Indeed, the early post–World War I fall in primary product prices had been instrumental in soliciting farmers' lukewarm support for the protection of infant indus-tries. Yet the impact of the Great Crash had a quite different outcome for the country as a whole. The South African government's first response to the Depression was to reassert its economic nationalism, most notably by refusing to follow Britain's departure from the gold standard in September 1931. With the South African pound vastly overvalued by comparison to the currencies of other peripheral producers, the country's economy quickly contracted as exports plummeted and capital fled.[102] Under these condi-tions the government moved toward coalition, and then "Fusion" with the political opposition. At the same time, the government, recognizing the inevitable, departed from the gold standard in December 1932. This effec-tively doubled gold prices overnight.

Revaluation resulted in an immediate expansion of gold mining and industrial production in South Africa, and vastly enhanced revenues for the state. Net (deflated) industrial output grew by 60 percent during the next five years, matching the 63 percent expansion between 1924–25 and 1929–30.[103] Expansion in the industrial and mining sectors of the economy, however, did not lessen the difficulties of disposing of the products of South Africa's settler farmers; protection and marketing boards were put in place to regulate the market and assist local white farmers. The dilution of economic nationalism after 1933 led to a curtailment of any new protectionist policies. No advances in protection for local industry were to be added to those achieved between 1924 and 1933.

This transition took place quite early in the Fusion years, as seen in the recommendations of the Customs Tariff Commission of 1934–35. While admitting that "a great deal of industrial development which took place after 1925 . . . is directly due to the stimulus given by the protectionist policy inaugurated in that year," the commission's report argued strongly against any attempt to create a "secluded economy," seeking instead to "maintain [South Africa] in equilibrium with the world economy."[104] The fruits of protection, in its view, were a high cost of living, inefficient industries, and ultimately a lower national income. South Africa's economic advance would, the commission argued, rest on primary industries exporting to the world market.[105]

Yet what had been created and fostered as a result of the 1925 Tariff Act and related measures could not be easily stripped away. As the commission itself argued, "If we had considered it possible to call a halt to the process of extending protection without detriment to the work which has already been undertaken under the protective policy, we would have preferred to recommend that no further protection be granted."[106] While protection was not to be extended in the 1930s, the inability to roll back the gains of the previous government's policies allowed the continued expansion of the country's manufacturing community. This became especially important as the world trading system collapsed amid the coming clouds of war. By initiating protection much earlier than competing states, South Africa was well positioned to weather the effects of a deepening world-economic crisis. Far from the windfall profits due to the gold boom being expended on imports, South Africa turned to the consumption of locally manufactured consumer goods and processed foodstuffs.

Regional Divergence—and Integration

By contrast to conditions of their counterparts in neighboring territories, white South African producers in the 1930s experienced very good years indeed. Alone among the states of southern Africa, South Africa would industrialize during the period between the world wars. These divergent outcomes directly reflected the global racial dynamics of those who held power. South Africa's international standing and power were directly attributable to its large white settler population, as was the case for Britain's other white settler colonies. Surrounding territories were still held firmly in the grip of a highly racialized colonial order, where colonial authorities had power and subject Africans did not. Where there were significant numbers of white settlers, matters were more complicated. In Southern Rhodesia, for example, forces seeking to follow South Africa's protectionist model existed. Yet the voices of primary producers held sway, and in the end Southern Rhodesia fell back within the role of privileged primary producer within the British Empire. Thus Southern Rhodesia would remain "in the late '30s, after nearly two decades of self government . . . a typically colonial economy with no industrial sector apart from the railway workshop and small firms engaged in wholly subsidiary activities."[107] Other colonial territories lacking the authority endowed by Responsible Government status, such as Northern Rhodesia, similarly followed suit. Portuguese territories, areas without independent settler voices of any magnitude, followed a path of forced enclosure within the folds of the Portuguese Empire. While South Africa broke with the colonial division of labor, other territories remained subject to colonial power and bound to produce primary products at low cost for their respective colonial powers.

These political trajectories were coupled at the same time with increasingly unequal and interdependent relationships across the social and economic landscape of southern Africa. Rather than a continuous decline in trade across the board—as might be extrapolated from trade rivalries and increasing levels of colonial control—a quite different pattern began to coalesce in the late 1920s and firmed up in the 1930s. For the Rhodesias, the percentage of their total exports taken by South Africa generally rose through the mid-1920s and then fell until the effects of World War II took hold. Imports from South Africa, however, followed a quite different pace and trajectory. While peaking during World War I, they remained at substantial levels through the 1920s and 1930s, and then accelerated as war again broke out in Europe.[108] Rather than Rhodesian markets being consistently severed from South Africa, South Africa was able to retain access for its goods, with South Africa coming to supply ever-increasing volumes of manufactured goods, and taking in lower levels of primary products in return. While southern African markets were thus segmented during the interwar period, this indicated not a unilinear, downward spiral, but rather increasing and linked disparities. For the Rhodesias, South Africa became a far greater supplier of imports than a consumer of Rhodesian exports, accelerating South Africa's emergence as a regional center for manufactured goods. Center-hinterland relationships that had previously been sustained between southern Africa and overseas core areas now began to be encapsulated within southern Africa itself.

Relationships between other southern African territories and South Africa varied, largely due to their different locations, export and import needs, and the timing of trade agreements. Official statistics for distant Nyasaland show very low levels of trade with South Africa, especially after 1930. For Mozambique the crucial turning point was 1928. Of the colony's exports, 37 percent went to South Africa in 1928; in the next year only 27 percent did so and the 1928 level was not reached again until World War II disrupted links with overseas suppliers.[109] Imports from South Africa peaked in the late 1920s and early 1930s, and failed to expand in the 1930s. This was a divergent trajectory from the Rhodesias, reflecting the imposition of the *Estado Novo*.

Of far greater importance to Mozambique, however, was the link provided by migrant labor. With the gold boom of the 1930s and the transition to a Fusion government the mines developed a strategy to expand foreign sources of labor, with little immediate success. The number of migrant miners that came from southern Mozambique had peaked in 1927 at the level of 76,000 miners (36 percent of the African portion of the mining labor force), falling to less than 40,000 in 1932 (19 percent of the African portion of the mining labor force).[110] While numbers rose during the boom years, regaining the 1928 peak in the 1940s, Mozambicans would never again represent as high a percentage of the mines' African labor force as they did prior to the 1928 agreement. While increasing numbers of migrants came from the High Commission Territories, the greatest expansion during the 1920s and 1930s came from within South Africa's borders. For the first time the majority of African miners were recruited from within the territorial boundaries of South Africa itself.

Meanwhile South Africa's imports from the region fell right up to the outbreak of World War II, while her exports to the region boomed, a gap that widened steadily in the 1930s and accelerated up to the war. Even more striking than trends in shares of trade is the relative importance of the trading relationship. It might be assumed that as the largest economic power in southern Africa, South Africa was inextricably bound into regional trade. Yet by comparison to surrounding territories, regional trading and labor relationships were *less important* for South Africa, since they formed a far smaller share of the country's total export-import trade, labor supply, and state revenue. Both export and import levels with surrounding territories were less than 10 percent until the eve of World War II, levels of regional trade significantly below those of the Rhodesias and most other surrounding territories.

As Hirschman stressed long ago, national power as expressed through trade correlates positively with the degree to which trade is heavily concentrated for only one of two trading partners.[111] A state with diverse trading partners has far more alternatives and is far more powerful in bilateral negotiations, for example, than a state whose trade is concentrated with just one or two states. The processes at work in southern Africa during the interwar period indicate the birth of this relationship within the region. For territories surrounding South Africa, South Africa's market was important for exports, imports, and often labor remittances and taxes. Yet southern Africa was far less important a trading arena for South Africa for both imports and exports. This reality sustained the hard bargaining position of South Africa vis-à-vis regional trade. As South Africa industrialized, and surrounding territories turned toward the closer and more readily available manufactured goods of South Africa, this relationship was only further enhanced.

This transformation could not have been imagined, let along predicted, during the opening decades of the century when southern Africa's place in the world economy seemed assured as a zone of low-wage primary production serving core markets. By the end of the interwar period regional markets had, however, become increasingly segmented and integrated, while industrial production blossomed in South Africa. Behind these developments, and the often bitter interstate struggles that accompanied them, stood a new reality: the South African state was acting in increasingly independent ways in relation to European powers, particularly Great Britain, *and* surrounding colonial territories. And at the root of this transformation stood the independent white power of the South African state as it operated in an increasingly racialized colonial order.

3

State Enterprise

When stock markets crash, banks default, speculative bubbles burst, and unemployment accelerates, calls for state intervention against the brutality of unfettered markets invariably follow. This was particularly true between 1914 and 1945, a period marked by the collapse of the international financial system, a "thirty years war" of sorts between the great powers, a deep global depression, and rolling waves of labor and social unrest. It would be, as Karl Polanyi eloquently argued, an epoch where widespread social and economic unrest eventually led political authorities to shelter their citizens from highly competitive and destabilizing market forces.[1] In rich, core areas of the world economy this led to corporatism at home and the pursuit of colonial monopolies abroad.

What was possible for the core states that Polanyi was writing about was rarely feasible, however, in poorer zones of the world economy. In these areas neither territorial conquest nor the state expenditures necessary to incorporate wide social strata was possible. Indeed, core states' ability to respond to the interwar crisis rested in no small part on their ability to block political and economic initiatives in peripheral, particularly colonial, zones and impose their own self-protective policies and programs. State formation in one zone and state deformation elsewhere was again the rule: as core states expanded their powers in the battle for hegemony, racialized, colonial control was extended and intensified elsewhere—especially by rising powers Germany, Japan, and the United States. As crisis moved toward war, this colonial process would be extended to subject populations within their home state boundaries as well.

By contrast to colonized peoples across Africa and Asia, South Africa's white citizens were able to respond to economic crisis by expanding local state power. This capacity would extend from the regulation of trade and tariffs to the building of great state enterprises. There was no natural national road to this outcome as is commonly asserted. The most detailed and penetrating study of the economic arms of the South African state for this period,

Renfrew Christie's study of the electricity generating industry, argues, for example, that both the state and private capital moved hand in hand to assure supplies of cheap energy, and that cheap energy and the political alliances it generated inexorably led to mechanization, and mechanization to industrialization.[2] Nancy Clark's work on South African state firms similarly stresses the felicitous alliances between the state and both national and foreign capital.[3] As Christie argues, "Electricity was not used in twentieth century South Africa to serve the common good, but was used by the capitalist state and by owners of private property to serve their own interests."[4] Or in the words of Clark, "The state corporations did not so much challenge private capital nor work as a 'tool' of private enterprise, but rather they provided a growing link between the state and the private sector."[5]

To accept both the capitalist nature of the state and its advocacy of capital accumulation hardly leads, however, to the universal conclusion that the state continuously acted in concert with dominant capitalist classes to promote industrialization. In South Africa as elsewhere producers of raw materials and primary products consistently worked against a national industrial project. Electricity, transport, or education may advance primary production; they hardly guaranteed in the first half of the twentieth century a transition from primary to industrial production. South Africa's interwar history of state intervention reveals these dilemmas very well. At issue was neither the capitalist nor interventionist character of the state; both had been evident since the earliest days of colonial rule. The question was rather quite different: what *kind* of capital accumulation would the state foster in South and southern Africa? Would South Africa escape the role of a low-wage, primary-product producer?

This debate was especially vociferous and volatile over the role for local state enterprises. Three key areas demonstrate the debate and different outcomes: the railway system, the creation of the South African Reserve Bank, and the founding of the Iron and Steel Corporation of South Africa (ISCOR). Both the railway system and the Reserve Bank were established prior to the election of the Pact government, which makes these cases particularly suitable for assessing whether long-standing state institutions led to industrial development. The case of ISCOR allows us to examine a totally new state enterprise.

Developing or Underdeveloping Rails

One of the most basic teachings of economic history is that modern economic growth is often driven forward by revolutionary advances in transport technologies. From the British industrial revolution to the industrialization of continental Europe, North America, and China today, modern transport systems have been deemed essential to economic progress. With no area farther than seventy miles from the sea, Britain's early industrial advances could initially rely on water transport for both the internal and external movement of light and heavy commodities alike. Across the larger land-masses of areas like North America, Asia, and Africa, it was the railroad that made possible the rapid spread of new production processes, the diffusion of market forces, and substantial population movements. The evidence from economic history seems inescapable and is often proclaimed: modern transport networks have been a powerful initiator of rapid economic advance.

Yet these are lessons from and largely for core areas of the world economy. They do not hold elsewhere: railways in nineteenth- and twentieth-century Africa, Asia, and Latin America invariably served as engines of extraction and underdevelopment. As Walter Rodney pointed out long ago, transport networks in Africa "had a clear geographical distribution according to the extent to which particular regions needed to be opened up to import/export activities. Where exports were not available, roads and railways had no place."[6] Under colonial rule roads and railways served to send primary products, produced by coerced and low-wage colonial labor, to feed the factories and populations of core areas, and facilitated the import in return of the mother country's high-wage manufactures. Some have claimed that in Africa "the railway was the pioneer of all development . . . providing means of access and egress at all seasons and promoting settlement, economic growth, social intercourse and political security";[7] however, this "development" was quite unlike that of core areas of the world economy.[8] Southern Africa did not escape this complex, with early roads and rails linking only concentrated centers of primary production. How South Africa escaped the fate of underdevelopment via extractive transport networks, and how this offered a hothouse setting for industrial development, remains a puzzle to be solved.

Southern Africa's lack of navigable rivers and high plateau interior posed considerable obstacles to the exploitation of areas beyond the coast, and the high escarpment rising along the coast was not breached by railroads until the exploitation of the Kimberly diamonds fields in the 1860s and the much larger Witwatersrand gold fields in the 1880s. The extension of rail lines into the interior was fraught with colonial rivalry, with the two British colonies of the Cape and Natal competing vigorously over the lucrative traffic to the Rand. The Afrikaner government of the South African Republic for its part discouraged rail links from British colonies to the Rand, and pursued an alternative and much shorter rail outlet to the sea through Portuguese-controlled Mozambique to the port of Lourenço Marques (present-day Maputo). In the end, lines reached the Rand from the Cape (1892), Lourenço Marques (1894), and Durban in Natal (1895). Fiercely competitive railway wars ensued, with the Transvaal government holding the master card of access to the Rand. Such conflicts played no small part in the events leading up to the Anglo-Boer War of 1899–1902.

One of the primary aims of the postwar British administration of the Transvaal and the Orange Free State was to unify southern Africa under British hegemony. Conferences to resolve fights over the division of the spoils of the Rand traffic were held in 1903, 1905, and 1906. Each meeting was followed, however, by a fresh outburst of quarreling among the representatives of the Cape, Natal, and Central South African (Transvaal and Orange Free State) railway systems. As the 1907 British memorandum to unify these territories reported, "Of all the questions fruitful in divergence of opinion or of interest to the Colonies of South Africa, there is none so pregnant with danger as the railway question."[9] As the memorandum argued, a single railway system would secure empire and white supremacy: "This divergence, this conflict of railway interests, this cloud of future strife, would vanish like a foul mist before the sun of South African Federation, but no other force can dissipate it. . . . The wealth of the Transvaal would be used, not in enriching a foreign port and a foreign country [i.e., Lourenço Marques and Portugal], but in building up a great white population in the British ports of British South Africa with interests identical with our own."[10]

The merging of the colonies' separate railway lines into the South African Railways and Harbours (SARH) created a network of more than 7,000 miles of line that linked all the major cities, towns, and ports. SARH was a financial giant: net profits during the initial year of the railway's operations alone topped £3.5 million.[11] Total operating expenditure of the railways in the early years of the Union averaged around £7.5 million; the total ordinary revenue of the Union government *and* its constituent provinces fluctuated by comparison around £12 million.[12] During the first year of the Union, over £1.5 million was contributed to the Union treasury out of railway profits—and this despite rate reductions.[13] British officials sought to make these resources independent of the South African government. According to the South Africa Act, a board of three commissioners was to be "free of political interference"; rates were to be based on "business principles"; and railway finances were to be kept totally separate from the authority and abuses of the treasury.

These restrictions did not last long. Increasing assertion of government influence culminated in a 1916 act that turned the Railway Board into an advisory body and vested real power in the minister of railways. Old political priorities resurfaced, particularly in the construction of new lines and the setting of "uneconomic" rates. From 1910 to 1916 over 2,000 miles of new track were also opened for traffic.[14] Checked by World War I and the early postwar economic crisis, new construction programs were again set in motion in 1922 and 1925, and South West Africa's rail network was absorbed in April 1922. Not counting the South West African lines, government railway mileage increased by 37 percent between 1910 and 1920, and by 66 percent between 1910 and 1930—an extraordinary achievement.

Such impressive advances created a rail system far beyond the typical colonial network that served only concentrated centers of export production. One could predict, however, which rural areas were bypassed by rail lines: hardly any area with independent black farmers was served by the railways. White farmers, an overrepresented political force even among the small, male, and white voting population, benefited mightily from the lines and, especially, their subsidized rates. Like railway administrators worldwide, managers of the South African railways could charge either "what the traffic will bear," or "the cost of service" for each specific commodity class. The principle of charging "what the traffic will bear" had long been enshrined in southern Africa. In the early days of the operation of the coast-to-Rand routes no other choice seemed possible: the Witwatersrand imported massive stores from overseas via distant coastal ports, yet generated little in the way of return traffic flow. The result was high rates on mining supplies destined for the Rand and low rates to encourage return traffic, with the coastal colonies adding low "preferential" rates for the few products of their own land and labor.

The new South African Railways attempted little in the way of rating reform: the Rand gold mines were charged high rates on all their stores and needs; white farmers, including those of the inland provinces, were charged low rates for their supplies and low rates on the movement of their output to local markets and ports (in the case of export products); high rates were set for imported manufactures except for agricultural machinery; and, finally, low preferential rates were charged on the movement of selected South African products from coastal to inland areas. These rating policies acted as a powerful stimulus to the expansion of local commodity production. Between 1910 and 1920, the Union became increasingly self-sufficient in basic foodstuffs. At the same time, agricultural and raw material exports boomed.

Quite unintended developments soon arose. The expansion of agricultural production after 1906, and to a lesser extent the blossoming of industrial production during World War I, completely undercut previous rationales for the railroads' revenue structure. Far from rail traffic being marked by heavy traffic to the Rand, by 1920 the problem was to find loads on the inland journey from the coast. As the general manager of the railways put the matter, "In former years, thousands of trucks had to be worked empty to the ports to carry imported traffic to the interior. To-day the position is completely reversed and train loads of empty trucks are hauled daily from the ports to the interior to carry the large export trade in coal, grain, etc., that has been developed. What has happened is that *high-rated traffic has materially decreased, while low-rated traffic has enormously increased.*"[15] The result was that "the position has now so changed that low-rated South African products and minerals have become the main traffic of the railways and high-rated traffic a diminishing quantity.

Over ninety per cent. of the railway traffic to-day is of South African origin, and over eighty per cent. of the total traffic is conveyed at very low rates."[16] "These changed conditions . . . ," concluded the GM, "altered fundamentally the economic position of the railways."[17]

This new pattern solidified in the years after 1920, with low-rated agricultural traffic maintaining its growth as local sugar, corn, maize, butter, and tobacco displaced the imported products that had fed the Union's urban population during the early years of the century.[18] Exports also continued to grow apace. In 1925, a year of good harvests, exports of maize alone reached a value of £5.7 million, becoming South Africa's fourth-largest export after gold, wool, and diamonds.[19] The main beneficiary, and indeed instigator, of transport development was quite clearly white agriculture. Export of maize from interior provinces in large quantities and the consumption of coastal Natal sugar in the interior (while Natal itself consumed imported sugar) were unthinkable without railway subsidies.

Manufacturing: Seizing Precedents

The principle of low rates for white farmers offered significant opportunities for nascent South African manufacturers—if they could seize them. Following the example set by white agriculture's support for low rates for goods produced domestically, South African industrialists pushed for correspondingly low rates for the movement of their inputs and finished products. Manufacturers were assisted by pre-Union preferential rates on the products of manufacturing. While these benefited coastal industries at the expense of inland industries, and thus caused dissension between coastal and inland manufacturers, low rates to assist all manufacturers slowly evolved under successive railway administrations.[20]

The advent of the Pact government in 1924 inaugurated a new phase of assistance to the development of national industry. Rates on a wide variety of South African manufactured goods were reduced, particularly in 1925. In contrast to previous rate reductions, goods destined for manufacturing purposes were singled out for tariff reductions. Many of these were agricultural products, indicating the promotion of new intersectoral linkages between agriculture and manufacturing.[21] SARH also moved to privilege local producers for its own considerable operations. The railways purchased large amounts of capital goods and road construction supplies, consumed vast quantities of stores in daily operations, and operated railway workshops that were among the largest industrial units in the Union. The railway administration was also one of the largest employers in the Union, with 70,000 employees in 1924.[22] And in 1925 a new program of branchline railway construction was announced, totaling over 900 miles.

The new government's desire to break the country's dependence on Great Britain and promote local producers quickly became apparent. Tenders by South African firms were granted a preference of 10 percent on articles produced in South Africa from South African materials, and a preference of 5 percent on articles produced with partial South African content. Great efforts were similarly made to utilize South African materials, such as wood, within the railways' own workshops. The practice of requisitioning supplies directly from Britain through the High Commissioner was terminated, with local purchases rising accordingly.[23] Placement of orders for new mechanical equipment also altered radically, antagonizing those who valued the Union's enduring alliance with imperial Britain. The editors of the *South African Mining and Engineering Journal*, noting that the railways under the Pact government had spent the astonishing sum of more than £3 million on tenders, pointedly noted that "from 55 per cent. to 65 per cent. of the Union's products have been going to Britain, but that country has had to be content with less than 20 per cent. of our Railway's expenditure abroad.[24] In addition, the activities of railway workshops were expanded, with more rolling stock being built or erected in South Africa itself.

As the largest state employer, the railways also became the centerpiece of the government's "civilized labour" policy that promoted the replacement of low-wage black workers with whites at higher levels of pay. In the first two years of the Pact, almost 12,000 white workers were added to the employment rolls of the railways. When previous governments had directed the railway administration to use small numbers of whites on relief works, the increased costs were duly noted and taken out of general state revenues. Under the Pact this practice ceased.

The Pact's swift reorganization of the railroads served to refocus attention on the Union's transport system. Mine owners, having been burdened with high tariffs from the earliest days of service to the Rand, were galvanized into action. The opening salvo in the mining industry's response to Pact initiatives came in a study commissioned from S. H. Frankel, senior lecturer in economics and economic history at the University of the Witwatersrand. Frankel's *Railway Policy in South Africa* was published in 1928, and was immediately hailed in prominent pages of the *South African Mining and Engineering Journal* as an "outstanding book."[25] It would remain for over two decades the touchstone for liberal attacks on government manipulation of the railways.[26]

Frankel set himself the task of proving that the state's intervention in railway management ran counter to constitutional principles and had retarded the economic development of the Union by placing undue burdens on gold mining, the primary industry of the land. Losses on branchlines, for example, were estimated by Frankel to have run to over £500,000 in 1926 alone, while the additional cost to railway accounts of the "civilized labour" policy was placed at a figure of at least £300,000 per year and "most probably equal to more than twice this figure."[27] Railway rates came under particularly heavy attack, with Frankel quite easily illustrating that the rates on goods consumed by the mining industry exceeded the cost of their transport by upward of an estimated £1 million per year.[28]

No matter how loud Frankel shouted, his arguments fell on deaf ears: the government was committed to use railways to pursue a "South Africa First" policy. Cost overruns and delays on a wide variety of projects such as branch-line construction, the scheme to extend electrification in Natal, and the erection of port facilities in Durban were well covered in the country's press but failed to change state policy. In 1930 and again in 1934 "investigatory" bodies appointed by the government rallied to the defense of the state.[29] Pact policies outlasted the government as well, for while the Fusion government in 1933 brought a substantial weakening of the thrust of state intervention, the upward revision of the international price of gold in the early 1930s undercut the case to reduce state expenditures and provide relief to mining firms. What the Pact introduced would remain a constant feature of the transport system well past World War II.

Struggle within the World Monetary System:
The South African Reserve Bank

In the critical field of finance there was no equivalent to the SARH: investment funds, loan capital, exchange rates, and monetary and fiscal matters were all deeply dependent on overseas markets and financial institutions. As the international monetary system began to collapse during the interwar period, ready channels of portfolio investment began to dry up, exchange rate volatility accelerated, sources of local credit tightened, and inflation began to increase. These effects were transmitted directly from the core to peripheral areas, threatening to disrupt the export-import trade, the development of more commercialized and mechanized sites of primary production, and the financial stability of local banking systems tied to distant British financial markets. Independent states often responded by searching for ways to exert national control over financial and monetary affairs, and South Africa was no exception.

One rather unexpected result of raising tariff walls was the encouragement given to direct investment, as foreign corporations sought to evade import tariffs; it was during the relatively prosperous 1920s that initial investments in South Africa by firms such as Ford, General Motors, and Firestone took place. These investments were largely restricted to factories assembling components shipped in from abroad. More importantly, this new form of investment did not address the decline in portfolio investment and the regulation of monetary and fiscal policy—much less enhance national financial autonomy.

One other possible route to national economic strength was precluded throughout the interwar period: the seizure or nationalization of the private banking system. Even if a South African government had desired to break boldly with *private* capital accumulation—and there were calls for the nationalization of the mines, for example, among the more militant sections of the labor movement—the social base, ideology, and resources for such an action were virtually nonexistent. Those calling for enhanced South African sovereignty over financial firms had a point, however, for the development of South Africa's monetary and financial system prior to World War I was the story of the growing command of the City of London and the empire.

The advent of World War I proved decisive in breaking the hold of British financial power. By the end of the war, not only were British resources seriously depleted, but the gold-pound standard that had underpinned the international monetary system—and with it Britain's preeminent position—had been set aside. This left the Bank of England, and British finance capital in general, fiercely scrambling to reposition itself at the heart of the international monetary system. It was an attempt that would ultimately fail. Key to the effort was South Africa, for any reassertion of London's primacy in global finance would have to rely on South Africa as the world's largest gold producer. The importance of privileged access to South Africa's gold output had been proven in World War I, when such control was instrumental in sustaining Britain's war finances.[30]

British domination of the South African monetary system was not a natural outgrowth of imperial expansion. Indeed, the early history of banking in South Africa was one of almost entirely local initiative. By 1861 there were at least twenty-nine local banks in the Cape Colony earning handsome profits.[31] By the end of the century, however, considerable concentration had taken place, especially during the 1873–96 Great Depression. South Africa's banking system came to mirror that of other Dominions such as Canada or Australia: it was dominated by the British-based "imperial banks." By the time of the Pact government, two imperial banks, the Standard Bank and the National Bank (which had merged with Barclays in 1926 and moved its headquarters to London), had absorbed no less than twenty-eight other commercial banks, while many local banks had collapsed during periods of economic difficulty.[32] As one assessment in the mid-1920s put it, "South Africa's grand total of about fifty banks established since 1837 has dwindled to five."[33]

By the 1920s over 90 percent of South Africa's banking assets were accounted for by the two imperial banks.[34] The banks' headquarters and a considerable proportion of their reserves were in London, while their general managers were drawn from Britain and were thus "less likely to be under the influence of either local politicians or local businessmen."[35] The imperial banks' extensive branch network and ability to control currency and foreign exchange stretched, moreover, across the whole of southern Africa. Foreign banks issued their own currency notes and set exchange rates through their control of London balances generated by the import and export trade. The imperial banks were not, in the words of one of their defenders, "attempting to force the pace of economic development and were very definitely not development banks."[36]

The financial disruptions attendant upon World War I and its immediate aftermath shattered this finely tuned network. During the war a semblance of stability was maintained by the fiction that war prevented the free movement of gold and thus the convertibility of British pounds and gold. South Africa for its part supported an embargo on the export of all precious metals. The formal relationship between the British pound, the South African pound, and the prewar gold parity of both was thus maintained. Yet sterling, once detached from an open exchange to gold, floated against neutral currencies, making gold pounds more valuable than paper ones. It was a condition fraught with jeopardy for both South African banks and British financial interests.

Such a situation could only be maintained if strict controls on the movement of gold were secured. For England, surrounded by water and under wartime regulations, this proved to be feasible. The prevention of smuggling out of South Africa was, however, an altogether different matter. South Africa not only had open land borders, but was home to numbers of foreign migrant miners (who by custom demanded payment in gold sovereigns), and an Indian population with extensive connections to foreign markets where gold was now worth more than in South Africa itself. And neither of these segments of the population, disenfranchised as they were of political rights, was likely to be persuaded to place "patriotic" duties above familial ties and economic motives.

The Armistice revealed for all to see the fiction of Britain's ability to maintain the prewar international monetary system and, with it, control over the finances of the whiter parts of the empire. When the British government was forced to end support for the sterling-dollar peg after March 1919, the pound (free of both dollar and gold) dropped in value against foreign currencies. The gold price in sterling thus rose, with immediate effects on both the value of the South African pound and gold production. The mines were able to realize an increased gold price, or "premium" in the coinage of the day (although this occurred only after much appealing to the Bank of England).

For the banks, Britain's newly revealed weaknesses portended disaster. They were committed to pay gold sovereigns for their South African bank notes, while gold sovereigns were now worth much more in foreign currency. Under these conditions, they could be forced to expend their London reserves for specie to be sent to South Africa to meet local demands. Such transfers could only take place at a considerable loss, given sterling's depreciated value and the maintenance in South Africa of the prewar gold standard rate. In short, it was no longer possible to sustain publicly or privately the belief that South Africa's monetary and commercial exchanges would move in concert with London's.

By the end of 1919, the situation of the imperial banks seriously deteriorated as assets hemorrhaged, threatening to trigger a financial crisis. Out of this conjuncture was born the South African Reserve Bank, representing, potentially, the strengthening of national financial power and the decline of British financial capital.[37] Among these possibilities it is the latter that deserves primary emphasis, for the Reserve Bank in its initial form actually represented as successful a defense of British finance capital's position as could have been expected in the early 1920s.

Imperial banking interests had long opposed the creation of a national public bank, and it was only worsening conditions in 1919 that forced their hand. Immediate relief was needed as events outpaced both the banks' ability to control the situation and the false hope for a reemergence of British financial power. At the same time, British interests feared the unregulated impact of the break in the sterling–South African pound link. As one bank historian put it,

> London . . . had become apprehensive of a serious break in the exchange, now that South Africa and the United Kingdom were no longer based on the same standard of value. If the Union Government would not, and the South African banks could not, effectively intervene, it looked as though the exchange rate would be forced to a point corresponding with the cost of importing gold, with the result that South African industry would be stifled and capital would go elsewhere—as appeared to be already happening in East Africa.[38]

Yet in opening the door to state regulation and assistance, both London and the imperial Banks were forced to confront long-standing calls for a fully empowered national bank, owned and operated by the state.

South Africans had legitimate cause for complaint with the imperial banking system. Continued shortages of capital locally were hardly helped by the flow overseas of profits and dividends, and by local banks' practice of holding their assets in London. Strong elements in both the Labour Party and National Party had long voiced resentment at the imperial banks' highly concentrated and foreign-oriented operations.[39] As the appeal for state support for the banking community grew, the structure and powers of a state financial institution became an arena of charged debate. When the Smuts government referred the banking and exchange issue to a select parliamentary committee, British-imperial banking interests moved with full dispatch to contain any such proposal.

The key figure was Mr. (subsequently Sir) Henry Strakosch, a London gold company manager, who completely dominated the committee meetings.[40] The outcome was a report that rejected a break with sterling and recommended instead a continuation of the gold embargo, which was to be sustained by declaring bank notes inconvertible into gold. This would relieve the imperial banks of the need to convert their London holdings into gold to meet local demands. In order to maintain the link with Britain, even the last remnant of the gold standard was thus to be removed. It was further proposed that the central bank would concern itself only with currency and consolidate note issue, and assist private banks as a lender of last resort.

These recommendations represented a complete rejection of the idea of forming a national bank that could break the monopoly of the imperial banks and the hold of the City of London. A minority report did forcefully advocate the more radical state-owned bank. The central bank proposed by the committee majority, they argued, "will not effectively control or restrict the power of private banks over the business of the country."[41] This conclusion by the Labour Party members of the Select Committee was astute. Not only had a national bank been rejected, but so too had the power of the state to regulate the operations of the imperial banks. Such assessments, however, fell on deaf ears. Following the issuance of the majority report, legislation was subsequently introduced and passed.

London was particularly well pleased with this outcome, for there were significant advantages to British financial circles given the form and structure of the Reserve Bank. Allied to the Bank of England, the Reserve Bank promised not only to resolve the hiatus in British–South African monetary relations, but to become an important ally in the struggle to secure the monetary and financial conditions that supported the sanctity of British investments in particular, and British–South African ties in general. The constitutional independence of the Reserve Bank from the government of the day, a principle continuously argued by the Bank of England, was especially important in light of the growing clamor on the part of the white Dominions for economic independence.[42] While the Reserve Bank centralized local financial and monetary policy, it did so in a manner calculated to isolate the bank from white nationalists' political intervention. As one historian of central banking in the Dominions has argued, the political independence of central banks would lead them to "be dependent upon traditional financial precepts, upon the trend of opinion in financial and business circles, and upon the advice of the Bank of England itself."[43]

The governor of the Bank of England, Montagu Norman, was especially pleased by this very first experiment in establishing a Dominion central bank. His chief accountant, W. H. Clegg, was appointed the first governor of the South African Reserve Bank, assuring a close relationship between the Reserve Bank and the Bank of England. The South African government's control over the Reserve Bank was further limited in the enabling legislation. Indeed, the form and management of the South African Reserve Bank suited Norman's hopes so well that he used it as a model for other Dominions: "The establishment of the South African Reserve Bank in circumstances that facilitated the closest contact with the Bank of England naturally encouraged the Governor in the idea that similar institutions should be established in other Empire countries."[44] This view accelerated as international financial markets collapsed. As A. R. W. Plumptre summarized in 1940 in his *Central Banking in the British Dominions*, "English advice played a central part in the establishment of all the Dominion central banks. . . . In no case has English advice been more influential than in the establishment of the South African Reserve Bank."[45] The driving force was also clear: "the desire in England for a chain of Empire central banks was a latter-day expression of financial imperialism. The terminology was changed and the word co-operation figured more than formerly, but the essential purpose was all the same: the maintenance of London's influence and control."[46]

The Early Years: Restraining the Bank

The advantages for London were not, however, so straightforward, for the creation of the South African Reserve Bank had contradictory implications. On the one hand, the constitution and powers of the South African Reserve Bank appeared to circumscribe local action quite severely, a substantial victory for hard-pressed British interests. On the other hand, the Reserve Bank reflected the very real decline of Britain's ability to dictate financial operations throughout the world economy and even the empire, which opened up the possibility of independent action—in this case by the South African government.

The operations of the Reserve Bank in its first few years of operation revealed these different possibilities. The limits on the Reserve Bank's powers were very real, and were extended by the first governor, W. H. Clegg. The Reserve Bank took over note issue and was empowered to act as a lender of last resort. Its officers, however, interpreted this as the limit of its delegated powers. As Clegg summarized the situation in defense of his inaction, "The Bank is allowed to do none of the main ordinary business of an ordinary banker. It may not make advances upon mortgages of fixed property, it may not allow interest on deposits, it may not grant unsecured overdrafts. It may not make advances on ordinary Stock Exchange securities, nor even on Union Government stock, unless the stock is due to be repaid in a few months' time."[47] Like his mentor Montagu Norman, Clegg preferred to interpret central banking powers in negative terms, supporting the views of the imperial banks and their London connections. As two South African economists noted at the time, the Reserve Bank's establishment "was strongly opposed by the commercial banks, who saw in it a possible competitor, and it is clear from the evidence before the Gold Standard Inquiry Commission 1924–25 that a 'gentleman's agreement' was effected with a view to limiting its scope of operations and curtailing its competition."[48] Given the Smuts government's own close ties to Britain at the time, the result was that "born in a time of financial stringency, disowned by the banks, unutilized by the Government, its functions completely misunderstood by the public, it is not surprising that the Reserve Bank during the first two or three years of its existence was a somewhat ineffective institution."[49]

The Reserve Bank under the Pact

When the inconvertibility of South African gold certificates was due to come up for renewal in June 1925, however, the newly elected Pact government used the occasion to reassess South Africa's monetary and financial policies, institutions, and overseas linkages. The mechanism for this was a "Gold Standard Inquiry Commission." Unlike the Select Committee of 1920, whose parliamentary members had little financial expertise and were easily swayed by the influence of London, the 1924–25 commission consisted of two internationally prominent, non-British monetary experts: Dr. E. W. Kemmerer, professor of economics and finance at Princeton University, and Dr. G. Vissering, president of the Netherlands Bank. Furthermore, the appointments were made without any consultation with London, something unthinkable under the previous government. As such they came as a total surprise to Governor Norman of the Bank of England, who had attempted to maintain close surveillance of Dominion banking matters and who had cultivated a close relationship with Clegg in order to ensure the alignment of the Reserve Bank with the Bank of England and the London financial market.

Norman was not pleased and was startled into action. When Vissering and Kemmerer passed through London on their way to South Africa, Norman and his colleagues, in a long private conference as well as at private dinner parties, pressed the case for South Africa remaining tied to sterling and not gold. South Africa, the visitors were told, should only return to gold if and when London did.[50] In South Africa, similar efforts were made by those committed to the imperial system, with the imperial banks and the pro-British press in particular being adamant that South Africa was much too weak to sustain a return to a gold standard ahead of Great Britain.[51]

Much to the imperial banks' and the Bank of England's dismay, the commission recommended a quick return to the gold standard, especially in light of the fact that the South African pound was already close to prewar gold parity. Even worse for the opponents of such a move, the commission recommended that the Reserve Bank act forcefully both to sustain the gold standard and to take its rightful position as the arbiter of financial markets. As the commissioners stated, "The bank must be affected with a great public interest and must enter the open market when the public interest demands that it should. It must be able to cover its expenses, build up a reasonable reserve and pay adequate dividends on its capital in normal times."[52]

Four days after the report was issued (January 12, 1925), the government announced that it would not extend inconvertibility, which was due to lapse on June 30. South Africa would return to the gold standard regardless of Britain's course of action—a complete reversal of the decision taken by the Smuts government in 1920. Norman was so incensed that he refused to see Commissioner Kemmerer on his return passage through London, while a "conspiracy of silence" greeted the report in London.[53] In the end, Britain returned to a modified gold standard in May, preempting South Africa's move announced for July 1, leading at least one scholar to argue in detail that South Africa "forced Britain's hand."[54] The settler state tail could indeed, at least this once, wag the imperial dog.

Returning South Africa to the gold standard was well within the government's powers. By contrast the government could not easily compel the Reserve Bank to assume an interventionist stance vis-à-vis financial and commercial markets. In this area Norman's strong intellectual alliance with Clegg served to forestall such action. At the next general meeting of the Reserve Bank in June 1925, Clegg reaffirmed his noninterventionist stance. As one commentator noted at the time, "It is one thing, apparently, to invite an expert commission to advise this country on its currency policy, but quite a different thing to get those recommendations carried into effect."[55]

Even in the face of Clegg's obstinacy, the government was able to enhance the local financial and monetary powers of the Reserve Bank by extending its powers, prestige, and realm of activity. In 1925 the Reserve Bank took over the handling and marketing of the mine's gold output; the disappearance of the gold premium made it cheaper for the mines to sell gold in South Africa, rather than ship it to London for sale. With the Reserve Bank accumulating large balances in London as a result of gold sales, it could effectively control exchange rates. Thus, "exchange policy ceased to be partly in the hands of the commercial banks and could no longer fall into the hands of the Chamber of Mines."[56] Branches of the Reserve Bank were also opened in five cities in 1926, while the government in 1927 transferred its accounts from Barclays and Standard Bank to the Reserve Bank. This considerably increased the latter's resources and power, a move that had been resisted by Governor Clegg for some time.[57] In 1930 the Reserve Bank's ability to control credit rates, and thus the commercial banks, was further bolstered when the government passed into law most of the remaining recommendations of the Kemmerer-Vissering Commission. Most important here was allowing the Reserve Bank to deal in long-term securities. After this date, the commercial banks followed closely the Reserve Bank's discount rates.

The limits of local financial independence became, however, all too clear at the end of the decade. When Britain was forced off the gold exchange standard in September 1931, the South African government pointedly refused to separate the South African pound from gold. As was acknowledged at the time, the decision to let the South African pound float against the British pound was an assertion of national prestige and independence, without reliance on any technical advice. As one of Prime Minister Hertzog's closest allies within the cabinet at the time, Oswald Pirow, later related, "General Herzog, who was assured by his economic and financial advisers that it was technically possible to maintain South Africa on the Gold Standard, saw in this policy a glorious opportunity to prove to the world South Africa's economic independence."[58] Hertzog was to be rudely awakened. For at this juncture it was not only the British pound and South African pride that were in jeopardy, but the very structure of the international monetary system. Pirow only later admitted that Hertzog and his advisers "had not the faintest notion of what they were up against."[59] And South Africa would prove to be very vulnerable.

For South Africa this crisis flowed through the channels linking it to Britain. With Britain still South Africa's largest export market, and sterling at a 25 percent discount against the South African pound, South Africa could only watch as other competitors' currencies depreciated and South Africa was priced out of export markets—as, for example, by Australian wool. Under these conditions South Africa's decision soon proved to be unsustainable. Mounting economic pressure on South African producers was matched by the accelerating flight of capital from South Africa in anticipation of the depreciation of the South African pound. Intense economic difficulties gave way to a political challenge from outside the National Party, leading not only to a decision to go off the gold standard in December 1932 but to a coalition government in March 1933. The government's inability to resist world-economic forces surrounding the 1931–32 gold standard crisis illustrated quite well the limited possibilities of independent monetary policy along the periphery of the world economy. Much was achieved: in the years from 1925 to 1930 control over currency, credit rates, and foreign exchange rates had been substantially transferred to state institutions. The eclipse of Britain's financial power had moved hand in hand with local initiative. National monetary and financial independence could not, however, be attained simply through the establishment of new institutions. Together with the Reserve Bank's timid leadership, structural conditions entrenched by long dependence on Britain posed considerable obstacles to the development of local financial markets throughout the interwar period. Among the most important problems were the country's total dependence on foreign exchange earnings and sources of credit and, especially, the almost total lack of any local market in both short- and long-term loan capital. In these and allied areas South Africa remained tied to core areas of the world economy, the City of London, and the imperial banks. The largest capital market in the country, the Johannesburg Stock Exchange, was completely dominated by the mining houses, whose own shares were traded in London and Paris as well as on the local exchange.

The lack of a loan market was more limiting for local entrepreneurs. The banks and the big trading houses drew on their London connections, while the mines had always turned to Europe for their large capital needs. The establishment of a fully empowered national bank such as the Commonwealth Bank of Australia could have addressed the need for local credit facilities. Manufacturers had, however, little political clout to push for the provision by the state of loan capital to private industry, and indeed they played hardly any part in the deliberations leading to the establishment of the Reserve Bank. Manufacturers also did not want to open the door to the radical ideas of the Labour Party regarding state regulation and the nationalization of private firms. The other large private producers with loan needs, white farmers, hardly saw a national bank as a pressing need, for their requirements had long been met by state assistance. The Land and Agricultural Bank of South Africa, established in 1912 and fully under the control of the state, provided long-term, low-rate loans to white farmers, while facilities for intermediate credit were extended in 1926.

South Africa's financial and monetary system during the interwar years thus made limited advances. The central bank in the end turned away from London toward South Africa, enabling the Reserve Bank to assert control over credit and currency rates. This was a considerable achievement. It did not, however, lead to a local money market, particularly one that could assist local white entrepreneurs. This would be a project of the apartheid era. None of these efforts would, however, diminish South Africa's vulnerability to international financial crises and, especially, to volatile capital outflows.

The State as Entrepreneur: ISCOR

All of the state initiatives discussed so far fell within the institutional framework inherited by the Pact government. In this regard, the Pact ran true to form: it was most active in transforming existing state enterprises. As with previous Union governments, there was no intention of taking over private enterprise. Yet industrialization as desired by government planners extended far beyond what could be achieved by expanding the small manufacturing firms typical of the early post–World War I period. As the decade wore on, commercial firms to an increasing degree turned their energies and financial resources to industrial ends. But by and large, these too could not take on large industrial activities. A few select mining firms, most particularly De Beers and the Consolidated Gold Fields Group, also cautiously entered into the industrial sphere as it became lucrative to do so, concentrating their investments in areas related to mining such as engineering and explosives.[60] Yet such interest on the part of the country's only substantial private enterprises remained small and subordinated to the needs of mining operations.

The limits set by private capital and the need for reformation of existing state agencies became evident as the Pact government took up the long-standing attempt to foster a local steel industry. It had long been recognized that without an iron and steel industry South Africa would remain a dependent producer of primary products for overseas consumers. Steel at the time was a leading core industry: as late as World War I, with the exception of Japan, not a single steel mill of any significant size existed outside Europe and North America.[61] Nor did the war, which stimulated industrial activity in the stronger regions of the periphery, alter to any great extent the distribution of world steel production. Almost 90 percent of world steel production in 1918 was accounted for by only three countries: namely, the United States, the United Kingdom, and Germany.[62] It was a lucrative trade, particularly for Britain: in 1913, 65 percent of British iron and steel production found its way into export products worth over £55 million.[63]

South Africa with its mining complexes and ever-expanding rail system was a particularly valuable customer. In the years immediately prior to World War I, imports of raw or partly manufactured iron and steel approached £1 million, with metal manufactures and machinery fetching an additional £5 million.[64] Yet South Africa, like many countries outside North America and Europe, possessed all the natural resources necessary for a heavy steel industry. Unlike most peripheral areas, moreover, South Africa consumed large quantities of steel products, had a resident body of mining experts, and was endowed with extensive infrastructural support. More critically, the country was also politically independent, and ruled by white settlers with continuing, close ties to Europe. Independent political authority proved to be a crucial factor in the blossoming of steel production outside Europe and North America during the interwar period: the major advances were to be made by Latin American countries and the British Dominions. Of the colonies, only India, with its much larger home market for iron and steel, and located even farther from core markets than South Africa, would give birth to a local steel industry.

State assistance in the creation of a local steel industry came late, however, in the South African case. This was not for want of knowledge regarding the potential of the country as a producer of iron and steel. The existence of sufficient deposits of iron ores and coking coal were known by the late nineteenth century, and the Afrikaner government of the South African Republic even granted concessions in the 1890s to have them developed—without any results.[65] By the early twentieth century, the issue of local iron production had received wide discussion and groups such as the Transvaal Customs and Industries Commission (1907–8) repeatedly stressed the contribution that an iron and steel industry could make to the country's economic development. The new Union government followed these leads and signed an agreement in 1911 with a local consortium for the production of iron and steel from scrap metal. Investigation of local resource potential continued at the same time.[66] All such efforts, however, came to naught. In the years up to and through World War I, several small concerns were established by local firms, but all of them lacked the financial backing needed to establish an integrated iron and steel works using local ores.

At the end of World War I, high world prices for steel and the prospects of a postwar boom led many in South Africa to think that the time for full-blown steel production had finally arrived. As a review of iron and steel potentials in October 1920 put it, "As yet, there has been scarcely more than experimental production of iron or steel from ore in the country, but rapid developments are in progress and it is anticipated that production on a considerable scale will not be long delayed."[67] Such hopes were shattered by the postwar depression of 1921–23. As world steel prices dropped precipitously—falling in Britain from above £11 per ton in late 1920 to under £5 per ton in mid-1922—hopes of attracting capital to start a steelworks plummeted.[68]

In order to attract a private iron and steel firm the government had undertaken several investigations and offered financial inducements to local and foreign capital. There were, however, strict limits to the extent that the government would commit itself. When local firms tried to amalgamate in 1923 in order to combine capital resources and launch larger projects, the negotiations fell through due to a lack of governmental assistance. As Nancy Clark has shown in further detail, these efforts were promoted by Prime Ministers Botha and Smuts—but fell well short of endorsing the direct government participation that would prove necessary to launch an integrated steelworks.[69] Even H. J. van der Bijl, Smuts's scientific and technical adviser (and later the first head of the state steelworks no less), remained steadfast in his belief that the production of steel should be undertaken by private enterprises, not public ones.[70] With efforts by local capitalists failing, one of the last acts of the Smuts government was to invite European experts to South Africa in an effort to induce them to establish a local steel industry. In the middle of 1923, an offer was received from a German firm, the Gutehoffnungshütte, which in early 1923 sent out four technical experts to South Africa. Their report, issued in early 1925, would form the basis for the establishment of a local iron and steel complex—but only under a new government.

Reception of the Gutehoffnungshütte report led the newly formed Pact government to announce its intention to establish an iron and steel industry. As the governor-general announced at the opening of the 1927 session of parliament, "The history of the efforts made in the past in this direction has convinced my Ministers that direct Government assistance and participation are necessary to ensure the establishment of steel works on an adequate scale."[71] The resulting Iron and Steel Industry Bill, which established the government-owned South African Iron and Steel Industrial Corporation (ISCOR), was one of the most hotly contested pieces of legislation in the interwar period. As even C. S. Richards conceded, "The revolutionary feature from the point of view of South Africa was the Government's direct participation."[72]

The Gutehoffnungshütte report had been tendered on the basis of the establishment of a privately owned steelworks. The new bill, by contrast, posited full state control, although a minority of shares were to be sold to the public and a minority of directors of the new corporation would be elected from the private sector. The minister of defense justified such extraordinary measures by arguing that without a steel industry South Africa would forever remain outside the ranks of the industrial nations:

> There was a plain obligation upon the state to ensure both the conservation and the expansion of industrial power. The general trend of policy pursued by the great producing nations is to preserve and strengthen the native supply of certain fundamental products which, while in the first states of manufacture not highly differentiated, nevertheless form the indispensable bases of other industries. Prominent among these staple products are pig iron and ingot steel, and to raise to the highest power the production of these commodities is regarded as a vital function of national policy.[73]

While the bill easily passed the Pact-controlled House of Assembly, it was blocked in June 1927 by the South African Party-influenced upper house, the Senate. The government, in response, moved forward the 1928 parliamentary session to October 1927, yet once again, the bill was defeated in the Senate. It finally took the extraordinary measure of a joint session of both houses before the bill was passed in April 1928.

Debate over the bill in both parliament and the press revealed that the government had few supporters outside the ranks of the National and Labour Parties. The Board of Trade and Industries did come up to expectations, issuing a highly favorable report on the prospects of a state-owned steelworks. The board defended the financial prospects of the proposed plant, disputed the charge that the corporation would soak the mining industry, and finally went so far as to reveal that import duties and dumping duties would be imposed, if necessary, to ensure the success of the steelworks.[74] The South African Party, led in opposition by General Smuts, reaffirmed its support of a local iron and steel industry but staunchly and vehemently opposed any government undertaking.[75] The arguments were multiple and imaginative: technical and financial problems were certain to defeat the proposed plant; placing the government in control would lead to endless bureaucratic inefficiency; and railway rates, import duties, and employment policies would all be manipulated to the detriment of the country's consumers. Such a litany of charges by the South African Party were, of course, lent considerable substance by the Pact's actions from 1924 to 1928. Even van der Bijl, at the time chairman of the state electricity firm, opposed direct government control over steel production in his testimony at hearings on the bill.

Reactions by organized private capital were more divided, but hardly favorable. The *South African Mining and Engineering Journal* stated mining capital's consistent view: "To progress, to acquire capital and population, [South Africa] must look beyond her own borders, and build up a big volume of export trade especially in a certain few staple lines in which she has been favored by Nature. . . . We are especially moved to criticism by the new duties on iron, steel and engineering products."[76] Even assistance to private firms (as was initially expected) was denounced: "Recourse to Government backing [of a steel plant] in the way of capital argues convincingly that the scheme is unsound, and no Government free of socialistic aspirations would be willing to risk the taxpayers' money in it."[77]

The publication of the bill announcing full government control, rather than assistance to a private firm, triggered immediate and strong objections. Small private firms (some backed by mining interests), it was argued, already fulfilled all requirements that the local market demanded. Any larger facilities were surely madness: "Granted, heavy rails, plates and heavy structural sections have not been attempted [by existing private firms], but why? Simply because any mill laid down to produce such materials could satisfy Southern Africa's needs in about two months or less, and would thereafter perforce stand idle."[78] Estimates of annual losses of almost a half-million pounds were given wide coverage. When the government appointed a German expert as technical director of the works, and drew on Gutehoffnungshütte for consulting engineers, objections regarding the exclusion of British nationals were raised.[79] After the passage of the bill the mining community drew bitter solace by citing the words of its ideological ally, the London business magazine the *Economist*: "No doubt the South African Government adventure will be watched with interest, and perhaps by those who have not to pay for it, with mirth."[80]

Opposition by commercial firms (with the sole exception of those based in Pretoria, where the plant was to be located), was no less implacable. The opinion of the Association of Chambers of Commerce was blunt, announcing that "the Government had decided to embark on a scheme of advanced socialization of industry for which the country is totally unprepared. . . . If the Bill becomes law, it will alter the existing outlook of every industry in the country."[81] Like the mining community, commercial capital raised the specter of an economic disaster, asking why, if the German report was so favorable, hadn't German investment been forthcoming?

The introduction of the state as an entrepreneur posed serious problems as well for local manufacturers. On the one hand, if the door were opened to state industry, and a monopoly supplier of a commodity consumed by many manufacturing firms at that, where would the process end? On the other hand, local manufacturers were loath to bite the hand that had fed them so well. Manufacturers thus drew a careful line, represented in the official testimony of the South African Federated Chamber of Industries before a select committee that argued against "State interference by direct participation in any industry which is normally carried on by private enterprise."[82] If the government were to go ahead with the project, the chamber suggested, the bill should be revised to ensure that limits be imposed on the steel corporation's ability to "undertake the manufacturing of goods from iron and steel," and that assistance be given to private engineering firms and other users of raw steel.[83] It further proposed that the state relinquish control of the steel corporation to the private sector after the plant was set on a sound basis: "This would mean that, while achieving its object of developing the industry, the Government would not be utilising public money to inaugurate and support the socialistic principle of State control of, and managerial interest in, an industry."[84] These provisions were never adopted, and the steel act passed as proposed.

Subsequent failure by private investors to take up the shares in the corporation left the state in even fuller control than the original bill proposed. The journal of industrial capital, *Industrial and Commercial South Africa and Storekeepers Review*, now ran articles with such headlines as "The Iron and Steel Gamble: Possible Monopoly and Threat to Private Enterprise."[85] The president of the Federated Chamber of Industries proclaimed that "all over the world Governments seem to be flying to economy as the drug fiend flies to narcotics. I hope that South Africa will not pursue this course without grave reflection."[86]

The planning and construction of the ISCOR plant took six years, with the works being opened with great fanfare on July 11, 1934. In the words of the governor-general, it was a "red letter day" in the history of South Africa. In the words of the *Industrial and Commercial South Africa*, "The formal setting-in-motion of the plant by Lady Clarendon was the culminating point of a quarter of a century's efforts to establish an iron and steel industry in the Union."[87] Looking forward, ISCOR—more than any other state undertaking of the interwar period—set the pace for the acceleration of industrialization. There can be little doubt that if iron and steel production had been left to private initiative, South Africa would have been left without an integrated steelworks during the interwar period; the chance of successfully importing the required technology and machinery from Europe as world war approached would surely have been nil.

As it was, the timing of ISCOR's inauguration in 1934 could not have been more fortuitous. ISCOR started producing just as South Africa entered a boom initiated by the upward revision of the gold price in 1932. Multiplier effects from the mining industry spread throughout the economy, with demand now being met by increasing levels of local production. ISCOR played no small part in this. Although initially the ISCOR chairman, H. J. van der Bijl, had to struggle to find local customers, plant capacity, far from exceeding national demand as mining interests had predicted, quickly fell far short. And this happened even though ISCOR was designed to serve only the inland market, the distant coastal areas being fed by imported iron and steel. Two years after ISCOR began production, a second blast furnace was blown in, doubling production capacity. At national exhibitions ISCOR proudly displayed the variety of its manufactured products, from mining tubes to furniture to baby carriages.[88]

With ISCOR South Africa joined the privileged ranks of countries having steelworks. Former suppliers viewed the opening of ISCOR with dismay. As South African representatives of British manufacturers noted, "From the point of view of United Kingdom Steel Manufacturers, the commencement of local operations cannot, of course, be viewed with so much satisfaction. Inevitably, the British Iron and Steel Industry must suffer."[89] South Africa's gold boom, in the midst of depression elsewhere in the world economy, led, however, to increasing steel imports. By 1937 South African imports of primary and semimanufactured iron and steel stood at 592,000 long tons, an increase of 254,000 tons over 1933 figures. Imports, nevertheless, would have been almost 50 percent higher without ISCOR's contribution, which in 1937 reached 272,000 long tons.[90]

Depression and falling prices in major steel-producing countries in the early and mid-1930s soon led ISCOR to request protection against foreign imports. The Board of Trade and Industries responded favorably to ISCOR's demands, and dumping duties against foreign steel were imposed in 1935 and thereafter. In 1936 the chairman of ISCOR struck a deal with the British Steel Federation and the International Steel Cartel (Germany, France, and Belgium-Luxembourg) whereby 350,000 tons of local demand were reserved for South African producers. Shortly thereafter, dumping duties were imposed on iron and steel imports from the United States. The duties protected European exporters as much as ISCOR itself.[91] With the latter action, the safeguarding of the home market was complete despite continuing protests against this hallmark instance of state intervention.[92]

When the outbreak of war isolated South Africa from overseas suppliers, ISCOR flourished. At the end of World War II, the Smuts government would move to lessen government control, with support not only of liberal ideologues such as Richards but also of the new staff of the Board of Trade and Industries.[93] The election of the reconstituted National Party in 1948 put a stop, however, to any moves to reverse the course of state intervention. For apartheid's proponents of strict and broad state control of socioeconomic life, ISCOR provided a shining model of the benefits of state control over the economy.

Reprise

The three cases considered here chart the complex and impressive movement to enhance the South African state's power and industrialize the country. Indeed, the actions of the South African state formed but one example of the ceaseless struggle of states to transform the character of local production processes within the global division of labor. South Africa's independence and its status as a white Dominion made state intervention possible. Still, as we have seen, South African policymakers confronted strong opponents both nationally and internationally. In each of our three cases the intractable interdependence between core and peripheral areas was deeply and internationally rooted: capital, transport, and steel made up the foundation of South Africa's great mining complexes and were essential as well to agricultural production.

Attempts to transform these relationships had mixed results. Born of the breakdown of the prewar international monetary system, the Reserve Bank did lead to local control over exchange and credit rates. The country, nevertheless, remained woefully dependent on foreign sources of loan capital and openly exposed to the vicissitudes of international finance, while being constrained by the ties of local commercial banks and the big mining houses to the City of London. This situation stood in stark contrast to the evolution of central and commercial banking in the other Dominions, where a stronger position within the international monetary system was successfully established.

If there is one area where the South African state was able to marshal financial resources in the service of national industry, it was the transport system. By contrast to the Reserve Bank, the transport infrastructure proved far more amenable to state control. What had been designed to serve the open flow of primary products was, with but little tinkering, turned into a powerful stimulus for both the expansion of the exploitation of local resources and labor and the growth of interindustry linkages. In this case a strong set of local political interests—agriculture, manufacturing, and government officials—combined to push for the development of the railway system. Mining capital stood almost alone in opposition to such initiatives.

The ISCOR case stands as the crowning achievement of state intervention in the interwar period, a bold new entry by the state into the realm of what had hitherto been the privileged realm of private capital accumulation. As such, it raised cries of protest not only from the mining community but also from commercial and even manufacturing capital. The bitterness and length of the battle waged to create ISCOR marked a substantial but singular achievement for the state. International capital could do little to prevent the establishment of ISCOR; the loss of all or parts of the Indian, Australian, and South African steel markets was to continue during the interwar period.

The success of ISCOR raises one final question, however: why did the state not take similar measures to localize industrial production? Different combinations of local and international forces as sketched above are not sufficiently explanatory by themselves. Nor do specific characteristics of the government, such as the minister of finance's restrictions on state spending, provide a satisfying answer.[94] Central to any answer is the lack of a sufficient political and ideological impetus to force the industrialization issue.

Immediately obvious is the lack of a social and political alliance necessary to force the pace of state intervention. In no single case—the railways, tariff rates, the Reserve Bank—was the Pact driven by, or able to marshal, strong and continuing support from its racial and political base. The broad social forces most strongly committed to national action—white farmers and white workers—not only were driven by very different purposes but were even segmented within themselves. White farmers were often divided by the different markets—export, coastal, or inland—that they served, while white workers were split along skill and ethnic lines. In large part, such divisions were the legacy of a century of uneven development between the countryside and the city, and between "Boer" and "Briton" in the urban and global labor force. Their entrenchment in the political culture of the nation blocked the political alliances that elsewhere in the periphery most often drove state intervention forward. Neither radical "nationalist" projects nor radical "socialist" projects could obtain a solid backing of the class and racial strata that were, in the abstract, their most likely supporters and beneficiaries.

The Pact's strength, the combination of Labour and National Parties, was thus also its great weakness. The dissolution of the alliance—the demise of the Labour Party in the 1929 elections and then the coalition with the South African Party in 1933—arrested any further development of state intervention. A reassertion of white nationalist aims would await the consolidation of a truly unified social bloc of Afrikaners in 1948. The Pact's initiatives would assist this process in two fundamental ways: first, they set the stage for expanded state intervention; and second, they led to substantial transformations in the country's labor force, industrial base, and subsequently class and racial structures. These in turn made for new political crises, alliances, and projects in the postwar period.

4

1948

Semiperipheral Crisis

As World War II came to a close, the foundations of South Africa's impressive economic growth, which had seemed so solid, began to shake and wobble. Sporadic discontent by black and white workers erupted into a major strike wave. Alliances between employers and the state over labor policy gave way to increasingly acrimonious conflicts. Electoral support for the government, particularly by white workers and Afrikaners, collapsed. Seizing the opportunities created by these conditions, Afrikaner nationalists mobilized within the white population and across class lines and won the 1948 election. A new word, *apartheid*, would henceforth frame the construction and analysis of South Africa.

The parallels between the early post–World War II upheavals in South Africa and those accompanying the end of World War I have often been noted. Both periods were marked by strong waves of social and political unrest, and both led to a radical shift in the governing coalition and a further entrenchment of racial distinctions. Belying these apparent similarities, however, stand the radical transformations that took place in the local and international relationships among labor, capital, and the state during the interwar period. By the mid-1940s four great changes had seemingly resolved the post–World War I crisis.

First, there was an unprecedented burst of industrial activity based on the reorganization of relationships with nearby peripheral areas and with overseas core areas. Second, the almost two-decade-long intensification of the confrontation between white workers on the one side and the state and capital on the other gave way to a period of relative labor peace. Third, shortages of African labor were replaced by seemingly ample labor supplies. Fourth, the allocation of labor by race and nationality, pursued through the state policy of "civilized labour," gave shape to industrialization and increasingly to social and cultural life. Yet even as these transformations marked the resolution of the early 1920s crisis they planted the seeds for later challenges to capital accumulation, racial and class formations, and the legitimacy of the South African state. From these—and not simply racial animus or atavistic racial policies—would spring apartheid.

Racing Labor, Capital, and the State

Of all the changes that took place during and after the interwar period, scholars have focused most intensively on the entrenchment of racial segregation in South Africa's factories, labor market, and labor movement. Considerable debate has taken place over the sources and perpetrators of racial segregation. Liberal scholars target a white labor aristocracy that pursued a strategy of racial exclusion in alliance with Afrikaner nationalists. In this formulation free and nonracial markets were displaced by racially inspired state regulation that hindered both economic progress and black advancement.[1]

In the 1970s and 1980s neo-Marxists replied that capital, and the state on behalf of capital, not only profited from but promulgated racial segregation and apartheid. The seminal work by Frederick Johnstone argued that white miners' demand for a statutory color bar was only a *response* to mining capital's prior construction of an "exploitation" color bar. For Johnstone, the Pact government represented white workers' capture of the state: "The State, which in 1922 had served as the instrument for the repression of the white workers, was now in the hands of their representatives, and implementing a protectionist policy for them, reinforcing and extending the employment colour bars, to protect skilled and unskilled white workers from the negative effects of the exploitation colour bars of the employers on their conditions and prospects of employment."[2]

These conclusions were subsequently challenged by radical scholars on two grounds, with one line of argument maintaining that the large majority of white wage earners were not workers at all, but supervisors and thus members of a new "petty bourgeoisie."[3] This exercise in class redefinition merged with a second line of argument that maintained that the extension of segregation by the state was part of the process of mining capital being replaced by national (or industrial) capital as the hegemonic "fraction of capital"—with white workers playing a subordinate role.[4] This argument emphasized that it was capital, and not labor or even the white petite bourgeoisie, that drove the Pact government, and later apartheid, forward.

Previous chapters have demonstrated that a major component of the radical interpretation is mistaken: far from being under the control of a unified "national, industrial" capital, interwar industrial policies originated in the initiatives of a far more autonomous state responding to irreconcilable competition and crisis among peripheral production processes and class and racial formations. During the 1980s and 1990s labor and social historians

further undermined the liberal versus neo-Marxist debate by documenting a wide variety of working-class strata and antagonistic relationships
between labor and capital. Many white workers, particularly women, were,
for example, poorly paid, yet very "productive" workers. Complementary
work by labor historians challenged depictions of the terminal decline of
white worker militancy and the simultaneous formation of a segregated
labor force and labor movement, including significant levels of differentiation among African wage workers.[5]

Two important conclusions follow. First, South Africa's racialized labor
force and labor movement during the first half of the twentieth century
were far more heterogeneous and fluid than has been allowed by those who
have focused on the demise of white workers and the rise of a bifurcated
racial order in the 1920s, 1930s, and 1940s. Second, the state and capital
were not alone in setting the terms of the allocation and remuneration of
labor. This leaves open, however, the question of how to account for the
transition between the pre–World War I and post–World War II character
of secondary industry and its differentiated labor force. Having struggled to
undermine linear depictions of interwar industrialization and labor force
formation, existing scholarship offers us few means to grasp long-term labor
force and production patterns.

One major turning point has been pinpointed above: the economic and
national crisis that erupted after World War I took place as primary production and international alliances were shaken due to world-economic developments. The resolution of this crisis was reached not simply by entrenching
segregation in the labor force, but through state action to reshape racialized relationships with both overseas core areas and surrounding peripheral areas—including radical changes in the racial composition of the labor
force. It was the very success of these efforts that would lead, a generation
later, to intractable conflicts between the state, core-like and peripheral
enterprises, and new racial and labor force formations.

Industrial Production in the Interwar Period

Behind the South African state's promotion of industrial production after
1924 stood a belief that the growth of manufacturing would resolve the dangerous conflict that pitted white workers against capital and the state itself.
Above all, factory production offered the promise of increasing high-wage
employment for the growing and unstable "poor white" stratum, something
neither commercializing agriculture nor mining could offer. For the government and its supporters this was a bold prospect. During the interwar
period, however, industrial production did indeed grow, white employment
expanded, and white labor militancy diminished.

These developments had few precursors. Manufacturing's lot before World War I was very difficult and marginal, especially in the inland provinces. As one report on industrial conditions in the Transvaal just prior to 1910 noted, the deplorable state of industry was due to "the limited market for most goods, the want of local raw materials, the high cost of labour and unstable industrial and social conditions here, and competition from the Coast Colonies."[6] The situation was not much better in the Cape Colony, which led the region in manufacturing output. Throughout the nineteenth century manufacturing in the Cape had failed to reach beyond the production of handicrafts and the most minor branches of manufacturing suited to a distant colony. According to the 1891 census in the Cape, the gross value of manufacturing output stood at just £5,639,000, of which the value of raw materials (substantially composed of imported materials) amounted to £3,353,000.[7] Activities such as milling, baking, brewing, building, cart and wagon works, and the preservation of fish and fruit were the most important manufacturing activities during even the opening decade of the twentieth century.[8]

The formation of the Union of South Africa in 1910 did little to change the dismal state of manufacturing. World War I by contrast significantly stimulated manufacturing production as imports became difficult to obtain from Europe and North America, prices accelerated under wartime conditions, and freight and insurance charges considerably increased due to restrictions on shipping and dangers posed by conflict on the high seas. These elements acted to shelter the home market, providing, as in many peripheral areas, a protectionist environment for manufacturers. Between 1915–16 and 1919–20 the deflated gross value of private manufacturing grew by 70 percent and the number of employees rose from 102,000 to 178,000.[9] When the war ended, manufacturing output and employment stalled as global competition and transport revived. The use of South African materials, which had substantially increased during the war, was rolled back immediately, falling from 53 percent of the value of manufacturing inputs in 1918–19 to 43 percent in 1921–22.[10]

Intersectoral linkages were few, even for those industries that could have drawn on local raw materials and especially the output of local mines and farms. Clothing and textiles, metals, chemicals, and wood manufacturing all could have used local materials extensively but failed to do so.[11] Moreover, the very industries that promised to use ever larger quantities of local products were precisely those that felt most heavily the brunt of world competition after the war; the gross value of the production of foodstuffs, chemicals, clothing, and textiles, as well as the treatment of raw materials, was lower in 1924–25 than in 1919–20.[12] And it was precisely these industries that offered the greatest opportunities for increasing white employment.

Indeed, by the early 1920s white South Africans were dismayed to see how far South Africa had failed to keep pace with other, whiter, industrializing areas outside Europe and North America. South Africa's economic and

Table 4.1. South African percentages of Canadian, Australian, New Zealand manufacturing (in £)

	Canada	Australia	New Zealand
Value added			
1915–16	16	27	166
1919–20	13	49	226
1922–23	10	29	130
1924–25	16	26	131
Value added per employee			
1915–16	82	89	92
1919–20	52	91	86
1922–23	40	66	56
1924–25	43	61	55
Average wage per employee			
1915–16	94	85	89
1919–20	68	93	83
1922–23	47	64	62
1924–25	53	60	60

Sources: South Africa, *Official Yearbook*, 1917: 485; 1924: 555; 192627: 557.

political elites paid especial attention to their rank in the world economy and among Britain's white Dominions. Numerous state commissions and each issue of the *Official Yearbook of the Union* during this period included, for example, an international comparison of South African manufacturing with that of other settler areas. And these comparisons made for successively bitter reading. While it fared somewhat better than New Zealand, South Africa lagged far behind Australia and Canada, not simply in terms of gross value of production, but also on such measures as output per employee and wages. Furthermore, South Africa's standing was falling over time rather than improving, as table 4.1 showing South Africa's percentage of its competitors' industrial attainment demonstrates.

By the beginning of the interwar period South African manufacturers had still barely moved beyond the simplest processing of local materials and the finishing of imported materials. The commanding heights of the market created by mining and commercial agriculture had been successfully captured by overseas producers. The distance from Europe and North America did offer relief for some local producers, particularly in those service and maintenance operations that needed quick turnaround and on-site production facilities. A good example of the latter were the metalworking industries, which overwhelmingly comprised service shops on the mines and in the railway administration. But in general local manufacturers found survival in the fiercely competitive world market very difficult indeed. Manufacturing's prospects in the early 1920s were accordingly bleak: existing industries were struggling to sustain their positions, and no new developments seemed to be on the horizon.

Manufacturers' fortunes changed for the better starting in the mid-1920s. Industries whose future had been uncertain in the face of world competition—such as boots and shoes, textiles and clothing—found their position strengthened as the new government's industrial policies had their effects on the local economy. Such measures as tariff protection, favorable transport rates, and government tenders had a significant effect. Industrial production accelerated until it was checked by the world-economic crash and, especially, the gold standard crisis in the early 1930s. Such performance was all the more remarkable since it was not stimulated by the gold mining sector, which steadily declined during the 1920s. When the mining industry boomed after 1933, the result was an even faster pace of industrial expansion right through World War II—a twelve-year period of uninterrupted boom. The contrast between these periods of industrial growth—1924–30 and 1933–45—and the years preceding the mid-1920s is revealed in figure 4.1.

The impact of the war years and Pact policies in stimulating manufacturing is illustrated by the rising percentage of South African materials used in manufacturing (see fig. 4.2). As figure 4.2 shows, a steady ascent in the use of local materials might be checked, but not reversed, by the notable financial and trade crises of the interwar period.

Industrialization, Labor Force Formation, and the State

While the above figures document the rhythms of industrial production, they do not reveal the complex and volatile set of social forces that emerged as higher-paying, core-like, and lower-wage peripheral production processes began to coexist within a single state. Expanding industrial employment did not dictate any particular pattern of utilizing and rewarding white or black labor. This point was driven home for the Pact government as it sought to resolve the threat posed by militant white workers and the growing army

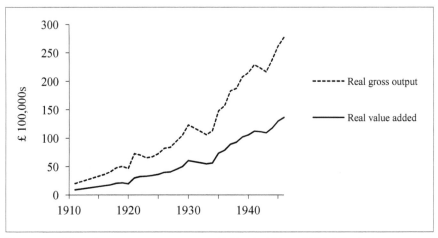

Figure 4.1. Manufacturing output 1911–46. South Africa, *Official Yearbook*, 1937, 911; and 1948, 970 (for values); *Union Statistics for Fifty Years*, H-15 (for Union goods; deflator: 1938 = 100).

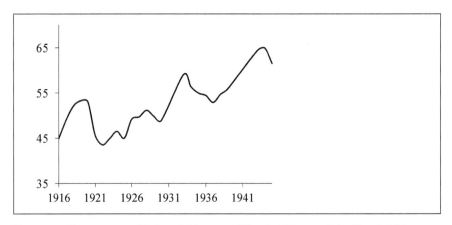

Figure 4.2. Percentage of industrial inputs of South African origin. South Africa, *Official Yearbook*, 1926–27, 554–55; 1931–32, 504; 1937, 919; 1941, 877–88; 1948, 976–77.

of white unemployed. This task required not only the taming of organized labor, but the creation of jobs for the growing number of poor whites. But was manufacturing capable of providing sufficient employment opportunities for white men and women?

At the time there was much debate and contradictory evidence. A clear-cut set of different views was expressed in the reports of the Economic and Wage Commission of 1925. The majority report espoused the orthodox free trade position: it attacked inefficient and ineffective industrial experiments and argued that the development of export agriculture and mining was the only solution to the problem of white unemployment. "The policy of developing manufacturing industry by means of protection," the majority concluded, "will have no effect on the employment of white labour so far as it merely diverts labour and capital from other industries."[13] Under attack was not only the protectionist tariff but the whole panoply of new state programs being introduced at the time, from the exclusion of foreign black labor, through the administratively dictated replacement of blacks by whites in the state sector, to state-imposed wage fixing in the private sector.

The commission's minority report, which primarily reflected the views of the Labour Party, was much more sympathetic toward state assistance to private industry and white labor. Improved prospects for white workers would come, it argued, not in mining—which was widely recognized to have been in a downward spiral since before World War I—but from the encouragement of the development of industry, and especially industries closely linked to agriculture.[14] Manufacturing's promise to expand the number of unskilled and semiskilled jobs was especially important, since it was assumed that the number of high-wage, artisanal jobs would never match the number of whites entering the labor market. The minority report noted a significant obstacle: high wages in industry for urbanized workers could not be maintained in the face of unrestrained labor inflows from rural areas. In order to restrict black jobseekers, the minority report recommended the termination of the admission of "East Coast" (Mozambican) Africans while providing assistance to African farmers in the reserves in order that the reserves could remain the home base for circulating migrant labor.

The reports of the Economic and Wage Commission thus posed divergent and mutually exclusive alternatives to resolving the problem of white unemployment: either the primary producing sectors of the economy must be expanded or manufacturing production would have to be favored in quite specific ways in order to increase the number of positions for white workers.

There was little doubt which path the newly elected Pact government would choose. Even under the most favorable conditions, neither mining nor agriculture held any prospect of rapid expansion using white labor. Commercial agriculture also offered few prospects for unskilled whites. Indeed, the very commercialization of white agriculture had produced the poor white, who, once displaced as a landowner—or, more frequently, a tenant—could not compete with African tenants for unskilled farm work. To save the poor white farming household would have required nothing less than the decommercialization of agriculture and, consequently, an attack on more prosperous white farmers. Prospects for white employment in the mining sector were equally bleak. Even presupposing a rollback to prewar white-to-black employment ratios, the fortunes of a mining industry tied to declining world prices provided little prospect for jobs for poor whites.

The creation of an industrial structure, and especially one that would employ whites, was fraught with unknowns. Even if protectionist measures led to industrial expansion, this by no means ensured that whites would fill the new positions that were created, or that white workers would be engaged at the high wage rates that had become the norm in mining and in those industries based on artisanal labor processes. It is necessary to emphasize these very different prospects in light of the common assertion that racial employment patterns in mining were simply extended to industry.[15] Like settler agriculture, mining capital had struggled to organize a very low wage bill. Established with great urgency during the last two decades of the nineteenth century, the mining sector relied on both the importation of trained white miners from core areas of the world economy and the employment of Africans completely unfamiliar with mining work. As the mining industry was more firmly established, mine owners moved to lower wage costs by localizing and regulating labor supplies: white South Africans, predominantly Afrikaners, replaced imported labor, while the Chamber of Mines set in place recruiting organizations to ensure a stable and large flow of African labor from across southern Africa. This labor force structure was firmly entrenched by the time of World War I.

Even in its earliest days, the structure of industrial production and its labor force were already diverging from patterns that prevailed on the mines. Manufacturing's many small producers faced a consumer market that was localized within the country and the region—and thus a market susceptible to price manipulation by such measures as the 1925 Tariff Act. Unlike mine owners, therefore, manufacturers did not necessarily face the international cost pressures that dictated mining companies' drive to lower their labor costs. This situated manufacturers in a quite different position than employers in export-oriented mining and agriculture. Manufacturing, even when dominated as it was in its early days by craft production, showed little tendency to replicate the reliance on low-wage labor that characterized export-oriented, primary production in the mining and agricultural sectors. Between 1915 and 1925 white employees constituted at least one-third of the manufacturing labor force—three times the prevailing percentage in mining—and by the early 1910s *more* white workers were employed in manufacturing than in mining.[16]

White workers in manufacturing did, however, share one key problem with white miners: despite their proportionately greater numbers, they still faced competitive pressures in the labor market due to their potential replacement by low-wage black, particularly African, workers. And it was this potential that worried the authors of the minority report of the 1925 Economic and Wage Commission. If manufacturing were to grow behind tariff walls and favorable transport rates, would it continue to employ white workers? Or would the ratio of white to black workers descend to that prevailing in mining? On this point the fall in the white proportion of the industrial workforce during World War I and its failure to recover in the immediate postwar years were revealing precedents.

The Pact government's policy of promoting what was called "civilized labour" was designed to solve the problem of maintaining and even expanding the white worker's position in all sectors of the economy. The policy's application and effects, however, were uneven. In the state sector unbridled replacement of unskilled black workers with unskilled whites was applied with all due speed. This was most evident on the railways, where more than 15,000 whites were added to employment rolls between 1924 and 1927. This immediately increased the white share of the labor force from 45 percent to 58 percent, and by 1933 that figure had risen to 64 percent.[17]

The gains for white workers in the state sector were not achieved in private industry or mining. This did not mean, however, that state intervention was lacking. In the mining sector, where the color bar had been declared ultra vires by court action in 1923, the government passed the Mines and Works Amendment Act of 1926. This measure, which was only passed by an extraordinary sitting of parliament, reestablished the reservation of skilled and supervisory positions for whites in the mines. No such color bar was, however, to be imposed in private industry. If state-directed segregation and high wages were, as many have charged, a key to the expansion of industrial production, we have to look elsewhere for evidence.

Most studies identify that "elsewhere" by pointing to the Pact government's enactment and extension of industrial legislation. Just prior to the Pact's election, parliament passed the Industrial Conciliation Act. Building on previous legislation and modeled after Canadian and Australian law, the act was designed to regulate disputes between organized white labor and capital. Conciliation boards arbitrated between labor and capital, with provisions that made a legal strike very difficult; black workers and trade unions were excluded by the terms of the act.

Complementary to the Industrial Conciliation Act's coverage of organized white labor, the Wage Act of 1925 aimed to fix wages for unorganized and unskilled workers. While this act did not preclude its application to black workers, it was clearly designed to raise wage levels and secure white workers a place in the expansion of industrial production. As the minister of labor stated in introducing the Wage Act, the government believed that "the tendency of modern industry unless controlled and checked simply leads to larger and larger sections of the population being sweated down below the level of dignified life." And in South Africa the problem was that "we have not got a homogeneous population. We have two races separated by the wide gulf of history and civilization. . . . In the competitive wage production system in a situation such as we have here in South Africa, the lower civilization will gradually drive out the higher civilization."[18]

It was toward the newly emerging industries employing semiskilled and unskilled labor that the Wage Act was especially directed, for it was here that the competition between blacks and whites was especially sharp. As the minister continued, "If our civilization is going to subsist, we look upon it as necessary that our industries should be guided so that they afford any men deserving to live according to the European standards greater opportunities for doing so. . . . It is mainly, at all events in its earlier years, in regard to unorganised labour of the sweated industries, and where men can hardly look after themselves, that this Act will find its main field of work."[19] The Wage Act was potentially revolutionary. High-wage determinations by the Wage Board, coupled with the ambiguously broad areas of employment covered by the act, portended an intensified state role in the allocation and remuneration of labor in industry. The state, as guardian of the white worker and the poor white alike, was thus poised by 1926 to fix in stone a racial order in the labor market.

The burst of legislative activity in 1925 and 1926, which indicated to white workers the seriousness of the "civilized labour" policy, was soon followed by the creation of a new system of industrial relations. As numerous studies have shown, workers' representatives in the most organized, and hitherto most militant, sectors of the labor force soon became entrapped in the machinery of industrial conciliation. As the professional negotiator became increasingly more important than the shop steward or trade union organizer, the steady bureaucratization of white trade unions proceeded apace. Yet this did not mean the death of organized labor: trade union organization among white workers actually grew during the interwar period, as did challenges to capital by semiskilled, operative workers. Labor militancy did not, however, spill over into the mass political movement mounted by white labor between 1907 and 1922.

The achievement of labor peace through government intervention was indisputably of great importance to underwriting the success of industrial growth. Yet white workers won only limited economic concessions as a result of state intervention. The state's failure to intervene in the mining sector, where neither the ratio of black to white employment nor white wage levels were fundamentally altered, was also the pattern in other sectors including manufacturing. White wages in the industrial sector, for example, advanced only slightly during the Pact period, with wage determinations under the Wage Act following existing rather than higher wage rates.[20] The white proportion of the labor force in private industry did, however, increase 40 percent in the next ten years, from 131,000 employees in 1924–25 to 177,000 in 1933–34.[21] Where white gains were few, as in the engineering and metal industries, labor processes remained dominated by the division between white artisans and a black army of unskilled workers.[22]

The largest recorded increases in white employment significantly took place in consumer goods industries, often employing mass-production techniques. Wages in these factories were lower, well below the pound-a-day standard for the white miner and skilled artisan. Of the total increase in white employment between 1924–25 and 1933–34, over 60 percent occurred in the categories of food, textiles, and especially wearing apparel.[23] It was precisely in these areas that low-wage operative positions were filled by white workers—and most notably by newly proletarianized whites, including women. This was a highly gendered system: the Wage Board set women's wages at two-thirds the rate for men. Such wages never approached male artisans' pay rates, but they were well above rates paid to unskilled African workers. While no highly paid labor aristocracy was thus created during the Pact period, a white working class was promoted in key industrial sectors—an achievement of considerable importance for both the growth of the industrial labor force and the course of the white labor movement.

By the late 1920s, the Pact government's initiatives in the field of industrial labor legislation had run out of steam, in large part because of the government's failure to maintain any organic link with white workers. Labour Party members, who had formulated labor policy and manned the highest ranks of the new industrial order, became a less coherent political force and less of an influence in the councils of state. The failure of the Pact to deliver radical change in favor of white labor also quickly led to dissension within the Labour Party. By the time of the 1929 elections, the Labour Party had split, leaving those members who remained within the government without any substantive political base. A poor showing in 1929 accelerated the decline of the Labour Party as a power within the Pact government.

The real setback to white labor's political strength occurred after the "fusion" of the Pact and the opposition South African Party in 1933. After that date, the Pact's industrial policy, and with it the "civilized labour" policy, was largely shorn of substance. Just as the 1936 Tariff Commission questioned the value of tariff protection and the protectionist drive ground to a halt, so too did the 1935 Industrial Legislation Commission report against continued government intervention in the Union's wage and labor force structure. The Wage Act, originally the centerpiece of the "civilized labour" policy for private industry, lapsed into disuse. In 1937 a new Wage Act was passed, reconstituting the Wage Board as an instrument designed to regulate black wage rates. This marked both an end to the encouragement of operative positions for whites and, especially, a recognition of the increasing numbers of black workers who posed new challenges for industrialists. By the mid-1930s, the demise of state regulation had given businessmen an increasingly free hand in manipulating the labor market.

Even more dramatic policy reversals occurred in the state sector. While the Pact government vigorously promoted the employment of unskilled whites in the public sector, the Fusion government ended this policy, despite an influx of poor whites into urban areas due to the agricultural depression that ensued in the wake of the Great Crash of 1929. The percentage of whites employed on the railways fell from 63 percent in 1933 to 54 percent only four years later.[24] Much the same course was followed at steel giant ISCOR, which had been promoted, designed, and established with an almost completely white labor force. This ended with the Fusion government: in 1936 ISCOR announced a new policy of employing unskilled black labor. This was immediately challenged by white employees, who set in motion the industrial conciliation machinery. The arbitrators appointed under the Industrial Conciliation Act not only fully supported ISCOR's radical shift in employment policy but roundly condemned "civilized labour" employment practices. As C. S. Richards summarized the findings, "The arbitrators characterised the excessive wages paid for unskilled work as 'unjustifiable on economic grounds,' completely upheld the policy of ISCOR that 'general labourers' (natives) should be employed on unskilled work and on most of the semi-skilled work where the degree of skill is low, and condemned any attempt to introduce a purely white labour policy and the attitude of the men that each was entitled to continuity of employment irrespective of the work available."[25] The government did assist poor and unemployed whites, but this now took the form of temporary poor relief. This was, in fact, a reversion to pre-Pact policies, which held that poor whites should be the recipients of social charity rather than beneficiaries of state intervention to ensure permanent employment opportunities.

The effects of these changes in state policy were less direct insofar as the private sector was concerned. Offsetting the need for such intervention was the uninterrupted economic boom from 1933 through World War II. As the state reaped massive revenues from a windfall profits tax on mining, it even became possible to subsidize the export of white farmers' crops despite rapidly declining world prices throughout the 1930s. From the mid-1930s onward, almost every agricultural commodity produced by white farmers benefited from state marketing boards.

The state offered no such assistance to manufacturers although the tariff structure set in place during the Pact years largely remained intact. Given the interruption of world trade after the Great Crash, industrial production for the national market accelerated, with growth rates in the industrial sector from the end of the depression in 1933 up to World War II similar to those from 1924 to 1930. The direction of industrial expansion also shifted toward the engineering and metals sectors, which remained locked into a dependent service role to primary production and transport. If manufacturing was to move from craft production toward mass-production labor processes, metals and engineering were poor examples of advancing industrial growth.

The industrial labor force, however, did change markedly during the 1930s boom. While the white percentage of the labor force rose throughout the Pact period, increasing from 36 percent of the total industrial labor force in 1924–25 to 43 percent in 1932–33, this trend was drastically reversed during the course of the 1930s as the percentage of whites employed in the industrial sector steadily declined from a peak of 43 percent in 1932–34 to 31 percent in 1944–45.[26] This trend was exhibited across the whole spectrum of industrial activity, from the consumer goods industries to basic engineering and metals.[27] Far from industrialization in the 1930s opening up positions for white workers, the industrial labor force was becoming increasingly African. If the Pact had succeeded in stimulating industrial expansion and white manufacturing employment, continued expansion under a less interventionist government opened the door to a radically different and more highly differentiated labor force.

The Rise of a Black, Urban-Centered Labor Force

Discussions of the displacement of white workers often proceed as if black workers were always available and willing substitutes for white workers. This was not, however, the case: neither rising demand by employers nor state action alone explains the supply of black workers. It is clear that a radical shift after 1930 in the employment of black labor did take place. Employers' cries of a black labor shortage, so prevalent in the 1920s, disappeared, even as black wage employment accelerated. Behind this transformation stood two developments that would fuel a social and political crisis: first, the transformation of black household structures, and second, increasing competition between high-wage production processes typical of core areas of the world economy and low-wage production processes typical of peripheral zones.

Agents of the state recognized the crucial impact of the first factor. As argued in the minority report the Economic and Wage Commission of 1925, employment of white labor, even under the most "civilized" of labor policies, would only succeed in the long run if black workers did not exert undue competitive pressures on the urban labor market. Two ways to reduce, if not halt, this were proposed. On the one hand, African agriculture in the Reserve Areas was to be promoted by expanding African landholdings and encouraging more productive agricultural practices. This policy, it was hoped, would stem the permanent flow of African labor toward urban areas. On the other hand, more rigid controls were proposed over the movement of African labor and the urban African population. Yet neither of these alternatives was seriously pursued in the interwar period, opening the door to a rapidly expanding urban black labor supply. Unimpeded by state intervention and facing a growing black labor supply, industrial firms by the 1930s were able to utilize black labor on an extensive and continuing basis.

The growth of African industrial labor in the 1930s marked the emergence of a very different type of labor force than South Africa had yet experienced. During the late nineteenth and early twentieth centuries, the development of a black labor force centered on the demands for unskilled African labor in the mines, on settler farms, and in urban domestic service. Different forms and locations of labor control were developed across the territories of southern Africa to meet these needs. Mining and settler agriculture came to rely on two different pools of black labor: white farmers controlled a coerced, on-farm tenant labor force, while the mines drew migrant labor from rural African communities. This pattern led to a forceful attack on, and the remolding of, the conditions of rural African life, particularly for women locked into nonwage activities. The ability of many rural Africans to withdraw from participation in labor markets—as occurred after the Anglo-Boer War when African wages were reduced—was disappearing by World War I. By that time restrictions on access to land and markets had intensified, as exemplified by the infamous 1913 Natives Land Act, which allowed Africans to own land in only 13 percent of the country. For an increasing number of Africans, participation in the labor market had become not discretionary but necessary on a continuing, part-lifetime basis. Throughout the interwar period the primary industries of the land would continue to rely on this low-wage labor force structure.

These geographical and household configurations were not well suited to the requirements of industrial production. In the early years of the twentieth century, the average yearly wage for black industrial workers was roughly equivalent to the annual African wage in mining, with similar large wage disparities between unskilled African and skilled white workers apparent in both mining and manufacturing.[28] The *Report of the Economic Commission* of 1914 could conclude that competition between white and black—as understood as between skilled and unskilled workers—was restricted: "none of the evidence proved that the sphere of white labour was being absolutely restricted in the Union, and the wages of the whites have not fallen."[29] The commission thus recommended that "the rising generation of the whites should fit themselves to fill supervisory and highly skilled positions, so that such competition as may be felt in the future may force them upwards rather than downwards."[30]

As industrial production blossomed during World War I, the question of who would fill new semiskilled, operative positions became a lively debate. The new semiskilled positions transformed the nature of industrial labor, for they entailed skills that, though rudimentary, were usually incompatible with the high turnover rates of African migrant labor. Poor whites, and often newly proletarianized women, came to fill the operative positions opening up in the consumer goods industries. Among the black labor force the more highly urbanized and stable "Coloured" population came to occupy a large number of semiskilled positions in factories in the Cape.

By the time of the election of the Pact government in 1924, attention was thus increasingly being paid to whites' ability to fill semiskilled positions. White workers were stable urban residents with some formal education and were generally suited to the new discipline of the factory. A stable black urban population, by contrast, was still in the process of formation. Needless to say, wages paid to semiskilled workers were often less than half of artisan wages.[31] The "civilized labour" policy was an attempt to expand and secure such positions for whites. And such positions did indeed expand. As the *Report of the Industrial Legislation Commission* of 1935 noted, the character of the industrial labor force had changed considerably over the past decade: "Since the passing of these Acts [the Industrial Conciliation Act of 1923 and the Wage Act of 1925] a considerable change has taken place in the composition of labour in industry. Owing to the greater mechanisation of industry, more scope is offered for so-called semi-skilled labour, and there is a growing tendency to reduce the field for artisans."[32]

The formation of a black urban proletariat in any large numbers threatened to undercut severely the advantages white labor enjoyed. In order to forestall such a development, the Pact government proposed to channel black labor into the agricultural and mining sectors as well as restrict urban industrial employment to whites. The "civilized labour" policy was designed to achieve the latter. What has often gone unnoticed, however, was a parallel program to achieve the first end by controlling not only the movement of labor and urban rights for blacks but also the decomposition of rural black communities. And these were not simply the repressive measures that we have come to associate with apartheid, but measures designed to enable black households to be anchored in rural areas under invented tribal controls.[33]

By 1923 the South African state already possessed considerable powers over urban residency rights and the movement of labor. In addition, Prime Minister Hertzog proposed to parliament in 1925 a new "native" policy intended to maintain the cohesiveness of rural African communities and thus, it was hoped, preserve urban industrial employment for whites. The key elements of this legislative program were land acquisitions for Reserve Areas and the institutionalization of new tribal authorities by empowering African chiefs and applying a newly invented code of "traditional," "native" law. Africans were at the same time to lose their voting rights in the Cape area, while voting rights were to be extended to Coloureds throughout the country—Hertzog had always maintained that Coloureds were part of the heritage of *European* civilization. The bills were never passed, however, running aground on the removal of Africans from the limited Cape voting franchise, which required a parliamentary majority of two-thirds.

In the early 1930s the pace of African proletarianization rapidly quickened. As late as 1930 the *Report of the Inter-Departmental Committee on the Labour Resources of the Union* could, for example, refer to "the shortage of non-European and the surplus of European labour."[34] Yet the increase in both mining and industrial activity after 1933 did not generate labor supply problems. The number of black miners, which had risen but slightly in numbers between 1924 and 1933 (from 271,000 to 313,000), increased rapidly between 1933 and 1938 to 409,000.[35] Black employment in private industry showed a similar trend, rising slowly from 88,000 employees in 1924 to 104,000 employees in 1930. After 1933 this growth accelerated: between 1932–33 and 1937–38 the number doubled.[36]

Neither state industrial policy nor industrial capital's willingness to employ black labor can adequately explain this transformation in the supply of black labor. Prevailing wage rates also do not explain the attraction of urban life and wage labor. Mining wages remained, for example, at constant real levels throughout the period, and while manufacturing wage rates rose above those prevailing in the mining sector, they hardly reached levels sufficient to sustain life in urban areas.[37] What did change, however, were the conditions of household reproduction in rural black areas. When combined with the emergence of industries utilizing semiskilled operatives, these transformations generated the conditions for the creation of an increasingly stable, urban-centered black working class.

Of prime importance were the declining conditions of rural life and the attractiveness of urban employment by comparison to rural or mining wage labor. Reserve Areas in the 1920s were already marked by serious overcrowding and falling agricultural production levels per capita. At the same time, grazing and tilling rights granted to labor tenants on white farms were being cut back as commercialization proceeded apace. The sharpest blows came, however, in the 1920s, when the prices paid for agricultural surpluses fell dramatically just as several bad agricultural seasons ensued. Protected by a panoply of state credit and price supports, white farmers were sheltered from natural disasters and the ill winds emanating from the world market. African farmers, by contrast, found no such relief. At the same time, an expansion of recruiting activities by the gold mines created new channels of entry into the sphere of wage labor. But what was crucial was not simply the increase in demand for labor created by the expansion of primary and secondary industries but the decline in the ability of African households to couple appreciable returns from agriculture with returns from intermittent wage labor. The flip side of an increased supply of urban labor was, in fact, the impoverishment of the countryside, which in many cases led to permanent out-migration to urban areas and not simply an increase in circulating migration.

The 1930s were, by most accounts, a period of considerable decline in the ability of most Reserve Areas to supply foodstuffs, leading to the importation of grain in large quantities and the necessity for Africans to find wage work.[38] The same story could be told for large areas of Botswana, Lesotho, and Swaziland, which were all territories that the Union government assumed would be incorporated into the Union. As Murray observes, for African famers in Lesotho "the early 1930s were disastrous."[39] The push to create a black labor supply for white farmers and the mines had thus moved well beyond making participation in the wage labor force discretionary; by the 1930s continual wage labor force participation was becoming the norm and not the exception for many South and southern African households. Far from the reproduction of rural communities over time being supplemented by wages, rural survival was being underwritten by wages. This was even evident on the mines, where wages bore less and less relationship to demand.

The implications of these changes in the conditions and reproduction of black labor, and thus its supply at even flat wage rates, were exactly what had been feared by the minority commissioners of the 1925 Economic and Wage Commission. By the mid-1930s, many reports highlighted the intense competition in the urban labor market, as blacks increasingly became urban residents. Speaking of the "influx of natives," General Smuts told a group of municipal authorities in 1937 that it had "become a movement of enormous dimensions" and that, if left uncontrolled, it might "lead to revolutionary social and economic changes in South Africa. . . . In fact, the figure shows that in the last 15 years, from 1921 to 1936, the native population in our urban areas has practically doubled from 587,000 to 1,150,000."[40] On top of that, in the next ten years, the urban African population would increase by more than 700,000 persons.[41] Figures for Africans engaged in industrial pursuits followed a similar trend, rising from 220,000 in 1921 to 276,000 in 1936 to 457,000 in 1946.[42] Africans were filling openings for both unskilled and semiskilled work.

To be sure, the process of black labor force reproduction and labor force participation was not as homogeneous as has been suggested so far. Still, an increasing number of urban Africans were attempting to survive without substantial rural support, while facing wages influenced by the continuing inflow of migrants from the countryside. In 1937 the Native Affairs Commission observed: "One of the primary factors in our economic life— often overlooked—is that natives employed in the basic [i.e., mining and commercial farming] industries who come from the reserves receive a wage subsidy from their resources in the native reserves, whilst completely detribalised and urbanised natives [in urban manufacturing], without such resources, are compelled to keep their wives and families on the wages they receive without any such assistance.[43] While urban residents faced ever higher costs of living, wages in urban areas were held in check as both the permanent black population and the migrant inflow grew.

One major effect of this transformation was to undercut the strength of the labor movement. Strikes by black workers outnumbered those by white workers by the 1930s, a trend matched by new attempts at organizing African labor—as in the growth of the Industrial and Commercial Union.[44] Yet the success of such actions was limited by four factors. First, as noted above, competition in the labor market was rising due to the expansion of supply. Second, blacks commanded few skills that enhanced their market-place bargaining power. Third, the expansion of industrial employment did not take place through the expansion of workers' bargaining power in the workplace (as would occur elsewhere due to Fordism and mass-production labor processes).[45] And finally, state power, and the willingness to use it, was employed without hesitation against black workers. White workers' organizations during the 1930s faced similar difficulties, as the value of unskilled and semiskilled white workers in the labor market was dramatically undercut. As the social character of the labor force significantly changed, the strength of both black and white workers vis-à-vis capital declined.

The Mounting Contradictions of Semiperipheral Development

As a response to the post–World War I crisis in the primary sectors of the economy and a political challenge by white labor, the promotion of industrialization was certainly a success. But this very success generated a new wave of unrest in the late war and early postwar years. At the forefront, yet again, was an increasingly unruly labor force. As gold boom gave way to war boom, simmering discontent by both black and white workers broke out into a series of major strikes. At the same time, increasing conflict erupted among those who ruled in industry, agriculture, and mining. In the face of such developments, the Smuts government vacillated, opening the door to the appeals of the National Party, which won the 1948 election by calling for "apartheid."

While the political details of this transition are well documented, explanations of the social forces underlying the emergence of apartheid are less satisfactory. Even if one leaves aside accounts based on the simple dichotomies of rigid caste and racial groups, following for example van den Berghe's *South Africa: A Study in Conflict,* support for apartheid and the National Party is frequently depicted as resting on racist and nationalist appeals to whites marginalized by the process of economic growth.[46] For others the secret behind the transition to apartheid is to be found in the construction of new mechanisms to ensure a continued flow of "cheap labor" given the emergence of an urban-industrial order,[47] or the emergence of exclusionary and split labor markets.[48]

There are, to be sure, partial truths in these various accounts. Yet focusing on white workers' fears or models of cheap labor too often reduces apartheid to essentialized racial or class groups, or the functional needs of national capital. Racial and class forces were far more fluid and far more deeply entrenched in regional and global networks than the dominant national models suggest. The changing class and racial composition of the country's labor force following the early post–World War I crisis had slowly generated unexpected fractures within the manufacturing sector and between the state and workers in mining, farming, and manufacturing. Still, as long as the number of unskilled and semiskilled positions expanded and whites were recruited to fill them, labor peace among the enfranchised seemed assured.

Toward the end of the interwar period these conditions were undermined from several directions. As industrial production expanded employers began to replace white unskilled and operative workers with black workers, leaving white workers struggling to move up the occupational hierarchy.[49] At the same time, the formation of an urban-industrial complex, when coupled with the impoverishment of many rural African households, threatened to undermine the structural conditions that reproduced the part-lifetime and coerced labor force for the mines and white farms of the country. This was not, it must be emphasized, a process of the homogenization of the labor force, but rather the dissolution of boundaries between very different streams of household, labor force, and thus racial and class categories—and this holds even if we restrict our view to African workers and households. Neither mining companies nor commercial white farmers would accept the higher cost of urban-industrial labor, especially as wages for Africans in manufacturing rose by over 30 percent between 1940 and 1946.[50]

By the end of World War II it was thus not simply white industrial workers who had reason to fear changes in the industrial sector. At war's end, labor unrest in mining and industry was compounded by open conflicts between primary producers and employers in the increasingly weighty and core-like industrial sector. As unruly workers exacerbated these tensions, employers were divided and state policymakers were bedeviled by the competing claims and requirements of industrial, agricultural, and especially mining capital.[51] Time and time again white farmers' organizations and mining companies protested against the untrammeled effects of manufacturing development, focusing especially on the corrosive downside of rising African wages, the flight of rural Africans to urban areas, and the threatened recognition of black trade unions. Confronted by such mutually exclusive demands, and unwilling to abandon the promise of continued manufacturing development, the government could see no resolution of the problem and offered no new policies to address it. The results were openly revealed at the end of the war: acrimonious and dissatisfied employers, an open challenge from labor, and a withering away of support for General Smuts's United Party government, which had itself emerged in 1934 as a fusion of Hertzog's National Party and Smuts' South African Party.

The National Party in 1948 would thus face a similar task as had the Pact government in 1924: any resolution of the country's economic and social crises would require resolving contradictions inherent in the racial distribution and reward of black and white workers among low- and high-wage, core and peripheral, production processes. In 1924 these were traceable to competing peripheral production processes and their different relationships to overseas forces and markets; in 1948 competing networks of accumulation now included core-like industrial as well as peripheral mining and agricultural production processes. State policies after 1948 were thus not simply a matter of protecting white labor and privileging nascent Afrikaner entrepreneurs. As segregation gave way to apartheid, the inner secret of this process was the construction of segregation between the requirements of white farmers, mining companies, and urban-industrial employers. And this required segregating racial relationships along core-peripheral lines—with the region now spatially marked by these relationships to an unexpected and striking degree.

The post–World War II crisis was thus quite unlike the earlier post–World War I crisis, for while the latter arose from the difficulties faced by primary producers openly integrated into a crisis-stricken world economy, the post–World War II crisis reflected conflicts engendered from the localization of industrial accumulation in the midst of a worldwide depression, which had generated competitive and increasingly mutually exclusive relations across core-like and peripheral production processes. Apartheid would seek to resolve these competing demands, particularly in relation to racialized labor and household structures: coercion would assure a captive agricultural tenantry, mining's migrant flow would be narrowed to foreign workers and separated from flows to industry and agriculture, and urban employers would be assured a disempowered, stable, and controlled black labor force. This was, moreover, a process that relied on and expanded the racialized center-hinterland relationships across the region and the world economy that had arisen over the course of the interwar period.

Seen in this light, apartheid was not an extension of segregation. Even if we restrict ourselves to the industrial labor force and segregation, apartheid policies were poised to control an existing and expanding black urban proletariat—a strikingly different set of conditions from those that prevailed at the end of World War I. The extension of apartheid power across regional boundaries would also offer manufacturers markets and investment opportunities. Far from the isolation and segmentation that marked regional markets and production processes as was the case during the interwar period, in the apartheid era the South African state, on the basis of its unassailable industrial power, would promote an ever-denser set of center-hinterland relationships across the region.

By segregating core-like and peripheral production processes along these lines, the apartheid state sought to resolve the bitter conflicts among dominant classes that in other semiperipheral states, particularly in Latin America, led to constant political upheavals. Under apartheid conditions, accumulation could thus proceed profitably regardless of vast differences in labor sources, production and labor processes, and markets for inputs and outputs. This innovative reorganization of regional and national economic spaces was central to apartheid's resolution of the contradictions of semiperipheral development as they appeared in 1948. The final demise of British power, the rise of US hegemony, and a global boom all offered, moreover, seemingly golden opportunities to South Africa's rulers for not only regional but continental domination.

5

A Mad New World

At no time in the twentieth century did South Africa stand taller on the world stage than at the end of World War II. It had been part of the winning war coalition, was a linchpin of the world financial system, and had a prime minister in Jan Christian Smuts who was a confidant of Churchill and had been a member of the Imperial War Cabinet in both world wars. Smuts, like Cecil Rhodes before him, saw the world as his oyster: throughout the war he had spoken to prominent audiences of the problems of postwar reconstruction, and with the end of the war he became a leading figure in postwar deliberations. At the founding conference for the United Nations in San Francisco in 1945, he was appointed president of the Commission on the General Assembly, and drafted much of the preamble to the UN Charter.

The specific postwar order that Smuts and his British allies had expected and planned for did not come to pass. Smuts had promoted a central place for Britain and the British Commonwealth, composed at war's end of just five white-dominated states: Australia, Britain, Canada, New Zealand, and South Africa. Britain was to lead in the reconstruction of Europe and, through her empire and the Dominions, manage relations between Europe and the rest of the world. Recognizing Britain's economic weakness, Smuts proposed the reorganization of Britain's many colonial territories into "less costly" regional groups, which would then be placed under the tutelage of one of the white Dominions. As Smuts explained in 1943 to the Empire Parliamentary Association:

> In this way, instead of the Dominions being a show apart, so to say, having little or nothing to do with the Empire, and taking very little interest in it, the regional Dominions will become sharers and partners in the Empire. You will tighten up your whole show; you will create fresh links between the Empire and the Commonwealth, and create a new interest and life in the system as a whole.[1]

This was nothing less than a claim for a true "subimperial" role. Smuts, of course, did not use the term: the Dominions were to be "sharers and partners in the Empire," and were "to take both interest and pride in the Colonies within their sphere, and in that way to create, in our great world-wide Commonwealth, a new 'esprit de corps,' a common patriotism, and a larger human outlook."[2]

Few, however, were deceived. Smuts's pursuit of a place in the world through an alliance with Britain and his desire to expand South Africa's control over at least southern Africa were very well known. These efforts had ranged from his attempt to persuade white Rhodesians in 1923 to join the Union, to his oft-stated desire to dominate Mozambique, and his recurring attempt, repeated at the beginning of the war, to incorporate into South Africa the British High Commission Territories of Bechuanaland, Basutoland, and Swaziland.

Still, Smuts's vision for postwar Africa was not far-fetched. His proposals were a plausible extrapolation of the interwar colonial system, now operating under conditions of peace, with British leadership of Europe and a growing global contest between the United States and the Soviet Union. White domination at home was not considered any obstacle: racial exclusion was the rule for immigration, citizenship, and, especially, the right to vote in Europe, North America, and all settler states. The overwhelming majority of Africans lived within colonial empires, and were denied voting rights as natives—setting aside the very few that could prove to French or Portuguese authorities that they were "assimilated,"—that is, évolués or *assimilados*, respectively. In the British Empire of roughly 500 million persons, even this was ruled out: citizenship rights were rigidly controlled by race and place.

Nor was Smuts's patriarchal and colonial hubris unusual. The South African government, like Britain and the Dominions, was boldly expecting the fruits of victory in war. After all, was not Europe, as Smuts put it, "the motherland of our civilization,"[3] with Britain destined to lead it and the world—with the assistance of the white Dominions and especially South Africa? And the ties to England were quite strong: when King George VI and the royal family made their first postwar overseas tour in 1947, it was to South Africa. As the king put it to white South Africans at the end of his tour: "Are we not one brotherhood—the greatest brotherhood in the history of man, a brotherhood that has been strengthened not weakened by past differences?"[4] Is it not true, as he put it to the British public upon his return to England, that "the faith of South Africans in Britain is not only unimpaired but has become stronger on account of her unflagging effort in war and in peace"?[5] Indeed, the king reassuringly reported to his British subjects that "South Africans are convinced that the mission of Britain in the world is not ended but is only entering upon a new phase."[6]

The king, Great Britain, and Smuts were to be sorely disappointed. Three factors intervened to undermine their expectations. One, rather than revive British power and hegemony, victory in the war ushered in its final demise. Two, the world economy boomed, alleviating fears of a return to the interwar depression, but did so under the leadership of the United States and American multinational corporations. Third, the racial definitions and hierarchies that had underpinned the concept of a worldwide European community and the European colonial system were recast—and were done so not by choice, but in response to the victory of anticolonial movements, the emergence of the "Third World," and the dictates of US hegemony.

These three factors emerged after World War II. The forced independence of India (and Pakistan) and the transition under Britain's Labour government to a policy that accepted self-government for the colonies were particularly bitter disappointments for South Africa's white leaders. Smuts had thought Britain's departure from India was an "awful mistake" and upon hearing Ceylon was to become independent could only remark, "Ceylon a Dominion this year? Am I mad or is the World mad?"[7] At the United Nations, Smuts's and South Africa's racial policies came under direct, unremitting attack in 1946 and 1947, and Smuts found that no European power, much less the United States, was willing to defend the Union. On white rule Smuts would not, could not, yield; on this he held his ground with the far more conservative Afrikaner nationalists in opposition parties. As he reported back to the South African parliament, "As a minority [we whites] have maintained our position here for three hundred years. We have built up something in this country, which, in my opinion, is a monument among the nations, something we cannot sacrifice."[8] By the time of his death in 1950, Smuts was thoroughly disillusioned: not only had he lost the 1948 election, but his lifelong struggle to ensure South Africa's place in southern Africa, the British Empire, and the world was in shreds.

The National Party in the Postwar Order

In the early postwar years Afrikaner nationalists, like Smuts, faced the fitful emergence of a new postwar political and economic order. Most accounts of the early nationalist years stress that the new government paid little attention to foreign affairs, bereft as it was of foreign allies and experience, and focused on institutionalizing the idea of apartheid and countering African resistance at home. In large part this is true. But this also reflects the ad hoc nature of postwar planning worldwide, where newly elected governments lacked any guiding framework on how to handle the reconstitution of trade, production, and social relations after the war—not to mention the pressures, especially pertinent for Africa, of anticolonial movements.

What became apparent after the war was that there would be no return to the prewar, much less a British-led, world order. But what might stabilize the world economy was very uncertain to even European and North American governments. In retrospect it is possible, of course, to recount mechanically the steady ascent of the United States to global hegemony, the regional power of the apartheid system, and the felicitous partnership between these two forms of domination. Yet whether or how this would take place, in what form, and when were very much open questions in the first decade after the war. Indeed, for South Africa, as for other parts of Africa, the rise of the United States had little if any direct impact during this period. The Roosevelt, Truman, and Eisenhower administrations paid little attention to Africa, seeing the continent as a sphere best left in the colonial hands of its allies Britain and France; up to 1956 relations with South Africa were still handled by the State Department's Bureau of European Affairs, after which time South Africa was placed under the Bureau of Near Eastern, South Asian, and African Affairs. It was not until 1958, after Ghana's independence, that a Bureau of African Affairs was finally created in the State Department.[9]

For the United States, as for almost everyone else in Africa and Europe, the National Party's electoral victory came as a great surprise, and threatened to upset the easy reliance on Britain, Smuts, and the slowly evolving colonial order. Immediate evaluations were sharp and negative, building on the still-fresh memory of many Afrikaner nationalists' support for the Nazi regime. In 1941 the *New Republic* called the National Party, for example, a "full-fledged Nazi movement aimed at the creation of a dictatorship by Afrikaners," with its victory in 1948 illustrating that "out-and-out Nazis in the ranks of the Dutch nationalists who run South Africa are beginning to throw their weight around." *Time* similarly reported that South Africa "had suddenly embarked on a perverse, isolationist, acutely race-conscious road under a party tainted with anti-Semitism and pro-Nazism," while the *Nation* noted that the "Nationalists are not easily distinguishable from Nazis."[10] At the time many expected Smuts's party to regain control in the next election; after all, the National Party had won in 1948 with only a plurality of the vote. The new government, for its part, had little reason to deal with the United States: South Africa's international and trade relations, as for the rest of the continent, were far more bound up with Britain and Europe.

And here were new challenges and opportunities. The postwar years saw war-weary and impoverished Britain—South Africa's dominant economic partner for more than a century—struggling to regain its position in the world economy and its hold on South Africa. In 1937 Britain took 41 percent of South Africa's exports (excluding gold); by 1948 this had fallen to but 28 percent. South Africa's imports from Britain similarly fell from 42 percent of the total in 1937 to 31 percent in 1948—with the 36 percent share coming from the United States exceeding Britain's for the second straight year.[11] And while Britain hungered for South Africa's food and raw materials, it was unable to provide South Africa with the capital or capital goods that South Africa's postwar economy needed. The steep downward slide in the importance of the British market was eventually halted as the British economy recovered and, more dramatically, as South Africa ran short of dollars, suffered a balance of payments crisis, and imposed import controls that limited access to dollar-denominated goods. By 1955 Britain again accounted for 33 percent of South Africa's imports and 31 percent of its merchandise exports; the US shares by contrast stood at 21 and 8 percent, respectively.

Behind these shifting trade figures stood substantial rivalries among great powers, radical shifts in Europe's and North America's changing relationships with Africa, Asia, and Latin America, and unsettling transformations in the international division of labor. As Smuts and his successors had found out, there would be no return to the interwar system whereby the territories and peoples of Africa were, with few exceptions, encapsulated within colonial markets and political blocs. But what would replace this system? Clearly Britain and Europe as a whole were weakened, but just as clearly the United States was not significantly challenging, much less replacing, European power in Africa. What kind of world economy was to emerge from the ashes of war was most uncertain in the 1940s and 1950s.

South Africa's interwar policies were no guide. They had rested on the foundation of a major worldwide depression, the collapse of primary product prices, and the pursuit—as in other independent, especially Latin American, states—of protected markets and state enterprises. Clearly these conditions did not hold in the late 1940s and 1950s: world markets were booming, primary product prices were high, and isolated national markets were waning. Meanwhile wholly new features such as the European Union, the World Bank, the International Monetary Fund, and GATT were emerging—not to mention the burgeoning weight of the Soviet Union and increasingly unruly anticolonial movements. Clearly the revived world economy was coming to depend on institutions, states, and alliances that fit neither the colonial system of the first half of the twentieth century nor the free trade system of the nineteenth century. For South Africa's prime ministers, as well as the country's businessmen, this seemed to offer golden opportunities across Africa.

Reaching Outward: Malan's Africa Charter

Shortly after being elected in 1948, Prime Minister Daniel François Malan charted South Africa's relationship to the rest of the continent in glowing, positive, and highly racialized terms:

We are part of Africa . . . and our actions here in South Africa are largely influenced by what takes place in the rest of Africa. Not only do we wish to be on friendly terms with the territories of Africa for that reason, but we also have a growing trade with these territories. South Africa also has the right by virtue of its population as a white man's country, and its experience during the course of years in connection with the native problem and the coloured problem to aspire to leadership in this matter and to act as adviser to the peoples of the Northern territories.[12]

This was not a new ambition. During the war Malan had spoken of an African charter, whereby Africa would be protected by South Africa from rapacious Asians, preserved for Africans, developed on Western and Christian lines, and kept noncommunist and nonmilitarized (by which he meant "natives" would not be armed). Like Europe, the United States, and even Smuts, Malan assumed Western rule would continue, and that "Africa should be safeguarded for the European in so far as he settled here permanently because he has borne civilization on his shoulders."[13] South Africa might be condemned in the United Nations by newly independent Asian powers, but in Africa, thought South African politicians, things would surely be different.

In Rhodesia, especially, South African whites and businessmen saw an ally, a bridge to exercising shared power over African peoples and markets to the north. To answer the question it posed in 1950 of "Whither Rhodesia?" the *Industrial Review*, the official journal of the Transvaal Chamber of Industry, began by stressing a settler, racial alliance over Africans:

It cannot be said that Union and Rhodesian conditions are completely similar, but they have a kinship. . . . It must never be forgotten, also, that Southern Rhodesia, like the Union, has a northern neighbour, or rather northern neighbours. Were it not for the presence of Southern Rhodesia as a buffer state, these neighbours would be our own. . . . Looking southwards, Southern Rhodesia sees a former colonial land able to sustain an independent sovereign role. She looks northwards and sees land where the "policy of trusteeship" is perhaps the best description of the position for a long time to come.[14]

By the early 1950s signs of growing African power could not, however, be denied.

Yet even as Britain granted independence to its former colonial territories, the vision of European leadership and trusteeship being exercised by white settlers persisted. Speaking in 1957 on the eve of Ghana's independence, Eric Louw, influential first minister of external affairs appointed in 1955, envisioned South Africa's role as "a permanent link between the Western nations on the one hand and the population of Africa south of the Sahara on the other."[15] After Ghana's independence Louw reported back to parliament that Nkrumah was "perfectly happy" with South Africa's low-level representative to independence celebrations, and that Nkrumah and Prime Minister Johannes G. Strijdom had exchanged "cordial" messages.[16] Nkrumah vowed to continue to trade with South Africa, and later invited South Africa to a meeting of independent states in Addis Ababa. Prime Minister Strijdom refused to go to the conference, on the basis that the meeting unjustly excluded colonial powers. Speaking to the House of Assembly in 1959, Eric Louw addressed his audience on the difficulties of the white man dealing with independent Africa, where "some of these leaders are not yet one generation removed from the primitive conditions of their forefathers. There are many of them whose fathers and mothers were completely primitive, barbaric people."[17]

From Region to Continent: South Africa as the Workshop of Africa?

Such views were hardly restricted to Afrikaners engaged in implementing the vision of apartheid. Similar expectations of Africa and the country's relations with colonial powers were rife among South African businessmen and foreign investors. Indeed, the weakness of Britain, France, and Germany after the war and the gradual but steady opening of closed markets and colonial empires seemed to offer a vast new field of expansion for South Africa. By contrast to the situation after World War I, in 1945 South Africa was now producing many manufactured goods that were unavailable from war-torn Europe or even North America. This offered the opportunity to expand into Africa, and in so doing extend the southern African region far to the north—with South Africa at its controlling center.

Such sentiments ran right across the economic spectrum, from commercial houses represented by the Association of Chambers of Commerce to domestic and international manufacturers located in South Africa. Manufacturers would benefit the most, and were the most exuberant promoters of such possibilities and their benefit for white South Africa. In a 1951 editorial the *Manufacturer* argued, for example, that "Africa is the last continent awaiting full development. The potentialities are enormous." And who would lead this? The answer was clear: "Birmingham was once the workshop of the world; the Union might become the great powerhouse of Southern Africa south of the Sahara. This bid for industrial supremacy will not go unchallenged by territories anxious to develop local industries. . . . But the Union starts the race with a great advantage of years."[18] Indeed, it was the industrial progress of the interwar and war years that made this possible. As the *Manufacturer* argued, "An increasing output of high quality manufactured goods entitles the Union to enter the export market. This is a step in our industrial development that must be faced and turned to good account just as Great Britain did more than 150 years ago."[19]

The *Industrial Review* went even further, noting that South Africa's new position as industrial supplier to African territories was the basis for yet further industrial investment in South Africa by both domestic and foreign firms. Foreign firms, it argued in September 1949, increasingly "regard the Union as a base for an export drive in the African Continent. Meanwhile, South African manufacturers are not neglecting the market to the north themselves. South African business men are meeting each other in all parts of our great continent."[20] The same issue reported on a new General Tire factory established in the Union, while the August 1949 issue reported on trade exhibitions in the Belgian Congo as well as the new Kellogg factory, shipped entirely from the United States, which ended the import of commercial breakfast foods.

The coming of independence to the north did not shake the expectations of South African leadership. Indeed, the end of colonially enclosed markets was celebrated as a great opportunity. The *Commercial Opinion*, published by the Association of South African Chambers of Commerce, heralded Ghana's independence in 1957 and Nigeria's coming independence by touting: "Forty million potential customers! That is what Ghana and Nigeria offer to manufacturers and exporters in the Union."[21] This was not, its readers were told, a poor native market. Indeed, "any comparison with the requirements of the native territories of the Union should be dismissed for ever. In Lagos and Accra the African ladies drive up to the departmental stores in their chauffeur driven limousines and buy Paris model gowns."[22] The president of the South African Federated Chamber of Industries, at the organization's thirty-ninth annual convention, called for formal negotiations with Africa and told his members to "take the lead in arranging a Pan African Conference on Trade Relations Between African Territories. . . . The Continent of Africa will be our natural market when we make it so."[23]

South Africa's commercial press contained similar sentiments, such as the argument of former World Bank employee Edward Jeal in the *Commercial Opinion* that South Africa should push for an African trade bloc in opposition to colonial powers:

> Today the need in Africa is for the States South of the Sahara to come together in trade reciprocity. . . . The difficulty lies, more particularly, with the mother countries, which have sought to integrate African "possessions" with their own economies, or to apply some preference scheme or other. . . . In this situation, some country should assume the initiative. The country to do that is the Union—with its three hundred years of history within Western Civilization.[24]

This would mean, moreover, replacing Great Britain: "The position of the Union of South Africa in relation to the subcontinent of Africa should be similar to that occupied by Britain last century in relation to the world. It will be remembered that from the end of the 18th century Britain became the world-workshop and its main source of capital supply."[25]

Progress toward these ends was much slower than hoped for in these ambitious statements of the 1940s and early 1950s. Still, as even reported in the *Finance and Trade Review*, the official journal of the Afrikaner savings bank Volkskas, South Africa was becoming the mother country to poorer areas even as it continued to export raw materials to overseas core countries: "Union exports to less developed countries and territories have increased more than four-fold between 1938 and 1958. . . . Well over ninety percent of all exported raw materials still goes to industrialized countries, whereas the portion of the products of secondary industry going to less developed areas reached three quarters (74.5% in 1958 and 75.1% in 1948) of the Union's export in manufactures."[26]

Southern Rhodesia and Federation: Whose Region, Whose Continent?

Nowhere were the implications of these structural and geographical shifts more evident, and tension-ridden, than in the Union's exports to Southern Rhodesia—a central market for the Union's manufacturers. For Southern Rhodesia was no longer simply a producer of primary products, but increasingly envisioned itself as a manufacturer not only for its home market but for the large markets to its north. As Ian Phimister has deftly charted, "After September 1939 the conservative attitude of the Southern Rhodesian Government towards secondary industry was rendered untenable and irrelevant by world war."[27] During the war and especially during the early postwar years Southern Rhodesia's settler economy had boomed, with its primary product exports, especially tobacco, earning high prices on the world market and underwriting accelerating imports that fed a growing industrial sector. Factories increased in number from 294 in 1939 to 473 in 1948, with manufacturing second only to commercial agriculture as a source of the colony's income.[28] White immigration from Europe and South Africa leaped upward after the war as well, as did production to meet pent-up demand for capital and consumer goods. By contrast to the interwar period, by the end of the war the manufacturing sector not only was accepted; it was being heavily promoted by the government.

Still, Southern Rhodesia's industries and market paled by comparison to South Africa's, and trade relations remained contentious. As during the interwar period, the South African government wielded considerable bargaining power, controlling as it did access to a large market for Rhodesian tobacco and, increasingly, for Rhodesian consumer goods from clothing (often made with Indian piece goods) to radios. Yet the Southern Rhodesian government was not without bargaining power itself. As noted above, exports of South African manufactures went overwhelmingly to African territories, of which Southern Rhodesia was the best-valued customer by far. Moreover, for Rhodesian settlers, as for South Africans, the postwar period reopened the configuration of international and regional relations. Not the least of these changes were the opportunities offered by the weakening hold of European colonial powers.

Rhodesian settlers' allegiance to imperial Britain remained strong, however. Still, relations with South Africa also seemed to warm in the postwar years. Trade relations, in particular the April 1949 Trade Agreement, opened up the prospect of free trade from Cape Town to Salisbury, and then onward to the Northern Rhodesian side of the Copperbelt. Yet if the language of the agreement was to promote free trade, the prospect of a customs union or free trade area was clearly set aside. Under the agreement the Union freed from duty all Rhodesian goods except vegetable oils, wines, spirits, cigarettes, and manufactured tobacco, while quotas were still set for unmanufactured tobacco and cattle. In return Southern Rhodesia was permitted to retain nominal duties on seventy South African items that threatened the colony's infant industries, from furniture and clothing to processed foodstuffs and paints.

While the agreement was not a big step forward in terms of actual tariff duties and preferences, trade boomed, fed by domestic demand, a shortage of dollars and of goods from Britain, and South African import controls on overseas goods, all of which operated to advance trade between the two partners. As a Federated Chamber of Industry economist reported in the *Manufacturer* in 1953, trade between the two countries had risen between 1948 and 1952 by 156 percent, with Union exports reaching £24 million and Southern Rhodesian exports to the Union reaching £6 million. "The balance of trade between the two countries has been consistently in South Africa's favour, rising from £9.3 million in 1948 to £17.6 million in 1952."[29] This trend represented Southern Rhodesia's turning toward South Africa and away from the United Kingdom and even the United States: "In 1948 the Union accounted for 24.76 per cent of [Southern] Rhodesian imports compared with 45.9 per cent for the U.K. and 9.3 per cent for the U.S.A. By 1951 the Union had increased its share to 28.5 per cent, whilst that of the United Kingdom had dropped to 43.3 per cent and the U.S.A. to 4.9 per cent."[30] How long and in what direction such trade would continue and whether the boom in Southern Rhodesian manufacturing would continue remained, however, very much open questions. A 1954 review of Southern Rhodesia's impressive economic growth in the *South African Bankers' Journal* was "particularly suspicious of [industrial] progress made in artificial inflationary post-war conditions, especially when such progress is protected by tariffs and is inevitably limited by the restricted local market. Southern Rhodesia cannot hope to be a serious rival to the Union in the foreseeable future."[31]

The end of early postwar shortages also impacted South African export-ers. As the president of the Exporter's Association of South Africa noted in 1953 in the *Manufacturer*: "We are now fully entering the era of the buyer's market. The halcyon days after the end of the last war, when the world was starved of finished goods, foodstuffs, produce and raw materials of all kinds, and when the seller could virtually dictate his own terms, have now com-pletely gone."[32] In this climate competition among settler states and over-seas colonial powers over opening African markets could only intensify.

By the time of Ghana's independence, Europe and North America were fully engaged in Africa, overshadowing South Africa. As Foreign Minister Louw told parliament, these "metropolitan powers" had growing economic interests in Africa, expressed in a new wave of "outside financial and eco-nomic aid in the development of emergent independent territories in Africa."[33] While this was "welcomed," it was clearly a competitive effort to thwart South African economic expansion: "The territories to the North of the Limpopo are the natural markets for our large and expanding indus-tries and, whatever arrangements are made, whatever interests are secured by outside countries, we expect that no impediment will be laid in the way of our access to those markets."[34] Louw then told parliament that it was imper-ative that South African industrialists "take greater pains than they have done in the past, to secure a footing in these markets."[35]

These new challenges were highlighted by the creation of the Federation of Rhodesia and Nyasaland in 1953, which embraced the colony of Southern Rhodesia and the colonial territories of Northern Rhodesia and Nyasaland. The Federation was primarily designed by Rhodesian settlers to stake their claim to central Africa—and at South Africa's expense. As shown elsewhere, Rhodesian settlers gained access to booming Copperbelt revenues and mar-kets in the north, while directing capital inflows and industrial growth in Southern Rhodesia.[36] Of course, the great difficulty, as seen by white settlers, was to find a way to stem African nationalism while securing white domination and the benefits of the larger Federation economy. Here the white Rhodesians moved away from colonial and apartheid models, and gingerly toward the US liberal model, which could legally admit Africans to vote while privately pre-venting it. As the *Industrial Review of Africa* reported to its South African read-ers, no less an authority that Mr. Philip Mason, the director of Studies in Race Relations at the Royal Institute of International Affairs, assured an audience in Salisbury (present-day Harare) that the solution

consisted mainly in ensuring that the vote is given only to those capable of maintaining an unspecified standard of what to-day is called "civilisation." There is of course no racial discrimination in these matters—in other words Southern Rhodesia has a common roll on which members of all races, pro-vided they measure up to the qualifications, can participate. The difficulty of

course is to ensure that the governing of the country remains in the hands
of civilised people, without damping too much the ambitions of the African
population.[37]

Only in this way could the "long-term racial harmony" be sustained that
would attract "hard-headed businessmen" who would "finance major industrial activities in the future."[38] Toward South Africa the new Federation
authorities took a new, protectionist stance, cemented in a July 1, 1955,
trade agreement that was "designed to end South Africa's duty free access to
Federal markets so as to end its competitive trading advantage."[39]
     On the South African side of the border, this turn of events was viewed
with dismay, as it signaled not only a retreat to liberal racial policies but the
raising of barriers to manufactured exports to the north. The pages of the
Union's business press reverberated with deliberations over how such a state
of affairs could have come to pass. Speaking for South African industrialists,
the *Manufacturer* greeted the new trade treaty with dissatisfaction, publishing the report of a Federated Chamber of Industries economist that "there
is every possibility the large share of the Rhodesian market which we have
previously enjoyed, may well decline below its present satisfactory level. Such
a contraction in exports to our principal foreign market could have serious repercussions on the economic utilization of the expanding productive
capacity of many of our secondary industries."[40]
     The Union's own Department of Commerce and Industry agreed, releas-
ing an official note concluding that "the advantage in respect of customs
duties hitherto enjoyed by Union exporters in the two Rhodesias is now
appreciably reduced. . . . Suppliers of other countries may gradually increase
their shares in this important market at the expense of Union exporters."[41]
The commercial press reached similar conclusions, stressing that Federation
and the agreement signaled the final end to the long hoped-for and
expected common market. As the *Commercial Opinion* reported to its readers,
"The new trade agreement, signed last month, between the Union and the
Federation of Rhodesia and Nyasaland, puts an end to the grand prospect of
a larger free-trade area in Southern Africa."[42]
     Not all was as dire as these statements alleged; some South African pro-
ducers actually gained from the agreement. South African manufacturers
had long complained of cheap clothing imports from Southern Rhodesia
based on African labor and Asian materials. Even worse in their view, some
of these factories were set up by absconding South African manufacturers.
As an earlier Federated Chamber of Industry resolution put it, "Many of the
Rhodesian factories, paying wages [less than £1 to £2] a week to predominantly Native labour, had been established by South African clothing manufacturers who had emigrated. In the Union, wage agreements give workers,
predominantly European and Coloured, from £5 to £15 a week, with an

established ratio of qualified to unqualified workers lacking in Rhodesia."[43] New clauses in the agreement specifically targeted the importation of Indian piece goods altered in Rhodesian clothing factories and sent to the Union as Federal goods.

Overall, rising Rhodesian competition and assertiveness was met everywhere with disappointment, and exports to the Federation would indeed begin to slide downward. And more than just trade relations was altered. As the *Manufacturer* woefully reported in December 1955, Rhodesia's new outlet to the sea was opened—bypassing South Africa: "Few decisions ever made by Rhodesia disappointed South Africa more than that which resulted in the construction of an alternative railway line to Lourenço Marques instead of the anticipated second route through the Union. . . . She has chosen, rightly or wrongly, to increase her dependence upon her Portuguese neighbour than rely still further upon communications via the Union of South Africa."[44] And worse was the exclusion of South African manufactured goods: "Quite apart from the transport of Rhodesian imports from overseas, no doubt a point that was considered at the time was the undesirability of making too easy greater deliveries of merchandise from the competitive industrial areas of the Transvaal."[45]

To early postwar South African assertions of a natural hegemony over the region and the continent, Rhodesian settlers thus offered another vision, more attuned to the intimations of waning European colonialism: a Rhodesian-centered central African market, based on a liberal racial construct. As South Africa's *Commercial Opinion* reported in 1956, "Salisbury industrialists are after the non-European market."[46] South Africa's role in such a region might be like Britain's toward South Africa in the nineteenth century, but only insofar as it provided capital goods and financing, and left consumer goods for a mass market to Rhodesian producers. And South Africans, by the end of the postwar boom, were hardly likely to fulfill this role, feeling short of capital and markets themselves.

Creeping Control: From Trade to Direct Investment

At the heart of South African, Rhodesian, and British postwar ambitions was the issue of controlling colonial markets to ensure outlets for manufactured goods. If the prewar situation of protected colonial and national markets was not to be reimposed, what might replace it? As we have seen, colonial and settler powers pursued quite different visions to reshape and dominate African markets after the war. Behind these struggles was the assumption that capturing and controlling *trade* flows, as in the previous fifty years, would ensure a flow of wealth to centers of advancing industrial production. What became quickly and surprisingly apparent, however, was that cross-border flows of *capital* would be equally important to economic and political hegemony—and these were beginning to take new forms, with most unexpected consequences.

For South Africa the new importance of capital flows was driven home through successive balance of payments crises in 1948–49, 1953–54, and 1957–58, which arose from the extraordinary postwar demand for consumer and capital goods imports. The state responded by devaluing the pound in 1949, imposing import controls, and applying monetary and fiscal restraints. What normally served to offset shortfalls in the balance of trade was the inflow of private capital. Yet this flow was most unpredictable: a massive spike in private capital inflows in 1947 of £154 million (due largely to a preemptive flight from a threatened capital levy in Britain) was followed by a drop to well below half that level in the next two years. And this seriously complicated the purchase of capital goods. An article on "investment capital in short supply" in a 1949 issue of *Commercial Opinion* neatly located the problem: "the productive and development equipment primarily needed in Southern Africa cannot be adequately supplied from Great Britain. . . . Only from the dollar world can adequate assistance in the supply of capital goods be obtained; but the essential articles are limited, as are the powers to lend."[47] By late 1950, even after the devaluation of the South African pound triggered further expansion, the chairman of the Board of Trade and Industries was publicly warning of a shortage of capital resources.[48]

These fears proved unfounded: after the surge in 1947, private capital inflows settled into a steady stream, supplemented by the state's and parastatals' access to funds from new institutions such as the World Bank. From such sources came much of the capital to underwrite the expansion of private industry, the growth of state firms like ISCOR and ESCOM, and the development of the massive new Orange Free State goldfields. Long-term investment capital had, of course, been central to the development of South African mining and manufacturing for almost a hundred years, and postwar uncertainties appeared, at least for the moment, overstated.

Or so it seemed. It was not until the mid-1950s that the sources, destinations, and earnings of private capital inflows—and outflows—began to be tracked and reported. Indeed, the first survey by the South African Reserve Bank in 1957 was meant to address not only fluctuations in the capital flows that countered trade deficits and fed investment to mines, industries, and state firms but also a new concern over the *form* of capital flows. Here the slow emergence of another type of capital inflow was foremost: direct investment. If in the interwar period control over trade and tariffs meant control over the location of primary or industrial production, in the postwar period it slowly became clear to settler authorities that foreign firms could bypass tariff walls by locating branch plants inside such walls.

This was an issue not only between South Africa and overseas investors. By the mid-1950s Rhodesian settlers had hoped by raising tariffs to entice South African manufacturers to set up shop in Rhodesia to serve the central and even eastern African markets. For South African capital and the South African state, with an established consumer and heavy industrial base already in place, the prospect of a rising tide of foreign direct investment (FDI) in the South African manufacturing sector was a more serious concern. Foreign and particularly US firms had already begun to set up branch plants in South Africa in the 1920s, most notably in the automobile sector.

In the early postwar period such investments were still viewed as positive, foreign judgments on South Africa and its regional potential. As the Transvaal Chamber of Industries journal the *Industrial Review* commented in September 1949, "The spectacle of new factories being opened in South Africa by overseas industrialists, using, to the greatest possible extent, South African materials and South African labour, is, indeed, a heart-warming one. Not only are they manufacturing here . . . but in some cases they regard the Union as a base for an export drive in the African continent."[49]

Still, in the late 1940s and early 1950s industrial expansion remained very much a South African affair, whether it involved private capital or state firms. In succeeding years, however, FDI became increasingly visible. And when placed alongside the familiar and yet still growing dependence on foreign sources for long-term investment capital, such inflows challenged the economic nationalism central to settler, and especially Afrikaner, economic policy.

In the mid-1950s slowing economic growth, a substantial outflow of private capital, and a fall in export values focused serious attention once again on the capital requirements of the country. Afrikaner economists, most notably at Stellenbosch University and the "peoples' bank," Volkskas, began to make the case that foreign capital was a threat to hard-won economic independence and was not needed. The chief economist for Volkskas, publishing in the house journal *Finance and Trade Review*, boldly termed foreign investment as nothing less than a tool of "neo-colonialism": "Immediately after the war, and especially in the boom year of 1947, the amounts of foreign capital flowing to the Union assumed such large proportions that all previous yearly figures were dwarfed and it outwardly appeared that South Africa was again passing through a stage of neo-colonialism."[50] The writer was particularly emphatic that South Africa was not a colonized African or underdeveloped country: "Many people in Europe, America, and elsewhere are apparently under the impression that the Union of South Africa, like some other African territories, is still economically an underdeveloped country. This is, of course, quite a fallacious concept."[51] South Africa's per capita income, it was pointed out, was higher than that of Brazil, Mexico, Italy, and Japan, and about the same as that of Austria and Portugal.[52]

Responding to such charges in the same journal, Eric M. Louw, the minister of finance and of external affairs, stressed that before World War II South Africa had borrowed heavily from Britain. But these loans had been repaid during the war, and after the war "it soon became obvious that the United Kingdom was not in a position to export capital on the pre-war scale, and the Government was forced to seek new sources of capital overseas. . . . Loans totaling £29,000,000 were raised in Switzerland, the Netherlands, and the U.S.A."[53] Foreign capital, Louw continued, was both needed and diversified and could be controlled.

When private flows turned negative, however, other Afrikaner economists pressed the case further. J. L. Sadie, a professor of economics at the University of Stellenbosch, wrote a lengthy response to Louw, arguing that "domestic sources [of capital] will be able to provide not only the desired aggregate amount but also the desired types of investment funds."[54] Sadie thus concluded that "our economic development target can be accommodated by domestic sources of capital supply and by the Balance of Payments without resort to the importation of capital."[55]

In a second and even longer article, Sadie made the case that foreign capital led not only to a loss of capital, through the repatriation of dividends, but to a loss of control over national economic development and national economic policy—a charge to which the government, representative of Afrikaner nationalism that it was, was particularly sensitive and vulnerable. In a prescient fashion, Sadie noted that while Britons remained the biggest overseas investors in South Africa, with 80 percent of foreign assets, US citizens had rapidly become the second-largest group—and over 90 percent of US investments was in direct investments versus the British pattern of portfolio investment.[56]

Moreover, the influence of foreign capital and the drain overseas of remitted profits, interest, and the repatriation of capital was increasing. Sadie protested that capital outflows were steadily increasing as "the amounts of interest, dividends and profits that have been paid or credited have, however, also been expanding gradually to reach £73 million in 1956 or nearly 12% of the total debits on the Balance of Payments current account, in comparison with 9.6% in 1953."[57] Under such conditions, Sadie argued, foreign capital could come to control economic policy; even worse, "monopolistic practices" would be used, with political repercussions—as had happened in South African gold mining and commercial banking. Nor was this only a South African problem: Sadie was quite adept at documenting Australian complaints against the "excessive" profits of General Motors there, or complaints in Canada that the influx of American capital was leading to the country "losing its soul" and "making a mockery of its political independence."[58]

The reference to banking was especially pointed: this was precisely the area that Afrikaner nationalists and the state had targeted as the growth area for Afrikaner entrepreneurs. Defending his comments, Louw argued in the *Commercial Opinion* that "the significance of foreign investment lies not only in its amount but in the form it takes. I express my concern at the very large measure of control by non-residents of certain sections of our economy, a concern which I know is shared by many of my English-speaking friends."[59] He then advanced statistics to show that foreigners controlled 88 percent of South Africa's banks, 71 percent of the short-term insurance market, 60 percent of gold mining, and 40 to 50 percent of manufacturing.[60] Louw's conclusions were a blunt challenge to nationalists: "such a large measure of economic subservience (*onderhorigheid*) was unworthy of a country like South Africa, and suggested that steps should be taken to make this country more independent (*selfstandig*) economically."[61]

Writing in 1958, Louw contrasted again South Africa's path with that of the United States. Whereas the economic growth of the United States had been financed with the aid of British loan capital, the growth of "large financial and industrial corporations" in America had led to a radically new pattern: "foreign capital was no longer being provided to any great extent as loans, but rather as entrepreneurial capital" whereby "the parent company in the capital-exporting country would take up 100% of the equity of a subsidiary formed in the capital-receiving company, and thus obtain full control of that subsidiary." For a mineral-exporting country like South Africa this was particularly dangerous, he continued, for this trend had "as a natural corollary a policy which, for instance, frowns at the beneficiation of base minerals in the country of origin because it suits the parent company in the capital-exporting country to receive it in the form of unbeneficiated conditions."[62]

For Louw, the conclusion was inescapable: "Do not let us fool ourselves, for unless counteracting forces are set in motion the degree of our economic subservience will increase and not decrease."[63] Citing Canadian Lester Pearson, the 1957 Nobel Peace Prize winner, Louw argued that "U.S. firms ... should agree to invest more capital abroad in the form of equity capital. They should be content with less ownership and control in other countries." As for South Africa, Louw suggested the government take steps to favor equity investment at the expense of direct investment, and grant preferential concessions to South African firms and persons.[64]

The response of the government to such arguments, made at major meetings of business leaders and in the leading economic journals, was quick, sharp, and stoutly defensive: foreign capital investment was necessary, should be encouraged, and would not threaten Afrikaner or national independence. The response by the minister for economic affairs, Dr. A. J. van Rhijn, was typical: "It could perhaps be argued that foreign investments in the Union could deprive the country of a certain degree of autonomy. Under present-day conditions, however, such a statement is without foundation.

The days of deliberate imperialistic investment, as far as the Union is concerned, have long since passed."[65]

The appearance of positive inflows of private capital in 1958, after the recession and outflows of previous years, was welcomed and even seen as a support for South Africa's regional ambitions. As one financial writer for the English-language press put it in 1959: "A new flow of capital is coming into the Union of South Africa, much of it from countries which hitherto were very reticent about any form of investment in the African Continent. Now money is also readily available from the United States of America; Switzerland; and recently from Western [sic] Germany, after a lapse of about 44 years." Why did this take place? It was, he continued, due to South Africa's stature in Africa: "The reason for this welcome change is not far to seek. South Africa to-day stands strongly established as the metropolitan area of the African Continent."[66]

South Africa did, as Rhodesians themselves had expected, continue to invest to the north, just as Americans invested in South Africa. As the *Industrial Review of Africa* reported on a 1959 speech by South Africa's high commissioner to the Federation, "One could not fail to be impressed by his statements about the Union's investments in central Africa. At the end of 1956, he said, some £28,500,000 was invested in the manufacturing industry in Rhodesia and a sum total of £115,000,000 has been sunk in overall investment in the Federation."[67]

With investment following trade, it did indeed appear that a nested set of settler states and colonies was in formation, opening up the prospect of a regional economic bloc that extended from the Copperbelt to Cape Town. This was not to be the continental market dreamed of by South African politicians in the immediate postwar years. Yet neither was it a continuation of enclosed colonial markets, controlled from London or Paris. Rather a successive hierarchy of centers of production and capital formation was to reach from Europe and North America to a settler industrial core in southern Africa, and then to yet simpler forms of raw material and primary production in African territories. This might be far from the expectations of the years immediately following 1945, but it would be a major advance from the early-twentieth-century colonial pattern of primary production even in settler areas.

Contesting Colonial and Regional Constructs

Neither the vision nor the economic realities behind this apparent nested set of white metropolitan centers and subject peripheries held. The reason is well known, having little to do with narrow economic or class determinants and everything to do with the exercise of racial power. For neither

Rhodesian nor South African settlers were willing or able to exercise economic hegemony without direct and overt white political supremacy. This was not the case for core states and elites. Indeed, the structure of the modern world-system, with a single world economy yet many states, facilitated the continuing exercise of racialized power on an interstate scale after decolonization. This arrangement was, as many have charted, the basis of British and French neocolonialism. In short: in global terms decolonization proceeded without deracialization of the world economy. Settlers, however, were in a different structural position, forced to rely on national political power to exercise white supremacy. This was the crux of the white settler conundrum: they were, as they often noted, embedded in Africa and relied on African labor and markets. They could not, as the United States and Europe could, exercise economic and racial hegemony from afar.

South African capital and politicians in the postwar years symbolized well the settler complex and dilemma. Everywhere they saw new trading blocs and treaties emerging, most notably in the North, from the formation of GATT to the emergence of the European Union, which threatened to pull in Britain and eliminate Commonwealth preferences. Africa, it was thought early on, could pursue the same path, with local European men easily believing that the cry of "Africa for Africans" included their rule over "primitive" Africa. As Gordon Harper put it in an article in the *Manufacturer* in 1959:

> One finds a reassuring tendency—from our point of view in Southern Africa—for Africa to trade within Africa itself. African countries are getting very Africa-conscious and all things being equal they tend to trade with themselves. Thus the manufacturer in South Africa starts off with this immense advantage, as he seeks business from the seething masses of black people in this continent.[68]

Where difficulties arose, Harper told his readers, they arose from Africans' racism against settlers! "There are prejudices, of course, in some countries. West Africa, for example, is not too friendly with parts of Africa which stick up for any pretence of a permanent white civilisation—I discovered this to my cost in Ghana. The people of this country have little use for white people." Still, Ghana was, assuredly, an anomaly: "But not all Africa is like this. Most territories are very co-operative and interested to learn about industrial development that is taking place in Africa. Unlike the Union and Rhodesia, other countries in Africa are not destined to become industrial."[69]

The events of the early 1960s showed that independent African states were, in fact, "like this." White South Africans' and Rhodesians' expectations that they could garner the fruits of decolonization quickly proved false. Although conservative African leaders controlled the new Organization of African Unity, South Africa was excluded from this body, and by the

mid-1960s South Africa withdrew or was expelled from all continental and
UN bodies related to Africa.

The political isolation of South Africa had a direct economic impact.
By the late 1950s the South African business press was reporting boycotts
of South African products led by Jamaica and Ghana—giving notice that
the end of colonial markets would not mean an opening for the products
of South Africa's factories. The breakup of the Federation of Rhodesia
and Nyasaland in 1963, due to settler intransigence in the face of African
nationalism, led to the emergence of Zambia and Malawi as independent
states the following year. This forced a recalculation of regional economic
and political alliances. With "multiracialism" incapable of sustaining settler
hegemony, Rhodesian settlers openly declared independence from Britain
in 1965 and aligned themselves more openly with South Africa and its legal-
ized racist practices. Portugal's response to similar nationalist pressures in
its colonies, particularly the emergence of mass resistance in 1961, served
to advance new regional linkages. Determined to hold on to its colonies,
Portugal's authoritarian leaders sought new alliances with white settlers in
Rhodesia and South Africa. This meant dropping colonial protectionist policies and opening previously closed markets to South Africa. Newly independent states, including even close neighbors such as Zambia, decisively cut
their economic relations with Rhodesia and South Africa.

For the South African state and business leaders, the forces narrowing
the region to settler and colonial allies were also felt at home: nationalist
protests, led by the African National Congress (ANC) and Pan Africanist
Congress (PAC), accelerated under younger leadership. This threatened
even economic relations with rich powers to the north: boycotts launched
by African, Caribbean, and Asian states might have little effect, but the
massive capital flight that ensued after the Sharpeville massacre in March
1960 could not be ignored. The South African government's response, like
that of Portugal and settlers across the region, was to mount an unrelenting military and repressive campaign. The banning of the ANC and PAC
in April 1960 (the Communist Party having been banned in 1950) and the
arrest, imprisonment, or execution of the nationalist leadership were aimed
at securing the home front; the extension of vigorous support for white
Rhodesians evading sanctions and for Portugal fighting nationalist guerrillas
was aimed at securing the region.

1965–75: Boom—and Settler Success?

In large part political repression and military expansion met with quick success: by the mid-1960s resistance at home had been contained, while guerrilla actions were pushed far from South Africa's borders. Political alliances

among white settlers and Portuguese colonies strengthened, moreover, leading to increasing levels of trade as well as political and military cooperation across an admittedly smaller "region." For South Africa, as for its regional allies and the world economy as a whole, these were boom years: in the 1960s South Africa's GDP grew at an annual rate of almost 9 percent. For many local economists, on the left and the right, the decade of the 1960s brought the "most spectacular economic boom in South Africa's postwar history," one that "placed South Africa among the fastest growing industrial economies in the capitalist world at this time, ahead of those of western Europe and North America."[70] Later evaluations were more temperate; still, as Jones and Müller concluded in the 1990s: "It would not be an exaggeration to say that South Africa has undergone an industrial revolution in this [post-1961] period."[71]

Behind such inflated assessments of the national economy were, however, deepening core-peripheral linkages and dependencies that developed from the compromises of the 1950s and early 1960s. As will be recalled from the long-term data presented in the introduction, it was precisely in this period that the gap widened between South Africa's standing in the world economy and comparable "middle-income" or "semiperipheral" states." Trade with the North as a percentage of GDP expanded through the 1960s and into the 1970s—but continued to be dominated by raw material exports to, and manufactured imports from, core states, even though imports were increasingly of more advanced capital and consumer goods. Trade relations across the newly constrained region also deepened—but were most unequal and became increasingly so.[72] Central here was the nature of regional countries' exports, highly concentrated as they were and are on highly competitive agricultural and mineral products. Even South Africa, industrial heartland of the continent, imported relatively little from the region (or continent); South African exports to the region were also low as a percentage of its exports, but could be quite significant as a percentage of neighbors' imports.

This situation was a continuation, it might be noted, of the pattern of unequal trade and power that was fostered by the state policies put in place after 1925. In this period, however, these relations expanded; no longer was South Africa exporting simple clothing, textiles, and processed foodstuffs; by the 1960s and 1970s one found far more advanced consumer and capital goods being shipped north (e.g., machinery, chemicals, vehicles). And for many South African manufacturers even the geographically smaller region that emerged after 1960 was critically important. By the mid-1970s exports for key industrial sectors were almost wholly due to shipments to neighboring states, accounting, for example, for 56 percent of chemical exports, to 73 percent of footwear, machinery, and equipment, to 90 percent of plastic products.[73] Rhodesian manufacturers had long aspired to a similar pattern based on exports to their north; the Universal Declaration of Independence (UDI) decisively put an end to such hopes. Zambia's regional trade followed a similar pattern: rising import shares drastically fell off after 1960, as did the much smaller level of exports to the region, particularly to South Africa.[74]

Southern Rhodesia's 1964 trade agreement with South Africa, signed in the wake of the breakup of the Federation and in anticipation of the UDI a year later, had unexpected benefits, however. For while it cemented Rhodesia's economic future to its relations with South Africa, it did so on the basis of the two states allying against a common, nationalist threat. This formed the foundation for a greater openness to fellow settlers' exports, including even competitive exports. Trade in the 1960s and 1970s thus accelerated. As Pangeti summarizes:

> The good news for [Rhodesian] manufacturers was that most of these [exports] were products of new industries which had not been exported to South Africa before. As such, the agreement was also going to promote infant industries in Rhodesia. . . . On the whole, the Agreement affected seventy-five percent of total Rhodesian exports of manufactured goods going to South Africa, with clothes, radios and rod wire being the major beneficiaries. This was a significant percentage of Rhodesian trade, and, under sanctions, this Agreement was to turn South Africa into Rhodesia's lifeline, providing a market, source of investment capital, and much needed transit trade routes.[75]

The cost to Rhodesia of such an alliance, it must be noted, was a greater dependence on South Africa—breaking with the path sought under Federation. Pangeti's emphasis on the embrace of South Africa is thus entirely consistent with Phimister's assessment that the agreement marked the end of the attempt during Federation to chart a course independent of South Africa by dominating markets to the north.[76] For Rhodesian manufacturers, moreover, the turn to South Africa in the face of sanctions marked the beginning of a boom to match South Africa's: from 1966 to 1974 manufacturing output grew at an annual rate of 9 percent.[77]

As South Africa's changing relationship with Rhodesia and other regional states suggests, the 1960s boom was not simply quantitative: it marked the emergence of new forms of production and regional-core relationships in a smaller region. Shifts in the direction, reach, and content of trade illustrate these well. Behind trade statistics, however, were equally significant developments in the form and ownership of capital, especially foreign capital—as suggested above by the vociferous debate in the 1950s and early 1960s over new forms of capital flows to and from South Africa and the region. For economic growth in the postwar period was shaped and driven by direct investment, primarily in the form of branch-plant operations and primarily by US corporations. According to Seidman and Makgetla's estimate, "by the 1970s, transnationals provided about 40 percent of all capital invested in the manufacturing sector of South Africa," playing an "important role in the sophisticated, strategic sectors: iron and steel, chemicals, auto, machinery and electrical equipment."[78] For South Africa, as for other countries in the periphery and semiperiphery, no longer could state policies and especially the tariff walls erected in the interwar period protect a national market by raising the cost of overseas firms' products—US firms simply leaped over tariff walls and built local branch plants.

US firms were hardly alone in this. But they were the leaders. British firms, traditionally dominating the South African market for consumer and capital goods, lagged far behind. The British pattern was also distinctive, being far more an extrapolation of earlier forms of alliance with local British capital and, whenever possible, the state. As Seidman and Makgetla summarize, "British firms tended to merge their interests with those of the South African mining finance houses and government parastatals, often retaining only a minority share."[79] US firms by contrast established wholly owned subsidiaries and "concentrated their investments in newer, technologically more sophisticated industries, where their financial power and advanced technological expertise enabled them to compete most effectively with the British. In a number of industries—electrical, nuclear and computer technology, motor vehicles, and petroleum refining—US firms achieved a crucial, in some cases dominant, role.[80] Indeed, as charted by many as part of the antiapartheid and sanctions movement,[81] US firms and later European and Japanese firms came to carve out a third, new cluster of capital in South Africa: foreign firms that built or contracted branch plants locally, while centralizing in their home offices the planning and technological brains of their worldwide operations.

As this description suggests, neither South African firms nor the state were capable or willing to challenge the capture of leading industrial sectors by foreign multinationals. While the postwar period saw major new parastatal firms established, the apartheid regime did not follow the path of other semiperipheral states in launching state firms or local capitalists into areas of higher technology. There was not to be, in short, any new ISCOR. The state would not—as states did in postwar Northeast Asia, Brazil, or Israel—attempt to launch domestic auto, electronic, shipbuilding, or aerospace industries.

In large part this was very much the legacy derived from the post-1933 Fusion government and particularly the return to power of Smuts—which allowed South African parastatals, increasingly controlled by Hendrik Johannes van der Bijl, to advance their monopoly position through a compromise with British and mining capital. When the National Party was elected in 1948, it found itself confronting a cozy relationship that would have surprised those who pushed the founding of ISCOR in 1928. As Nancy Clark, whose central book on state corporations focuses on the career of van der Bijl, states, "Van der Bijl had cultivated relationships with private businessmen and, following the war, had enjoyed an especially close friendship with Ernest Oppenheimer [the first chairman of the Anglo American Corporation, and the iconic head of British–South African capital]." Van der Bijl was thus far less a state capitalist and nationalist than those who assumed power in 1948. As Clark notes, "Van der Bijl's connections with the representatives of mining capital and the British military were understandably resented by the Nationalist government."[82] Van der Bijl and his handling of ISCOR was thus personally attacked even as he fell ill with cancer.

ISCOR would, eventually, expand and come to supply almost all of South Africa's steel needs. But the lack of support even within the state for expansion into new leading sectors, in the face of domestic opposition and now vigorous transnational activity, was evident. Early postwar plans for the creation of new manufacturing complexes under the aegis of the Industrial Development Corporation (IDC) subsequently died a quiet death. And even successful cases, most notably Sasol (producing oil from coal reserves) and Foskor (producing fertilizer), were not what was at one time anticipated. As Clark summarizes:

> Both were a far cry from the industries that [managing director H. J.] van Eck had hoped to see the IDC establish at the close of the war. Instead of consumer-oriented industries that could help to lower the cost of living as well as provide jobs and develop skills among the unemployed—both black and white—these new industries followed the old: they were based on minerals (coal and phosphates), the production of industrial goods (oil and fertilizers), and the use of highly skilled technical workers and unskilled mine labor.[83]

In a key sense the National Party after 1948 was not able to be nationalist enough: it did not pursue the creation of a nationally owned and directed industrial sector or manufacturing class. Again, unlike in South Korea, Taiwan, or Israel, the party did not nurture a local capitalist class in leading sectors beyond finance, blocked as it was by local capitalists allied to London and the mining sector, and constrained by South Africa's increasingly defensive position in the US liberal world order.

This not to deny that the "the National Party's apartheid policies created the conditions for rapid accumulation."[84] They did. Yet support for capital could vary between local and foreign capital, mining or financial or manufacturing capital, and mineral extraction or advanced industrial processes. The introduction of direct investment and branch plants by multinational corporations further complicated these groupings, as we have seen. In the period up to 1975 the state's achievements were, however, largely limited:

first, it created the conditions for the growth of Anglo-oriented capital from mining to manufacturing and financial conglomerates, and second, it directly drove forward the creation of an Afrikaner capitalist class in the financial sector. Indeed, by the mid-1970s Afrikaner capital had expanded into mining and manufacturing, paralleling the demise of long-standing antagonisms between Afrikaner and British capital. In this sense, ethnic and economic divisions among local settlers increasingly disappeared during the 1960s and 1970s as the result of the success of state policies.

What such success did not do, however, is challenge the growing hold over the heights of the economy by multinational corporations operating according to the rules established by US hegemony. By the early 1970s, the South African economy was certainly flourishing, with apartheid generating high profits for local and foreign firms alike, and for both Afrikaners and British settlers. Local firms were locked into mining and related energy and manufacturing sectors, as Fine and Rustomjee have stressed, while more innovative sectors remained dominated by foreign multinational corporations.[85] The high cost of this compromise with foreign capital, the free enterprise system, and the increasing integration of South Africa into the world economy was, however, to be rapidly revealed as the last quarter of the twentieth century began.

6

Creative Destruction

As the 1970s dawned, South Africa's rulers were in a self-congratulatory mood. The swelling tide of African nationalism that had so threatened them ten years earlier had ebbed. Fears of an intractable recession and capital flight, so sharply etched following the 1960 Sharpeville massacre, had faded away as a new inflow of foreign capital investment fueled an economic boom. Even the power imbalance between Afrikaner and British elites receded as grand new Afrikaner conglomerates flourished and whites benefited from steady economic growth. The National Party, it seemed, had fulfilled the apartheid promises of the 1948 election.

Unrest in the mid-1970s failed to shatter this hubris: the surprising student revolt of 1976 was contained, guerrilla challenges were suppressed, and strong if discrete support from conservative governments in Europe and the United States continued unabated. Yet ten years later the house of apartheid was in shambles, facing an implacable tide of resistance, international sanctions, a faltering economy, and intensifying capital flight. There would be no turning back the force of this wave: by the late 1980s the transition to majority rule was under way, sealed by Mandela's iconic election victory in 1994. Apartheid's notoriety was quickly replaced by the international celebration of racial reconciliation and the building of a "rainbow" nation, the "new South Africa."

Despite its singular features, South Africa's path in the last quarter of the twentieth century was hardly unique: in this period entrenched dictatorial regimes fell all across Africa, Asia, Latin America, and eastern and southern Europe. And as had already occurred across decolonizing Africa and Asia thirty years earlier, the deracialization of the South African state after 1994 proceeded quickly, while black economic empowerment incentives were developed for the public and private sectors alike. Economic growth, so critical to meeting post-apartheid expectations, was expected to readily advance as international sanctions were dropped, peace blossomed across the country and the region, and the costly machinery and regulations of apartheid were dismantled.

What commentators failed to appreciate at great cost, however, were the world-economic legacies and inequalities of the late apartheid period—and how these would be transformed in the postapartheid, postliberal world context. For hidden behind the tumultuous years of local revolt and reconciliation was South Africa's increasing engagement with a newly emergent, neoliberal, and neoracist world economy. These new relationships with core states and international institutions were forged, moreover, *prior* to Mandela's release from prison in 1990. To the dismay of many social democrats and socialists within and outside of the ANC, they would be accelerated under majority rule as both the Mandela and Mbeki governments abandoned past nationalist policies. In their place continued policies developed in the apartheid period and now defended as the only "realistic" response to a purportedly globalized, postnationalist, and postsocialist world.

What both the late apartheid and early ANC governments seriously overestimated, however, were the benefits of "globalization" and a close alliance with the neoliberalizing North. Signs of trouble to come quickly appeared in the rendering of the new South Africa's place in the global political economy. For even while Mandela was hailed across the world and the local state was deracialized, the South African state's place in the world's hierarchy was reracialized. Paradoxically, this took place through the new government's commitment to "nonracialism," which served to protect the white wealth accumulated under colonialism and apartheid even as it separated South Africa's new black elites from those in the North. As the international treatment of its leaders and policies quickly showed in the decade after Mandela's release from prison in 1990, no longer would the South African state be a privileged, white partner of the United States and Europe. Far from favoring the South African state and fostering national development, as in the interwar and postwar, apartheid period, Northern powers would promote the demise of the very economic policies that had been practiced by and benefited white settlers under segregation and apartheid. Majority rule would thus bring about a South African state openly heralded by the United States, Europe, and the World Bank, but a state increasingly treated by Northern powers as part of a dysfunctional African world. Meanwhile many African elites and states would bristle at South Africa's newfound assertiveness. If the postapartheid state was far more legitimate at home than at any time in the previous century—as the ANC's continued popularity illustrated— it was to be far, far less favored than in the past by global capital, core states, and international financial institutions, and far less accepted by Africans to the north than might have been expected. And this fact would largely determine the prospects of reversing the inequalities created by over 400 years of colonialism, segregation, and apartheid.

The 1970s: The World Falls Apart

Two words describe the world of the last quarter of the twentieth century: creative destruction. This process began like Thermidor, as rich, Northern states drove back the radical movements of the 1960s. While the 1960s movements in the North were defeated, governments everywhere were badly shaken. In the United States the events surrounding 1968 were followed by stagflation, a phenomenon that proved startlingly immune to the Keynesian techniques that had supposedly ended the possibility of a recession accompanied by rampant inflation. When President Nixon was forced to abandon the dollar-gold standard in 1971, the frailty of the US-led world order was nakedly exposed. As profits fell and labor pressures increased, multinational corporations fled overseas, leading to deindustrialization and rising unemployment in their home countries. Liberal welfare programs and social-democratic governments subsequently fell to fiscal crises all across the world. By the time of the Iranian revolution in 1979, both Europe and the United States were in the midst of a seemingly interminable economic and political decline.

Equally startling were the prospects that these radical upheavals might include a reversal of the North-South balance of power as prices for key commodity exports, led by oil, rose dramatically in the 1970s. This quickly led to fears in the North that Third World cartels would implement permanent, across-the-board commodity price hikes at the expense of rich core states. Indeed, talk of a "New International Economic Order," one that would redistribute income from the North to the South, was widespread by the late 1970s and was even endorsed by leading social democrats in the North (as in the 1980 report of the North-South Commission chaired by Nobel Peace Prize winner and former German chancellor Willy Brandt).

Such fears in the North and hopes in the South were short lived. World commodity prices briefly rose and then resumed their long decline across the twentieth century, sharply falling in half over the two decades after 1970.[1] Faced by drastic budget shortfalls, "Third World" and particularly African governments took on ever-increasing loans from international banks and financial institutions that were seeking to recycle the burgeoning petrodollars flowing into their vaults from the newly enriched Gulf states. Meanwhile core states, first in Britain under the Thatcher government (1979–90) and then in the United States under the Reagan presidency (1981–89), radically reversed the social-democratic compromise at home and ended liberal development planning and aid for the South. This entailed a wholesale attack on developmentalist states and even the international institutions that promoted development planning, particularly UNESCO and the World Health Organization.[2] As international inequality accelerated,[3] the harsh realities of "neoliberalism" imposed themselves: gone were the days of national progress, developmental core-peripheral relationships, civil rights, and social welfare. Deindustrialization was joined by the deregulation and denationalization of state enterprises. For the vast majority of states and peoples in the Global South, debt and impoverishment, rather than development and wealth, would prove the hallmark features of the closing decades of the twentieth century.

For South Africa these phenomena were rendered all but invisible by the far more spectacular struggles against apartheid. Yet South Africa was hardly a world apart from these global processes. While the 1970s began with firm recovery from an early 1969 Johannesburg Stock Exchange crisis, by late 1974 instability in world financial and commodity markets began to ripple through the country, leading to a full-blown recession by 1976, the year of the Soweto revolt. At this point, however, an unexpected stimulus arose from rapidly rising gold prices.

As noted in the introduction, gold prices had for several centuries proved to be countercyclical, rising in long cycles of world depression and fiscal crisis and falling in periods of global boom. Events in the post–World War II period followed this pattern: under US financial hegemony gold had been fixed at US$35 per ounce, which under price inflation gradually undercut the profitability of South African mines in postwar decades. When the United States was forced to abandon the dollar-gold standard amid a global economic crisis, the price of gold rocketed to over US$150 in 1975, and then to over US$600 in 1980. Even rising oil prices contributed to South Africa's fortunes by raising energy prices—promising a significant expansion of South Africa's cheap, low-wage coal exports.

As world stagnation continued in the 1980s and 1990s, such gains were turned back: gold prices fell to below US$400 in the rest of the 1980s and below US$300 throughout the 1990s. South Africa's terms of trade, measuring the value of exports in relation to the cost of imports, faltered (with or without gold prices in the ratio) as indicated in figure 6.1. Bereft of the golden windfall, South Africa returned to an unrelenting recession in the 1980s.

The 1980s: The Contradictions of Semiperipheral Development

Escalating world-economic pressures were soon matched by accelerating challenges to apartheid. And these arose not from the quarter most expected—the national liberation movements now based in surrounding independent states—but from new internal movements, rooted in a new generation, with new aspirations and identities. As elsewhere all across the middle or semiperipheral zone of the world economy, these movements expressed the very success of semiperipheral development in the postwar period *and* the collapse of the conditions that made such success possible. By the mid-1980s the failure of the apartheid state's model of semiperipheral development was evident—while new, post-1968 forms of global resistance radically strengthened new movements inside and outside the country.

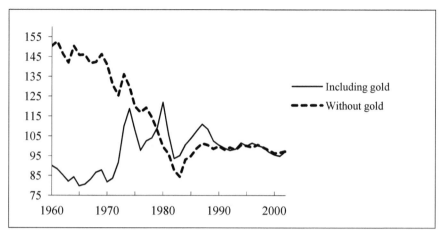

Figure 6.1. South Africa terms of trade 1960–2000 (1995 = 100). South African Reserve Bank, "South Africa's Balance of Payments, 1946–2000," table 4, B 35–40; and *Quarterly Bulletin*, March 2003, S-147.

Nowhere were these conflicting signals of the postliberal world to come more evident than in the domain of labor and capital. As argued above, apartheid had not simply rested on cheap labor, much less "monopoly capital," but rather a capital–labor force configuration that met, through spatial and racial differentiations, the very different needs of high- and low-wage, core and peripheral, production processes scattered across the urban and rural spaces of South Africa and the region. This entailed not simply the racial segmentation of labor supplies, but a division of labor among core-like and peripheral production processes that corresponded to the differentiation of very different household and gender structures across the region and the world economy. Simply stated, low-wage and controlled male labor flowed to mines from rural and female-headed households across the region; white farms were sustained by families forced to reside and work in rural areas; and higher-wage production processes drew on urban South African labor—with white labor, including immigrant labor, privileged for skilled and managerial positions. Under these conditions mining complexes expanded in the 1950s and 1960s even in the face of declining real gold prices, while industrial and agricultural employers drew on a stable, low-wage labor force whose cooperation was enforced by apartheid.

The conditions sustaining this differentiated labor force rapidly disappeared as the world crisis deepened in the later 1970s and 1980s. A key threat came from within the region: with the victory of the national liberation movements in Angola and Mozambique, it became most uncertain whether the regional labor supply complex, on which the mines had so heavily depended for almost a hundred years, would continue. While the new

Frelimo government in Maputo never severed supplies, the war in Zimbabwe and subsequently the formation of the frontline states and their regional body, the Southern African Development Coordination Conference, unnerved mining capital and South Africa's financial community. At issue was access not only to cheap foreign labor but to capital and regional export markets. As regional conflict between the apartheid state and its neighbors accelerated in the early 1980s, the pages of the *Financial Mail*, South Africa's most distinguished business weekly, continuously lamented lost trade and investment opportunities and called for quieter diplomacy.[4]

Much to their surprise, local manufacturers faced destabilization at home in the form of an outbreak of labor unrest, initiated by an unexpected strike of more than 100,000 unorganized workers in Durban and Pinetown in 1973. Since African unions were outlawed, management could not even find persons with whom to negotiate among the thousands of strikers milling around many factory gates. This would be the beginning of a long strike wave that accelerated in the following decade: of the 25 million workdays officially recorded as lost to strikes between 1910 and 1994, no less than 19 million were lost in the 1980s—and this number excludes workdays lost to political stayaways, which occurred with great frequency in the 1980s.[5]

Low wages and racial discrimination, which were constants for decades, do not alone explain this strike wave and its success. World labor phenomena suggest the source of workers' newfound power, for similar developments were taking place across older semiperipheral areas that, like South Africa, had industrialized in the interwar and postwar period. In states like South Korea and Brazil, for example, the labor processes associated with mass production had greatly enhanced labor's workplace bargaining power, leading to strike waves against both big business and authoritarian states. On the one hand, the accelerating movement of increasingly competitive—and thus less profitable—manufacturing activities from core to semiperipheral zones did result in the industrialization of southern Europe, Latin America, the Asian newly industrializing countries (NICs), and South Africa. Yet, on the other hand, it failed to bring the benefits of the Fordist bargain struck in the United States and Europe, where high productivity, high profits, and labor peace were matched to high wages and social welfare policies. And this was well before the flight of manufacturing production to locations in Asia with even lower labor costs in the closing decades of the century.

The explosive outcomes of this process were distinctively illustrated in South Africa. The analyses of this period that stress the "racial Fordist" nature of the postwar regime capture a critical element—namely, that postwar mass-production labor processes and management strategies, largely introduced by multinational corporations and copied by local firms, brought with them new sources of workplace bargaining power for an industrial workforce that had become overwhelming black.[6] Unlike in Europe or the United States, however, neither capital nor the state was able or willing to produce the high wages and social welfare benefits that had tamed labor in core zones. The result was entrenched labor unrest. In South Africa as elsewhere local and foreign firms urged the state to concede to workers' demands for the formation of representative unions. The spread of the unionization drive from manufacturing into the massive mining sector—where the large mining complexes with their labor compound systems concentrated workers and were thus particularly vulnerable to unrest—lent urgency to the recognition of African trade unions. Continuing industrialization under conditions of apartheid had generated a social force undermining capital from within the factory gates and the labor compound.

For its part the state feared labor's demands for what they would became: not business unionism, which could be incorporated into stable and subordinate bargaining councils, but a growing social movement unionism that called for the end of the apartheid state. And there was plenty of evidence from across the semiperiphery where that could lead: from South Korea to Brazil to southern and eastern Europe, old dictatorships and military regimes were falling one by one—with newly empowered workers playing a central role.

Seriously complicating labor's demands were those emanating from the families and communities built to provide increasingly skilled urban labor. Apartheid's policymakers had publicly proclaimed that black South Africans were to find their homes only in rural areas, and only a small, unskilled urban labor force would be temporarily resident in urban areas. This was always at odds with reality, and few had foreseen the degree to which economic success would demand skilled and managerial labor far beyond the capacity of South Africa's small white population to fulfill. As the economy grew in the 1960s, black, urban-centered populations and their concentration in townships rapidly accelerated. This meant increasingly large numbers of young Africans, consistently the main force behind eruptions of resistance, were living in urban areas—and this included increasingly educated youth as required by the growing economy. Indeed, black student populations dramatically surged, as figures 6.2 and 6.3 on secondary school and university enrollments reveal.

Black youth and particularly students became ever more radical in their demands in the 1970s and 1980s, pushing aside their elders as Mandela's generation had done fifty years earlier. In the 1970s, moreover, the older movements were banned and their leaders were either in jail or in exile. More critically, younger activists inside the country radically departed from the organizational and tactical attributes of the nationalist organizations of the 1950s. In what would become apparent only a generation later, the national liberation movement model, which had far too often led to a patriarchal and authoritarian state, was being abandoned.[7]

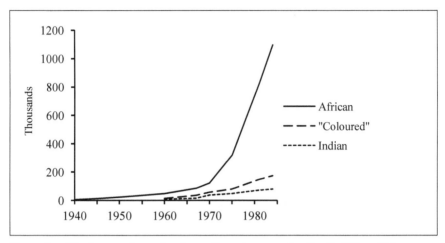

Figure 6.2. Black secondary school enrollments, 1940–84. South Africa, *Union Statistics* and *South African Statistics*, 1970, 1982; Horrell, *Bantu Education to 1968*; South African Institute of Race Relations, *Annual Survey*, 1981, 1985.

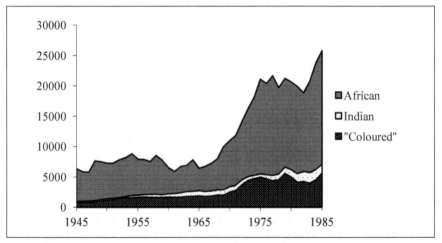

Figure 6.3. Black college enrollments, 1945–85. Calculated from Dreijmanis, *South African Government in University Education*, 117.

This was a global phenomenon in the late 1960s and early 1970s, a worldwide eruption of protest movements not only against exploitation, neocolonialism, racism, and sexism but also against the very labor, social-democratic, and nationalist movements that had come to power after World War II. In South Africa, the most startling expression was the formation and extraordinary influence of the Black Consciousness Movement and its immediate successors. Locally focused, committed to redefining black identity, and cul-turally oriented—as were their Black Power contemporaries in the United States, Brazil, Europe, and the Caribbean[8]—the Black Consciousness Movement provided the inspiration for the startling eruption and spread of revolts in the 1970s and 1980s, particularly the 1976 student revolt.

In their militant spontaneity these movements looked little like the orga-nized African nationalist protests of the 1950s, or the intermittent armed struggles of the ANC and the PAC in the 1960s and 1970s. While in the 1950s the ANC operated through an alliance of multiracial organizations, Black Consciousness groups by contrast strove to unite African, Indian, and Coloured activists under one banner. This meant rejecting the leadership of, and subordinate alliances with, white-led organizations, to the great dis-may of white reformers, scholars, and activists. Black activists also sought to recast "black" as a *political* color, encompassing all who suffered under white supremacy. This redefinition of oppression and identity, along with the new movements' spontaneity, community focus, and rejection of past national and organizational models were shared features of post-1968 movements worldwide. This made the institutional incorporation of the movements by the state more difficult—and their dissolution under repression more likely. In this the Black Consciousness Movement, pushing forward a post-liberal ideology and local community tactics, provided, even as it was being crushed, a sign of things to come.

One would not know this from the scholarship on the South African movements of the 1980s and 1990s, which has largely remained bound within national and institutional frameworks, reflecting both the triumph of the ANC and the predominantly white cast of South African historiogra-phy. To their intellectual and political elders, even decades later, the street forces behind the new movements and township revolts were and remained too local, too disorganized, too undisciplined. As Dan O'Meara put it in his chronicle *Forty Lost Years*, "The new political culture fashioned by [the 1976 revolt in] Soweto was voluntaristic, maximalist, and profoundly militaristic."[9] Likewise, Jeremy Seekings in his detailed history of the United Democratic Front (UDF), the national coordinator of resistance in the 1980s, concludes that student and youth protest was invariably militant but politically naive.[10] In this view their avoidance of formal political organizations based on the pursuit of state power left them without the institutional sinews necessary to undermine the apartheid state over time—something the UDF and its part-ner the ANC could and did provide.

Even Seekings has to concede, however, that the UDF and ANC's direct role in the major township revolts of the 1980s was minimal, with the UDF "on the margins of the revolt" and only later acting to contain and direct youth and student militancy.[11] This remains a central, unexplored feature of apartheid's demise: the historical roots and paths of the new, nonstatist forms of resistance that emerged in the 1970s and 1980s. The organizational quandary posed by the 1960s movements remains central, for while the new movements' attack on the bureaucratism of the Old Left expanded across the North and South in this period, they almost everywhere failed to find new organizational forms to carry their momentum forward. South Africa was no exception to this conundrum, as each successive eruption of township unrest led to a new flow of young exiles headed northward into the arms of the ANC, reinvigorating and strengthening the ANC itself. This would form a continuing dilemma, long into the postapartheid period: post-1968 movements could mobilize and destabilize, but would not replace dominant political authorities.

Imperial Dilemmas

While the eruption of student, youth, and labor unrest undermined apartheid at home, regional and international forces arose to undercut the apartheid state's support from above. Opponents of apartheid had long pointed out the contradiction between apartheid and the liberal principles of democracy and self-determination so central to postwar US hegemony. In the immediate postwar decades this contradiction was easily ignored by colonial powers like the United Kingdom and France. American political and corporate elites acquiesced, seeing little contradiction between professed liberalism and Jim Crow at home, much less abroad. Certainly the Western allies' 1941 Atlantic Charter, which had inspired young African nationalists to argue boldly for self-determination and independence, was not to be applied to South Africa—which in the eyes of the world's leading powers was already a democratic, independent state. Even the decolonization wave, moving down the continent in the 1950s and 1960s, ran aground when it reached the borders of southern Africa. Radical Pan-Africanists, meanwhile, were shunted aside in the 1960s by the middle-class nationalist leaders of Africa's new states, who embraced the promises and personal profits attached to the modernizing, developmental state.

The new forms of protest that emerged in South Africa during the 1970s, in concert with their counterparts elsewhere, openly called these arrangements into question. This was a dual indictment, against both the liberal world order established under US hegemony *and* the leftist nationalists who had come to power in many states in Africa and elsewhere. As Terreblanche summarizes for South Africa, the 1960s and 1970s generated a "new generation of revolutionary leaders" who arose amid three schools of thought: "The first was liberalism, whose popularity declined dramatically among the new generation of African intellectuals. Secondly, radicalized black middle-class students were inspired by the New left student movements in the United

States and Europe. And thirdly, again influenced by American trends, the Black Consciousness Movement (BCM) formulated a race consciousness in which the term 'black' signified an explicit and radical rejection of apartheid in all its forms."[12] While this evaluation seriously underestimates the influence of African theorists like Frantz Fanon and Amilcar Cabral on activists in the North as well as in Africa, it correctly points to the worldwide cross-fertilization of black movements in this period. Indeed, Africa became a focus of this process, as Northern activists sought out radical movements in the South.

Most prominent among these were the armed national liberation movements in Portugal's colonies, which promised to complete the decolonization drive through more radical, armed, and often Marxist popular movements. This promise was openly predicated on a second drive for independence, to surpass the neocolonial limits of "independent" Africa. The links among movements in the United States and Europe and those in the South, including South Africa, were extensive and deep. This relationship was, moreover, reciprocal, with radical movements in southern Africa stimulating radical movements in the North and vice versa, including strong ideological cross-currents between Black Consciousness and Black Power adherents in the United States, Africa, the Caribbean, and Europe.

While the 1968 movements were defeated in the North by the early to mid-1970s, southern African movements were not. The 1975 victory of the MPLA in Angola and Frelimo in Mozambique immediately narrowed the Pretoria regime's defense line and was a major inspiration for the 1976 Soweto revolt. Worse still for the South African government was the escalating war in Zimbabwe, which represented a much closer and more direct threat. To be sure, postindependence regimes in the states directly bordering South Africa did not grant the ANC or PAC military bases. Yet their open antiapartheid stances led South Africa to design and support counterinsurgency campaigns, leading to wide-scale war across the region in the 1980s—at a human cost estimated by UNICEF in excess of a million deaths.[13] As the wars accelerated, South African forces were stretched thin—as became apparent with the major defeat handed to the South African Defense Force at Cuito Carnevale in Angola in 1988.

Rising internal and regional challenges to apartheid in the decade after 1975 also emboldened European and North American antiapartheid activists. Their task was made much more difficult, however, by formative responses to the fiscal crisis of the liberal, postwar state. In the two states most heavily invested in South Africa—Britain and the United States—the difficulty of sustaining Fordism and social-democratic policies had given rise to the new, antiliberal ideologies and policies of the Thatcher (1979–90) and Reagan (1981–89) years. Both administrations were stronger supporters of minority rule than their predecessors, a development the South

African regime readily welcomed. Despite this, antiapartheid efforts grew considerably, escalating with each major outbreak of resistance in South and southern Africa. In the United States, pressure from local community, church, and student efforts built up until national sanctions were passed in 1986, despite the opposition of the leadership of *both* the Republican and Democratic Parties. This was the greatest foreign policy defeat of the two-term Reagan administration. In the United Kingdom, bank boycott efforts by supporters of the African National Congress movement began in the late 1950s and finally bore fruit in November 1986 when Barclays Bank succumbed and sold its stake in Barclays National in South Africa.[14]

The State and Capital Respond

As these local, regional, and international pressures grew they heightened the contradictions of the apartheid order, revealing the impossibility of defending apartheid amid the world crisis of the last quarter of the twentieth century. As this realization grew, big business and the state sought out new, increasingly "scientific" solutions to economic stagnation and new political insurgencies. The Anglo American Corporation, for example, set up a new research body, the Urban Foundation, while the state expanded the Human Sciences Research Council and launched a series of official commissions to investigate and propose solutions for key obstacles to further growth and stability. Sympathetic foreigners were roped in as well. Renowned US political scientist Samuel Huntington on successive visits to South Africa offered his own advice to the South African state, military, and big business on how to prevent revolutionary change. In 1981 he recommended reform from above to achieve a "quadri-racial polity congruent with a quadri-racial society."[15] In the midst of states of emergency in 1986, he advised that Mandela had few supporters and recommended agreements between big business and local ethnic chiefs, who were the "greatest hope for gradual reform."[16]

While such advice was welcome to white nationalist ears, it flew in the face of the political power being expressed by South Africa's growing labor, student, and civic movements. It also failed to address the underlying problems of the apartheid economy in a period of global stagnation. Prominent were the limits of local demand, constrained as it was to a small, white, middle- and upper-class group. Reporting in 1977, the Reynders Commission advocated a transition to export markets—just as regional and international export markets were about to be hit by falling prices and growing sanctions against South Africa. The official Kleu Study Group, set up in 1977 to investigate industrial strategy, was similarly bedeviled: reporting much later in 1983 (with a White Paper issued yet two years further on), it recommended mild liberalization and the targeting of key industrial subsectors for state support *and* a hesitant turn to the neoliberal policies being promoted in the North. The mounting labor and urban movements were more forcefully addressed by the Riekert and Wiehan Commissions, whose reports in 1979 recommended the end of statutory job reservation by race in manufacturing, the recognition of black labor unions, and legalization of urban black residents (but not the end of influx controls for Africans deemed to be resident in rural areas).

All these proposals signaled a real shift in official thinking, moving quickly away from the classic practices of apartheid. Yet the implementation of Wiehan and Riekert proposals only served to worsen the structural crisis. Once recognized, national trade unions grew into two large federations committed to political unionism; labor prices in manufacturing accordingly accelerated while gold mining firms came under increasing political and price pressures. Mining companies' movement to more local, stabilized labor—foreign migrant workers fell from over 70 to less than 40 percent of the labor force between 1973 and 1982[17]—corresponded to the rise of the militant National Union of Mineworkers and falling prices and production in the last half of the decade. In 1987 gold mines employed 500,000 workers; by 1993 the figure had dropped to 300,000 and would be less than 250,000 by the end of the century.[18] Foreign investment became increasingly rare; there was to be no repeat of the stabilizing foreign investment and loan inflows that took place in the 1960s after the international outcry over the Sharpeville massacre.

Indeed, as multinational capital fled in the face of shrinking markets and growing protest, South African firms, especially in sectors with heavy state involvement such as mining and finance, came to dominate the economic landscape. Rising world energy and mineral prices in the 1970s boosted this trend, leading to major new investments in fuels, coal, and platinum mines, most notably the coal-to-oil Sasol II and III plants, which came online in the early 1980s with considerable state support. This mineral-energy complex (MEC), as some have called it, fared poorly as energy and export commodity prices declined in the 1980s. There were, moreover, few multiplier effects. As even Fine and Rustomjee, proponents of the MEC framework, recount: "Since there was no structural or institutional basis laid down to diversify into non-MEC sectors, the latter declined according to the fortunes of the MEC, except for some subsectors driven by military and megaproject expenditure, whose buoyancy was prolonged until the late 1980s.[19]

Reliance on minerals and energy failed to provide a new development strategy: it promoted few industrial or technological advances, while the application of capital-intensive methods in the new mines and energy plants provided little employment for the growing numbers of unruly unemployed. Thus, while deindustrialization accelerated in the North, South Africa benefited little from it. While other, older NICs were replacing highly competitive manufacturing with more technologically advanced products, and shedding cheap manufacturing toward the periphery, South Africa experienced across-the-board losses in manufacturing and mineral employment.

Neoliberal Apartheid

In the face of fierce repression and failed economic policies, it was clear by the mid-1980s that the long-standing policies and practices of apartheid were gone: even the state was abandoning them. Hegemony over southern Africa had passed with decolonization in Angola and Mozambique in 1975 and Zimbabwe in 1980. Felicitous alliances with foreign capital and Northern governments had been rent asunder; such support as came from the Reagan and Thatcher regimes was increasingly restricted to covert military and intelligence matters. Internally, the implementation of the Wiehan and Riekert reforms in the face of militant black unions had overthrown apartheid strictures on black labor and, increasingly, influx controls. The admission of the necessity of reversing apartheid's political designs was finally made in 1983 in the form of a proposal for a tricameral (white, Coloured, Asian) parliament. Influx controls were openly abandoned in 1986. The "whites-only" signs of "petty apartheid" became increasingly rare.

None of these moves stilled opposition by the new unions, civic groups, and youth groups that arose in the 1980s. With the rise of the UDF in 1983, formed to fight the state's proposal for a tricameral parliament, these forces were linked into one organization that could coordinate national campaigns through the remainder of the 1980s—with close if unacknowledged ties to the ANC.[20] Together these forces, supported by a growing international antiapartheid movement, accelerated resistance amid successive township uprisings after 1984. The government responded with states of emergency, widespread detentions and bannings, regional destabilization, and the deployment of the South African Defence Force (SADF).

These measures failed: the country became increasingly ungovernable. And as repressive measures and political violence became fiercer there was less to defend: the controls over African labor and life that had been so central to apartheid had already been widely abandoned. Last to go was an exclusively white state apparatus. With President P. W. Botha's military "total strategy" offensive against neighboring states and rebels within South Africa headed to clear defeat, this too came to pass with the ascendancy of F. W. de Klerk in 1989. After private negotiations with Mandela and the ANC, de Klerk released Mandela in February 1990, removed the ban on the ANC and other political organizations, and entered into public discussions with the ANC and other political groupings over a new democratic constitution.

It would take four years of uneasy negotiations to reach democratic elections in 1994 and the installation of a government of national unity dominated by the victorious ANC. Negotiated transitions of this type had long been common in Africa—for example, after Nkrumah walked out of prison to lead the government of the Gold Coast colony in 1951, it had taken six long years to bring about national independence. Battlefield victories in southern Africa had shortened such delicate dances between colonizer and colonized: while it took several years to get Zimbabwe's warring parties to negotiate a settlement, in Angola and Mozambique the transfer of power took place with almost no negotiations at all, a case of "independence without decolonization."[21] The ANC was not, however, in a position similar to Frelimo's in Mozambique. The ANC's armed struggle had little impact by the mid-1980s; the local initiative had long since passed to independent unions and the uneven and uncertain upsurges of community, youth, and student groups that had created the conditions of ungovernability and economic disruption. The ANC in this sense rode a tiger to power, rather than an organization, union, or armed force of its own. This disjuncture between the institutional might of the ANC and the strength of the new social and civic movements would persist well into the future.

Bringing the ANC on Board

The four years of negotiations between the de Klerk government, the ANC, and big business would prove to be decisive in not so much cementing new economic policies as perpetuating existing ones. Big business and white farmers had long feared and loathed the prospect of ANC rule: for over two generations the ANC had celebrated the Freedom Charter of 1955, which called for a social-democratic state that would guide the economy, return land to the tiller, and place factories and mines in the hands of their workers. These aims were also consonant with those of the new unions: in 1985 the major federation COSATU formally adopted the charter, affirming the National Union of Mineworkers' long-standing call to nationalize the mines. Mandela himself, just prior to his release from prison in 1990, was quoted in the black press as confirming that "the nationalization of the mines, banks, and monopoly industry is the policy of the ANC and a change or modification of our views in this regard is inconceivable."[22]

Although Thabo Mbeki, the ANC foreign affairs spokesperson at the time, denied that the ANC had any formal "policy" of nationalization, business leaders were not convinced. As one account summarizes, "After 1990 the de Klerk government, private local capital and the international institutions came to form an informal 'triple alliance,' and in those early years they honed in whenever the occasion presented itself to attack and disparage any 'business unfriendly' ANC economic ideas and proposals."[23] The campaign against nationalization became especially blunt and unrelenting in the weeks and months after Mandela's release. As the leading business magazine *Financial Mail* proclaimed, "Whatever Mandela has been doing for the past twenty-seven years, he has not been studying either elementary economics or the SA economy." And nationalization of the mines and land? Perish the thought; the threat was clear: "foreign investors would disinvest. The rand would be devalued to a fraction of what it is now. . . . The country's financial services industry . . . would virtually collapse."[24]

"But there is even worse lurking behind nationalization proposals," the *Financial Mail* warned a week later, for "at the end of the road is the ultimate fear that they would be the thin end of the wedge, comprising the start of a process of complete delegitimisation of white property rights, including agricultural land. This would be the sure recipe for the complete ruin of the economy and mass migration."[25] In short: "The ANC is muddled and confused. It needs to be guided and educated."[26] Still, there were silver linings to be found. As the *Financial Mail* noted, "It is, therefore, fortunate that the Nationalists have laid the requisite stress on privatization and deregulation." Such comments ran uninterrupted for several years, triggering a long campaign to divert the ANC leadership from past commitments to the state intervention that had underwritten South African growth for over six decades.[27]

In the wake of the fall of the Soviet Union, big business and the media easily portrayed past ANC policy as a relic of a defeated socialist epoch. As even the *Sowetan* newspaper cast it at the time, "Most, if not all, of the ANC's leading economists were trained in the Eastern Bloc, and faced with the disintegration of the system they were trained in, they have simply not had the time to come up with a credible alternative."[28] The same could have been said, of course, of many Western economists and development planners, who had grown up and remained committed to state-led modernization—a program common to social democrats in the North, socialists in the East, and newly independent states in Africa and Asia. By the mid-1980s, however, this model was also fast disappearing. Many of the ANC's key leaders were well aware of this trend, having spent the 1980s in African capitals witnessing the end of state planning and the forced adoption of IMF structural adjustment models. This was notably true for Zambia, where the ANC in exile was headquartered and where Thabo Mbeki was resident throughout the 1980s. Bowing to these pressures, by 1993 Mandela and Mbeki removed nationalization from all ANC policy documents.

It was in this climate and against these experiences that the South African state passed into the hands of its first black government. For both the business world and the outgoing white government the international turn to neoliberalism was a godsend. For at the core of the neoliberal creed was a rejection of state planning, redistributive policies, and racial preferences—core elements of the apartheid state after 1948. These new beliefs would serve to ensure that no new government could abridge the rights of private property, capital, and those who had prospered under apartheid. And to these demands the ANC acceded.

Negotiating the Apartheid Inheritance

This convergence between the global forces behind neoliberal programs and local and international capital would forge the policies of both the late apartheid regime and the subsequent ANC government. Indeed, the transition started well over ten years before majority rule, beginning in the late 1970s when local capital and key bureaucrats, often after direct consultation with international financial institutions and governments, sought to convince the government that the resolution of their common difficulties lay in reducing state intervention in the economy, eliminating state-sanctioned racial segregation, and deregulating local markets.

Nowhere was this more evident than in the area of commodity trade, where liberalization began in the early 1980s with the relaxation of the quantitative restrictions that served as tariffs.[29] The real transition only became apparent, however, in the concluding stages of the final round of the General Agreement on Tariffs and Trade (GATT) negotiations that led to the formation of the World Trade Organization (WTO). Unlike previous GATT negotiation rounds, this last round aimed to combine both trade and new nontrade items, such as property and intellectual rights—with the mandatory acceptance of all measures to be enforced by the new WTO. Negotiations launched in 1986 led to an agreement signed by the apartheid regime in its final days.

The negotiations eventually took place with ANC participation and approval, despite open opposition by the ANC's allies and even among the ANC membership. As Hirsch recounts, "As the political transition advanced, the trade unions and the African National Congress voiced their own criticisms of the fact that the apartheid government was committing a future democratic government to a major long-term trade reform, without any proper process of consultation."[30] From this discussion emerged the National Economic Forum (NEF), which took over the task of revising South Africa's GATT submissions—and which included representatives of the government, business, labor, and, informally, the ANC. The advantage to the government was clear: "Minister Derek Keys (in charge of the GATT negotiations) enthusiastically supported the role of the NEF in the process, as he understood it would bind a future government to the GATT reforms."[31] The formulation and approval of proposals remained, however, firmly in the hands of the government since the NEF (not to mention labor or the ANC) lacked the technocratic and bureaucratic staff to develop GATT proposals.

In the end South Africa accepted GATT demands that it not only simplify its complex tariff structure but submit to major, mandatory tariff reductions in almost all key sectors of the economy, including agriculture. This portended disaster for manufacturers facing highly competitive, lower-wage imports from Asia, most notably South Africa's small and medium-sized textile and clothing manufacturers. When it became clear that GATT rejected South Africa's initial submissions and would force major reductions, Cape Town clothing firms immediately terminated hundreds of jobs. Mandela himself was led to intervene in the weeks before majority rule with personal, public support for the tariff reductions, and the ANC sent a senior official to the final signing ceremonies. Signing GATT also spelled the death knell for the state's interventionist export-promotion scheme, GEIS, introduced in April 1990. The long-awaited recommendations of the Kleu Study Group on industrial policy, which called for active state intervention, were also quickly tossed into the rubbish bin.

The Mandela government's commitment to continuing these late-apartheid trade policies was quickly confirmed when, under Trade and Industry Minister (later Finance Minister) Trevor Manuel, the new government lowered import tariffs *below* what the WTO required. The result was foreseeable as "deindustrialization hit key sectors—including clothing, electronics and appliances—once tipped as potential export success stories."[32] In the case of agriculture, the government not only drove down tariffs well below the bound rates negotiated in GATT but eliminated quantitative controls and subsidies, resulting in a sharp drop in domestic support from an OECD index of 13.69 in 1990–91 to 2.72 by 1997–98. By the late 1990s South Africa's level of support for agriculture was among the lowest in the world.[33] The result was lower employment and higher capital intensity—following the pattern in manufacturing.[34]

In retrospect GATT had always posed problems. When South Africa entered GATT in 1947, it was designated a "developed country" like those of Europe and North America and the other white Dominions. This act of racial privilege and hubris meant, however, that South Africa was ineligible for concessions offered to "developing countries." The new South Africa, now celebrated as part of Africa, was offered no release from this designation. When Manuel appealed to his personal friend US Secretary of Commerce Ron Brown to have this overturned, he was quickly rebuffed.[35] Throughout the postwar period the Board of Trade and Industries (BTI), the central agency dedicated to tariff protection, had launched few new initiatives. This changed as the national economy spiraled downward in the 1980s. For its part the BTI proposed a more active role for itself in promoting exports, and in 1988 it issued a report that, while accepting continued tariff reductions, argued the case for state intervention targeting select export industries. The stated aim was to follow in the footsteps of Japan and the East Asian NICs, whose successes had been forged by strong developmental states.[36]

The prospect of majority rule led both big business and the de Klerk government to foreclose any such enhancement of state regulation or intervention. The BTI's proposals were ignored. Initiative quickly passed to other state departments, particularly the Department of Trade and Industry (the DTI) and the Industrial Development Corporation (IDC): both publicly rejected the BTI's report as a continuation of failed import-substitution policies, and called for freer markets and less state action, a strategy suited more to exports of minerals and energy-related products than to advanced manufacturing exports. In 1989, the year before Mandela was released, the DTI in its annual report openly lambasted the BTI's proposals, and in the following year it withdrew ninety personnel seconded to the BTI, thus crippling its work. The trade and industry minister then forbade it to work further on its proposals. By 1992 the BTI's chair resigned, and the BTI was stipped of its powers by new legislation.[37] What had been put in place in the opening decades of the century, and had proven so critical in the interwar and even postwar periods, came to a quick, ugly end.

The Great White Capital Flight

Financial liberalization proceeded equally as fast—to a point. The apartheid state had long solicited and been supported by foreign capital, and after 1948 the state vigorously underwrote Afrikaner economic power in the financial sector. This made South Africa particularly vulnerable to the spread of financial deregulation and speculation across the world that so marked the neoliberal period. For local financial firms and conglomerates, endemic economic stagnation and rising political disorder propelled a scramble for safer and more profitable opportunities beyond South Africa's boundaries—which fit well with US policies aimed at attracting capital from abroad. At times flush with commodity price windfalls, South African capital sought to attach itself to the speculative financial winds circulating in the North, where Keynesianism had given way to free market policies, financial deregulation and speculation, and the unimpeded flow of capital and currencies.

A key obstacle to these new aims was the apartheid state itself, which had closely regulated capital and financial flows, increasing restrictions in the wake of rebellions and relaxing restrictions during periods of prosperity and political stability. The decade of the 1980s proved particularly difficult and spectacular. As gold prices rose and speculation ensued in the early 1980s, the financial sector was deregulated following the successive 1978, 1982, and 1984 recommendations of the De Kock Commission into monetary policy. There was a dangerous premise, however: "Policymakers tended to assume that the gold boom would be permanent, boosting the economy and raising state revenues in the long term."[38] And the gold boom was not permanent: prices (in current dollars) rose from US$35 per ounce in 1968 to over US$600 in 1980, only to fall to near US$300 by 1985. Yet this did not stop the introduction of new "market-oriented" policies. In 1983 the dual exchange rate system was abolished, lifting exchange controls for nonresidents, while the government itself turned to the IMF for a loan.

Such optimism became harder to sustain in the face of mushrooming revolts, stagflation, the depreciation of the rand, record high real interest rates, and an undeniable downward spiral in gold and natural resource commodity prices. Capital outflow accelerated: the South African Reserve Bank estimated that more than US$5.5 billion was withdrawn between 1982 and 1988.[39] Given the illegal nature of the flows, the figures were surely higher. Prime Minister P. W. Botha's draconian "Rubicon Speech" in 1985, which declared a military response to local unrest and thus acknowledged an uncontrollable situation, led to a real financial crisis. Annual capital outflows mushroomed, equaling 4.1 percent of GDP per year between 1985 and 1992 by one estimate.[40] At the same time, the US and European anti-apartheid movements successfully stepped up pressure on their home country multinationals, resulting in the departure of one-fifth of British firms by 1988 and more than a hundred US firms between January 1986 and April 1988 alone.[41]

As urban revolts mounted and the government declared a national state of emergency, financial liberalization sputtered to a halt. In 1983 the IMF, which had previously stepped in at moments of crisis, was forced to stop lending; it would be unable to help again. In 1985, faced by its inability to secure funds on the international market, the state declared a moratorium on debt repayment and reintroduced a dual exchange rate mechanism to stem the hemorrhage of capital (capital flows essentially took place via a lower rate of exchange, the financial rand rate, which would be abolished in 1995). As negotiations for a transition to majority rule started, state agencies tried to gain access to new foreign loans, but the ANC blocked the move in order to buttress its bargaining position.

The ANC leadership was by this time committed to fiscal and monetary orthodoxy, financial liberalization, and free movement for capital—all elements of what had become known as the "Washington Consensus" and key elements of the imposition of "structural adjustment" on much poorer countries. When Mandela visited the United States in 1991 he carefully and consistently reassured US investors who, like South African businessmen, had been worried by his early postrelease statements supporting the nationalization of industry. Directly addressing the business community he carefully declaimed: "Let me assure you that the ANC is not an enemy of private enterprise. . . . The rates of economic growth we seek cannot be achieved without important inflows of foreign capital. We are determined to create the necessary climate which the foreign investor will find attractive."[42] Mandela's promise was kept: ANC economic policy would be based on the assumption that free capital flows and foreign direct investment were the first necessity for economic growth.

At home business leaders and financial institutions were equally concerned over how the new state would exercise its financial power, for they knew from long, personal experience under apartheid how a strong state could control financial markets and privilege a particular racial group. Central was locking in the protection of private property, orthodox monetary policy, and, in particular, the independence of the South African Reserve Bank. As the transition to majority rule became apparent, calls for greater independence for the Reserve Bank were widely broadcast by international financial institutions— following a worldwide trend that saw at least thirty countries between 1990 and 1995 lessen democratic control over monetary policy by increasing the statutory independence of their central banks.[43]

While some semiperipheral states like South Korea were able to resist such appeals, the apartheid regime pushed forward central bank independence, and it was, like private property guarantees, enshrined in the new constitution with the ANC's blessing. Tito Mboweni, appointed as the first black governor of the bank in August 2000, was the very person who led the campaign for the bank's independence in volatile discussions among ANC economists in the early 1990s. It is thus hardly surprising that the Reserve Bank and macroeconomic policy under majority rule, in the words of one analyst, "arguably represents an extreme example of conformism to neo-liberalism," marked by little transparency and even less democratic control.[44] Fiscal policy became pinned to inflation targets, resulting in suffocatingly high interest rates.

The state's role in opening up capital flows and alliances with international financial institutions followed quite similar plot lines and timing. One of the first steps of the interim multiparty government in 1993 was to apply secretly for a US$850 million IMF loan, following ANC officials' visit to IMF headquarters in Washington the year before.[45] Leaked to the press in 1994, the terms of loan—accepted at the time by the highest ANC policymakers—included commitments to scrap import surcharges, control wages, and constrain government debt.[46] Reserve Bank economists and ANC economists also committed themselves in 1993 to paying back what international activists called "the odious debt" of US$20 billion in commercial bank loans contracted by the apartheid regime. These policies would continue as did close personal ties of South African officials with officials of the IMF and World Bank.[47]

Neoliberal state fiscal policies and South African Reserve Bank monetary policies imposed significant constraints and social costs. State spending was significantly restricted: there would be no "end of apartheid dividend" for social services, housing, or land reform. State budgets as a percentage of GDP were even smaller than the targets set by the World Bank, while the Reserve Bank's policies further constrained expansion and employment at home. Even on their own terms these policies failed to achieve their primary aim: a significant increase in long-term capital inflows and productive, direct investment. Capital inflows after majority rule did increase initially, but were largely concentrated in speculative portfolio investment on the one hand, and direct investment targeted at buying back market share lost during the period of divestment and sanctions on the other. This marked a global trend whereby investment funds flowed to financial fields and not productive ones in the closing decades of the twentieth century (and would lead to successive speculative crashes in the early twenty-first century). Even so, investment in new production facilities was especially sparse in the new South Africa, and by the turn of the century these flows subsided.

Even worse, large local corporations, which had so benefited from apartheid, used conditions of liberalization to accelerate their move out of the country. This was white capital flight with a vengeance. As Terreblanche summarizes, the liberalization of capital flows "enabled corporations—especially the large globalised corporations such as the AAC [Anglo American Corporation], Old Mutual, and SA Breweries—as well as wealthy individuals to move a huge amount of capital, and thus South African wealth, out of the country. These amounts are considerably larger than FDI [foreign direct investment]."[48] These large, early cases of capital flight were not the creation of overseas subsidiaries by South African firms spreading their tentacles outward from South Africa—as say Japanese *zaibatsu* and Korean *chaebol* had done after conquering local and export markets. Far from it: the largest movers closed their head offices in South Africa and opened new ones in London, and moved their primary stock listings to London. Six of South Africa's biggest companies shifted their stock exchange listing to the London FTSE, starting with the mining group Billiton in 1997, followed by SA Breweries, Anglo American, Old Mutual, Dimension Data, and Investec.

Subsequent mergers and diversification by these corporations led to their abandonment of their original South Africa identity, with only Old Mutual, in the words of a local financial magazine, "still predominantly South African in assets and earnings."[49] These moves were nothing less than a vote of no confidence in South Africa and a stunning riposte to the new government's promise that financial liberalization would lead to significant capital inflows and local corporate growth. Financial liberalization had, as Terreblanche notes, simply allowed "many corporations and individuals to 'escape' to foreign financial markets."[50] As trade unions put it: capital had declared an investment strike. As other critics sharply posed the matter: if local corporations would not invest in the country, why would foreign businesses?

Among the unintended effects of the liberalization of capital flows was difficulty in advancing the privatization of state firms. As with trade, labor, and capital deregulation, privatization preceded the transfer of power in 1994. On February 5, 1988, President P. W. Botha had announced a major reversal of apartheid policy: state firms, which had grown rapidly in the apartheid era, were to be sold off. This shift reflected not only the fear of a black state to come but the growing international call for privatization as recorded in the Kleu report three years earlier. More immediate and local pressures also impinged, most notably the difficulty of sustaining heavy state investments in a period of economic crisis—ESCOM's capital expenditures alone in 1982 were equal to nearly 42 percent of available savings.[51] The only state corporation fully privatized in this period was the steel giant ISCOR in 1989; Sasol, the oil and energy firm founded in 1950, had been privatized and listed on the Johannesburg Stock Exchange even earlier, in 1979. As Fine notes, prior to 1994, "at a time of international sanctions, the only major source of finance for purchasing privatized assets must have been the South African conglomerates. The limited extent of privatization that did occur reflected the unwillingness of these corporations to invest."[52] Pressure by unions, as well as ANC insistence after 1990 that privatization not occur until after majority rule, also played a leading role in preventing fuller privatization prior to 1994. The weakness of white workers and their lack of power or priority in the councils of state in the closing days of apartheid is striking in this area: in 1994 one-fourth of white workers were still employed by the state with another one-third employed by public corporations.[53] White workers with few skills might lose their jobs with the deracialization of the state, while white firms simply moved their capital, accrued over generations of segregation and apartheid, to London or New York.

On the eve of majority rule the ANC itself protested the effort to turn state-run firms into public companies, arguing that the policy of privatizing public-sector firms, "unilaterally imposed for ideological reasons, harmed basic services."[54] Once in power, however, the new government continued the policy of transforming parastatals into public corporations in preparation for full privatization when international market and local political conditions were optimal. Public services (e.g., electricity, water) were increasingly put on a "commercial" basis—thus pricing many out of the reach of the poor majority of the population. In 1997, 30 percent of Telkom was sold for US$1.3 billion to an American-Malaysian consortium, with an additional 25 percent floated in March 2003 despite a fourfold drop in the price the firm might have brought in more buoyant times.[55] Smaller state assets were sold off entirely.

By the opening years of the twenty-first century attempts to privatize large state firms ground to a halt. As *Business Day* reported, "Government strategy on parastatals has come full circle."[56] The slow and stalled pace of privatization was in part due to opposition by labor and the South African Communist Party, key partners in the ANC-led alliance. In larger part, however, there was a considerable lack of interest on the part of private capital and a growing opposition within the ANC and the state itself for the fire sale of assets. The bankruptcy of the government's equity partner in South Africa Airways (SAA), which forced the state to take back full control of SAA, was just one sign of the failure of privatization. By the 2004 elections, the government shifted to public-private partnerships, while promoting infrastructure investment by state-owned companies. In the midst of a global recession and speculative collapses in Asia, the Americas, and Europe, neither local nor international capital was willing to pay adequate prices for state assets.

Those with social capital built up during the apartheid era have been equally supportive of and benefited from neoliberal state policies. Under apartheid white South Africans had monopolized access to skilled positions and higher education, giving them the social and investment capital to migrate overseas. Historical connections to Great Britain and the white-ruled Commonwealth facilitated this: roughly 800,000 South Africans held British passports and were able to enter the United Kingdom and work there. As rebellion advanced in the 1980s and the prospect of majority rule strengthened, departures accelerated. To the surprise of many whites, however, the end of apartheid brought democratic rule, political stability, racial reconciliation, and the constitutional protection of private property. Fears of reparations, land reform, or prosecutions for apartheid crimes proved unfounded. Nevertheless, out-migration increased considerably.

Official South African statistics have greatly underreported this migratory flow as many skilled South Africans left as tourists and failed to declare officially their emigration. The numbers were, however, large and the financial losses great. Measurements of the number of South Africans overseas by the end of the century suggested that at least 10 percent of South Africans with university-level education lived in the United States or other OECD countries.[57] Estimation by migrant flows suggests similar trends, with a 2001 study indicating that official South African statistics recorded as emigrants only 35 percent of the more than 233,000 South Africans who appeared as immigrants in the official immigration statistics of the United States, United Kingdom, Canada, New Zealand, and Australia over the period of 1989–97.[58] The emigration of skilled labor and professionals was, moreover, higher in the late 1990s than earlier in the decade, and increased into the new century.[59]

The losses are particularly keen in the health field, and reveal the apartheid legacy of social capital inequality and the current character of professional out-migration. Statistics from the main countries of destination recorded the arrival of 23,400 health workers from South Africa, which is equivalent to one-tenth of all South African health professionals.[60] Between 1998 and 2001 more than 3,000 South African nurses went to work in Britain; by 2001 6 percent of Britain's health care workforce was South African. By 2006 the OECD was reporting that 37 percent of South Africa's doctors and 7 percent of its nurses had migrated to Australia, Canada, Finland, France, Germany, Portugal, Britain, and the United States.[61] Since it costs the South African government R800,000 to train a doctor and R340,000 to train a nurse, the losses are huge: the net training loss alone to South Africa was estimated in 2003 at US$1 billion.[62]

These are, moreover, highly *racialized* flows, reflecting enduring racial disparities in income, wealth, and education under apartheid. In 1996 whites were 11 percent of the population, for example, but held 77 percent of all doctoral degrees; Africans held barely over 10 percent of the doctorates.[63] Even more startling and inexplicable were mid-2003 census data that suggested that almost 1 million whites left the country in the preceding few years, out of a total white population of 5 million persons—with the number of English- and Afrikaans-speaking South Africans in the country sharply dropping.[64] Surveys of young South African doctors at the end of their required year of community service show this institutionalized racism with a vengeance: the proportion of doctors responding that they intend to leave South Africa and work overseas rose from 34 percent in 1999 to 43 percent in 2001.[65] By individual and institutional status there is a racial gulf: over half of the white doctors intended to leave as opposed to only 10 percent of African doctors. The majority of doctors trained at the historically white Stellenbosch University, University of Cape Town, and University of the Free State aim to head overseas, as opposed to the majority of graduates of the historically black universities of MEDUNSA (now the University of Limpopo) and Unitra (University of Transkei) who intend to remain in South Africa.[66]

Regional labor flows have *not* followed the pattern of these flows to the North. Here semiperipheral and highly racialized relationships give South Africa a distinctive profile that fits neither Northern nor African migration patterns. While labor flows from South Africa to the rich North remain predominantly legal, highly white, highly skilled, and facilitated by state policy, heavy flows into South Africa remain predominantly poor, undocumented, and increasingly attacked by the state and the media. This Janus-like pattern derives directly from the neoracist principles underlying neoliberalism: South Africa is acting toward its periphery as rich core countries act toward the Global South.

Since 1994 state policies have been steadily more restrictive toward regional in-migration; and while officially recorded migration numbers fell, the totals have clearly increased. Most of these migrants are undocumented, and estimates of their numbers range from the vastly overstated and later withdrawn figure of 2.5 to 4 million provided by state agencies, to estimates of 400,000–500,000 calculated by some migration experts. Whatever the actual numbers, immigrants are clearly coming from a wider range of African countries than during the apartheid era.

Grossly inflated figures by both the state and the media parallel steadily growing xenophobia and an associated crime panic stoked by both media outlets and government officials.[67] Independent surveys indicate that the citizens of South Africa were more xenophobic than any other national group in the world.[68] Attacks on foreign Africans grew steadily after 2000, exploding in May 2008 when scores were killed and tens of thousands fled South Africa's townships for hastily and poorly supplied refugee camps. For foreign Africans, including the increasing thousands fleeing the collapse of Zimbabwe's economy, South Africa had become not a refuge but a nightmare. Refugee camp residents went on hunger strikes, demanding that the United Nations intervene; others requested to leave, as some camp residents put, for a poorer but better "Third World" country. As one woman shouted, "Give us a place to live in Mozambique, Zambia, or Botswana. You can even send us to the bush there, if we can only live in peace!"[69]

While the government sought to find a "third force" behind these attacks, the postapartheid state had itself steadily isolated and increased the pressure on foreign Africans. Constructing the "rainbow nation" and a new South African identity had, since majority rule, been accomplished by sharpening the distinction between citizens and noncitizens, along with a panoply of new restrictive policies against newly "illegal" migrants. Attempts to apply Northern policies and restrict African immigration, as in the narrow amnesty granted in 1995 to long-term Mozambican residents, had been followed by tighter border controls, fiercer enforcement of immigration laws, the criminalization of foreign Africans, and rising deportations. Indeed, the stabilization and nationalization of the formal labor force that began in the 1980s, when the region was at war and unions were militant, showed signs of creating a group of illegal workers by the beginning of the new century. The reduction of foreign workers in the mining sector in the 1980s, for example, led to pressures for illegal migration by other household members, and particularly women, to make up lost income as they tried to replace lost male mining income—a possibility Davies and Head warned against in the early 1990s.[70] Employers for their part have sought to lower labor costs, and have begun to adopt policies pursued in the North of outsourcing and subcontracting work to smaller and nonunion firms, who more often employ vulnerable and cheaper foreign workers.

By 2000 there were clear signs that informal inflows were replicating old patterns of cheap labor, as employers in agriculture, construction, services, and even mining turned toward undocumented and, especially, short-term, subcontracted, migrant labor.[71] Where numbers are officially recorded, as by the larger mining companies' recruiting agencies, the reemergence of old apartheid patterns was clear: the proportion of the mining force composed by foreign migrant workers rose from 40 percent in 1985 to over 60 percent by the end of the century.[72] The implementation of the harsher 2003 Immigration Act may have moderated such flows in the contracted mining sector;[73] it certainly did not slow undocumented flows across the country's porous borders.

Rising levels of inequality, poverty, and unemployment inside the country have been exacerbating conflict between poor local and foreign Africans. While statistics for all three indicators are debated constantly, by the end of the first decade of majority rule the difficulties were clear to all. As the UN's *South Africa Human Development Report 2003* recorded, almost half of the population lived in poverty, and income inequality had increased from .596 in 1995 to .635 in 2001 (as measured by Gini coefficient). The official unemployment rate had risen sharply to more than 30 percent and would continue to rise.[74] African youth and particularly young African women were particularly hard hit: by 2011 over 50 percent of all young Africans were unemployed, three times greater than the rate of 15 percent among young white South Africans.[75] South Africa's scores on the UN Human Development Index would similarly fall from .644 in 1995 to .616 in 2000 and .610 in 2009;[76] its ranking among the world's nations over this period moved downward from 90 to 123.[77] Notwithstanding the expansion of the African middle class, poverty is at least as racially polarized as under apartheid if not more so, with the African share of South Africa's aggregate household income actually *falling* 5 percent between 1995 and 2000.[78]

Behind such statistics stand significant inequalities are job losses in manufacturing, a sector that shed 21 percent of its workforce between 1990 and 2002.[79] When added to losses in the formal agricultural sector and services, over 1 million jobs were lost in the 1990s, which the Department of Trade and Industry simply termed "unavoidable."[80] Altogether, nonagricultural formal employment declined by over 20 percent between 1990 and 2001, indicative of a long-term structural trend.[81] Privatization of state firms also had a part to play. Job losses at Telkom alone, even before its stock market listing in April 2003, were 25,000.[82] Slight falls in the official unemployment rate notwithstanding, fifteen years after the first democratic elections the state was still reporting a narrowly defined unemployment rate of 25 percent, with most economists agreeing that the real rate was closer to 40 percent. Work in the informal sector, often hailed as a viable alternative to formal wage work, rarely provided incomes to lift families to even the lowest poverty level. Indeed, according to the government's own 2005 data, 11 percent of the 2.8 million informal sector jobs provided no income at all, and another 35 percent provided earnings between R1 and R500 (US$83) per month.[83] Throughout the first decade of the twentieth century, less than half of adult South Africans had any income-generating employment at all, far below the world average. Indeed, South Africa ranked, according to the International Labour Organization, among the ten lowest countries in the world in terms of employment ratios—a group that primarily included Middle Eastern and North African states that effectively exclude women from the labor market.[84]

As South Africa's dismal record of unemployment and poverty mounted, it became increasingly difficult for the government and its supporters to defend an export-oriented growth model dependent on foreign investment. State policy, following in part the trade union federation COSATU's Industrial Strategy Project of the early 1990s, had promoted the creation of world-competitive industries and exports in the "post-Fordist" era. Export competitiveness was predicated not on abundant reserves of cheap labor—which South Africa lacks by comparison to East and South Asia—but on advanced technology and innovation, product quality and diversity, high capital and labor productivity, and high skills. This promised a route away from South Africa's dependence on cheap labor and primary product exports. It was a direct counter, moreover, to the early 1990s inward, redistributive development proposals by ANC economists and union analysts.[85]

The great difficulty, of course, is that this model was a failure, and an increasingly public one at that. In part this reflected its origins, having been imported from core areas like the United States and Europe, which had centers of technological innovation and were shedding manufacturing to semiperipheral and peripheral areas. In South Africa's case, the implementation of the model through the neoliberalization of trade, capital, and emigration flows undermined both technological innovation and manufacturing. On the one hand, it encouraged, as charted above, technological flight by both large firms and whites with social and technological capital. On the other hand, it undermined manufacturing employment while increasing the reliance on the devaluation of the rand to stimulate exports from declining manufacturing centers and primary product exporters.

None of this changed the state's strategy. As the independent, union-oriented Labour Research Service noted, the government refused to budge from "its export oriented growth model which relies on foreign investment." Indeed, "the government has bought into all the worst aspects of that model—namely creating industrial development zones, making labour flexible, privatization, an emphasis on highly skilled labour at the expense of labour at lower levels, targeting high export growth sectors of the economy at the expense of sectors producing for domestic consumption."[86]

The Exceptional Case: The Automotive Sector

Amid these competing claims it is worth looking at one large manufacturing subsector that has done better than almost all others: the automotive complex. As the Department of Trade and Industry celebrated, "The automotive sector has been a star performer in recent years. Since 1997, real value-added growth has averaged 8.2% and real fixed investment growth has averaged 8.7%. Export growth has been outstanding—averaging almost 30%. The success with automotive component exports is on a similar scale."[87]

This impressive growth is attributed to the government's Motor Industry Development Program (MIDP), introduced in 1995. The story is, however, more complicated. As described in chapter 3, Ford and GM began producing in South Africa in the 1920s; they accelerated their production in the postwar period, particularly after 1961 when the state introduced, as did other white and semiperipheral states, local content requirements. As the global economic crisis hit in the mid-1970s, consumption lagged and strikes exploded.

The world's major auto companies responded by reorganizing their global production lines, moving away from the national branch-plant model and toward leaner, globally organized and supplier-outsourced production strategies. While sanctions and the withdrawal of US firms delayed the impact of these changes on South Africa, in 1989 the late-apartheid government liberalized imports and promoted exports through new local-content regulations that lowered import charges for manufacturers in direct exchange for exports of cars or car components. This set the stage for the ANC government's MIDP, which enhanced import-export coordination by offsetting import tariffs in response to each manufacturer's export effort.

The impact of these changes has been significant. While local prices remained high and vehicle sales initially fell over the course of 1995–99, local sales eventually rose and, more significantly, vehicle exports did increase, particularly to Africa and Europe. Total vehicle production between 1999 and 2005 grew from 315,000 units to nearly 500,000 units, while exports more than doubled to 140,000 units. Significantly, components were a high proportion of total automotive exports, and were concentrated in the production of leather seat covers (for BMW) and catalytic converters (which used rare and expensive, but locally produced minerals). The big three German automakers who had never divested—BMW, Daimler Chrysler, and VW—all made significant new investments to sustain export production. BMW, for example, opened a plant to produce the 300-series car and by 2005 was producing 55,000 cars (7 percent of total world production of the 300-series), of which 80 percent were exported.[88] US and Japanese firms have, however, been far slower to invest, and have done so as part of rationalizing and integrating their global production network.

As this discussion suggests, there are no South African producers: the sector is completely dominated by the big multinational firms. Indeed, the end of apartheid and the reassertion of the international firms' control have led to the demise of local producers, even in subassembly, and the overall "death knell for South African technology in the automotive industry."[89] Local sales and production volumes remain marginal to international producers, even by comparison to operations in Latin America or Australia—South Africa accounts for less than 1 percent of total automotive output worldwide. This makes the future of local production uncertain.[90] Like the overall economy, output has grown while employment has not: at least one in every three jobs in the automotive sector was lost from 1995 to 2003.

Such figures sustain the case of free market critics, who argue that MIDP has only served to create a sheltered market that bilks consumers, due to unnecessarily high car prices, while providing large subsidies to automotive firms.[91] It is nevertheless evident that state action has made a significant difference in this one sector where it has been most prominent. Radical liberalization, as in the dropping of all tariffs and export subsidies, would have surely eviscerated local automobile production. By contrast the sector accounts for up to 8 percent of GDP and employs upward of 300,000 persons. A comparison with the fate of other consumer goods manufacturers, particularly the decimated textile industry, reinforces this conclusion. Strong state direction and an alliance with foreign multinationals has in this case retained South African production, while adapting South African facilities into the major firms' new global supply networks. Moreover, state policy could have been more interventionist; the endurance and growth of automobile production has not been replicated in other sectors. The new ANC government considered and rejected, for example, stronger incentives and penalties such as those followed in Australia. And certainly state policy cannot even begin to conceive of targeting and stimulating a local assembly firm. There is no prospect of stimulating a South African-owned firm, as there is no South African Mandelacar to match South Korea's Hyundai.

Among the costs of the failed bet on an alliance with the North have been falling employment levels, increasing inequality, white capital and social flight, and an increasing reliance on primary production. These have over time steadily eroded the legitimacy of free trade and free market policies. By the end of the Mbeki presidency the key architect of neoliberalism, Finance Minister Trevor Manuel, was openly challenged by other ministers who used the success of MIDP to call for a more comprehensive industrial development program led by a developmental state.[92] Lending urgency to these debates were continuing waves of global financial speculation and chaos on the one hand, and continuing attacks on neoliberalism by unruly popular forces across the country, the region, and the Global South on the other. These pressures contributed to the emergence of a much wider assessment of developmental strategies—under conditions that made harking back to past models even harder to imagine.

7

Looking Forward, North and East

In the late 1990s a new wave of protest began to ripple across South Africa. In the next ten years it would surge, with protesters all over the country demanding the basic necessities of life—from housing, land, and water to electricity, jobs, and basic health care.[1] Demonstrators aimed their barbs at a wide range of local, national, and global targets. In this respect the Cape Town protest of February 14, 2003, was larger than most I attended during those years, with more than 10,000 people in attendance, but its contours were typical of many such events before and after. Marching from the doors of the US consulate in Cape Town and moving up the hill to the doors of parliament, protesters aimed to pressure both the US and South African governments to finally act against AIDS. Young activists, many with little or no personal memories of apartheid—indeed, most must have been just entering school when Mandela walked out of prison in 1990—followed in the footsteps of their elders, toyi-toying through town, singing new words to old liberation songs. Standing in front of the locked gates of parliament, Treatment Action Campaign (TAC) speakers called on the ANC government to admit the reality of the AIDS pandemic, reverse neoliberal policies that undercut health care, and—along with the US drug companies, the World Trade Organization (WTO), and the US government—provide access to antiretroviral drugs and public health care. Peering over the shoulders of the speakers and protecting the doors of parliament stood the larger-than-life statue of the founding white father of the state: Louis Botha, immortalized astride a charger.

This juxtaposition was not without justification: it had been almost a century from the first days of South Africa's first prime minister, Botha, to the last days of the Mbeki presidency. Like Botha and Jan Smuts, Botha's partner in war and peace, Mandela and Mbeki came to power in the wake of a tumultuous war and bet their futures on racial reconciliation at home and an alliance with dominant powers abroad. For Smuts and Botha this meant peace with Great Britain and peace between, in the terminology of the day, the Afrikaner and British races. For Mandela and Mbeki this meant a developmental pact with Europe and North America, cemented by racial reconciliation between black and white South Africans. South Africa's new black presidents, of course, have had a major advantage over their white supremacist predecessors: they stand atop the fulfilled promise of the liberal twentieth century—a powerful, industrialized, and democratic state. To TAC protesters, however, this only accentuated the legitimacy of their demands: how could Africa's richest and most powerful state side with Western pharmaceutical companies and governments to deny treatment to the hundreds dying every day of AIDS?

As the new century dawned, protest by TAC campaigners, squatters, the landless, the unemployed and underemployed grew—bedeviling the stability sought by the ANC and big business alike. Whether the issue has been land reform, housing, access to water and electricity, unemployment, or meeting health and education needs, the ANC has increasingly found itself facing persistent challenges in the countryside and in the streets. The promised fruits of the neoliberal and racial reconciliation policies that had been embraced at the dawn of the postapartheid era have, quite clearly, failed to materialize. Yet neither the rule of the African National Congress nor the hold of neoliberal principles has been seriously shaken. Despite defections from the ANC and boycott campaigns, the ANC was handily reelected in the 2004 and 2009 elections.

This is an open conundrum, particularly for radical critics who have diligently tracked and protested the state's postapartheid failures: how does one reconcile the endurance of the neoliberal ANC despite increasingly harsh social conditions and rising social protest? How does one change state policies that have benefited so few, and produced so little development?

For longtime scholar-activists, the shattered expectations of what a postapartheid South Africa would bring marked a signal defeat. This is particularly the case for the many whose lives and publications spanned from the struggles for independence in the 1950s and 1960s to the more radical armed national liberation movements in southern Africa in the 1970s and 1980s. As John Saul bluntly put it in his assessment of the "post-apartheid dénouement": "A tragedy is being enacted" as South Africans "are being sacrificed on the altar of the neo-liberal logic of global capitalism."[2]

Younger scholars and activists, rooted less in past national liberation models and more directly engaged in recent local movements, are more optimistic.[3] But even here the lingering sense of dismay is palpable. Patrick Bond, director of the Centre for Civil Society and the most productive chronicler of South African neoliberalism, provided a typical summary in the 2005 updating of his volume *Elite Transition*. In conclusions that parallel Saul's, he restates the case: "During the early 1990s, a small corps of nationalist politicians emerged to hijack most of the country's mass popular movements," leading in turn to the adoption of disastrous neoliberal policies.[4] Racial apartheid may have passed; a new "class apartheid" had been cemented in place by petit bourgeois African nationalists.[5]

It is hard to perceive from these accounts the possibility of the ANC party elite reversing course and responding to calls to implement the central planks of the ANC's original Freedom Charter: redistributing land to the tiller and nationalizing the mines, banks, and monopoly capital. Particularly frustrating for social activists is the continuing alliance between the ANC and its partners to its left in the trade unions and the South African Communist Party (SACP), and the ability of the government to absorb civil society protests and reinscribe neoliberal values among even the poor.[6] For the Left outside the circles of government and the ANC, this raises the issue of the forging of an antineoliberal force and political party. As Bond put it in 2005: "In the coming five to ten years, my sense is that the regroupment of the left under some sort of anti-neoliberal party umbrella . . . is inevitable."[7] This is, as yet, a stark, unfulfilled hope.

ANC stalwarts and scholars for their part deride the "ultraleftists," arguing that there was no possibility in the early 1990s—after the fall of the Soviet Union and in the face of the global dominance of neoliberalism—of a return to either socialist state planning or the liberal import-substitution models of the 1960s and 1970s. Any prospects for expanding growth and income in today's world economy, they argue, require social peace and the cooperation of local and foreign investors—leading in turn to nonracialism and macroeconomic orthodoxy. Over time budget austerity and GDP growth will, it is argued, make progressive redistribution possible, a process heralded in recent years by pressures from within the ANC, most notably the populist framing of the ouster of President Mbeki in 2007 and the subsequent election of Jacob Zuma, with solid backing by the SACP and the trade union confederation.[8] The Zuma years, however, have failed to fulfill these hopes: macroeconomic and fiscal policy remains rigidly orthodox, while redistribution of land, wealth, and income remains far beyond the government's imagination.

Long-term analyses of the kind carried out here can easily reinforce these bleak conclusions. There can be no denying the terrible costs of neoliberal policies. Indeed, as has been argued in the preceding chapter, neoliberalism's tentacles were embedded well before majority rule, making them all the more difficult to uproot. ANC rule has, in this sense, only further solidified corporate wealth and the hold of Northern neoliberal powers, while creating a small, politically connected black elite at home.[9]

Moreover, the continuing global crisis reinforces these bleak structural trends. Many look for inspiration, for example, to the developmental successes of East Asian states, which blossomed after state-led land reform and heavy state investment in corporate and social capital. Yet both the global and local conditions that facilitated these successes in the middle of the twentieth century no longer hold. The long post–World War II global boom has turned to speculative bust, while development by the invitation of Western powers during the Cold War, which facilitated the East Asian NICs, is no longer promoted by core states, multinational corporations, or international financial institutions. Closer to home and the present, the South African state over the last twenty years has been stripped of key capacities that allowed it to facilitate accumulation among local firms, foreign multinationals, and the state itself. Further complicating any comparisons to East Asian nations is South Africa's heightened cost of urban, unskilled labor and the shortage of skilled labor, both due to apartheid's debilitating dispossession of rural producers and scant investment in African education, housing, and health.[10]

Wherever one turns, there thus seems little respite: both the political landscape and global conditions appear to militate strongly against any radical break with ANC rule and neoliberal policies and relationships. Calls for a developmental state may well continue to increase, as may demands to provide some redistribution of land and greater access to electricity, housing, and social services. But is the best we can hope for a slightly more activist state, one that tries to appease and incorporate protest movements, while expanding local consumption and aggregate demand through mild redistributionist measures? The rift between the pessimism of structural analysis and optimism of popular protest remains particularly daunting.

Crisis, Movements, and Ruptures

These are not conclusions we should accept. They are certainly not the conclusions to be drawn from this study of South Africa's developmental record over the course of the last century. Yet even as we set aside triumphalist extrapolations of protest events, we need to equally reject mechanical projections from models that hark back to another world-economic era or chart the future of South and southern Africa from fiscal crises and dispossession emanating from the North.[11] There is another way: to start by concretely situating South and southern Africa within historical patterns and ask: where and to what degree have postapartheid settlements and policies affected South Africa's actual relationships across the region and world economy? Set against the history of the last century, are conditions so difficult, and opportunities so few, in the years ahead?

My argument may be simply stated: postapartheid settlements have *not* imposed a stable neoliberal and nonracial order, but have created the structural opportunity for a fundamental break with both the political and accumulation regimes that have dominated the late apartheid and postapartheid periods. Indeed, sharp ruptures in the world economy are clearly under way—leaving short-run political choices in South Africa very much open. These are the lessons of a long historical view.

To perceive the possibilities in front of us requires placing today's dilemmas within the long histories charted in this book. As has been argued in detail above, the success or failure of developmental policies over the course of the twentieth century depended on shifting patterns of racial and capital accumulation that extended well across the urban and rural spaces of South Africa, the region, and indeed the world. And changing developmental paths have inevitably entailed radically altering these relationships. Models that ignore these dimensions and stress national economic spaces and macroeconomic factors invariably fail to grasp the transnational and spatial unevenness of capital accumulation, racial formation, and state power.

The most radical developmental rupture charted was in the 1920s, which led to a decisive industrial and technological leap forward. This was a moment of not simply global crisis and war, but of the collapse of the British free trade, competitive world economy. Global crises after World War I destabilized South African farmers and gold producers, leading to interminable conflict and, in 1925, the victory of radical, anti-imperial white nationalists. Their program entailed not simply protectionism and transformed macroeconomic policies but a wholesale reforging of the state, local forms of accumulation and labor force reproduction, and regional and North-South links. Global racial alliances were essential to this process: they permitted an independent white state to exist in a sea of colonial territories; defined, differentiated, and regulated exploitable black labor within the country and across the region; and allowed the settler state to claim a larger share of the wealth produced within South and southern Africa.

The years immediately following World War II opened a similar conjunctural opportunity, with global unrest and economic uncertainty once again intersecting local social and political protest driven by the very semiperipheral success of interwar industrialization and urbanization. In this instance, however, a newly victorious white party found itself facing a new world order led by the United States, new international financial and commercial institutions, and resurgent African nationalism. Strategies that underwrote interwar successes were less and less feasible as multinational corporations jumped protectionist boundaries and African nationalists closed off relations to the north. While the formal strictures of apartheid served to differentiate, reorganize, and stabilize national and regional labor and political forces, this came at considerable cost: it was not possible to construct a radical economic program that might counter underdeveloping forces from the North, in parallel if not alliance with newly independent states to the north. Adopting an open alliance with the United States and the institutions of the new world order did secure an uneasy place for white South Africa in the new postwar system, but this came at the cost of blocking further claims to wealth and standing in the world economy.

The post–World War II conjuncture and the opportunities it offered thus led to a very different outcome than that of the post–World War I conjuncture: where the earlier instance engendered a radical developmental state and a "leap forward," the second failed to sustain any movement within world-economic and world-racial hierarchies. The contrast with East Asia, where postcolonial, developmental states emerged to block multinational corporations' control and carried out local land reform and redistributive measures, could not be sharper. In 1945 South Africa was already a newly industrialized country; thirty years later it was lagging far behind East Asia and much of Latin America (as illustrated in figures I.1 and I.2 above).

There are lessons here for us today, for once again we live in a conjuncture marked by global economic crisis and significant political transitions. The working out of these processes has had signal effects: the breakout of new movements and global stagnation in the 1970s delivered both neoliberalism on the one hand, and the end of authoritarian rule, most notably apartheid, on the other. As the last chapter argued, however, this transition over the course of the 1970s and 1980s did not mark any radical rupture in South Africa's position in world development hierarchies. Moments of crisis and transition do offer, as has occurred in the past, critical opportunities as the hold of old forms of accumulation and rule are loosened or even broken. Studies of the transition to majority rule in 1994 document how continuity, rather than rupture, of neoliberal macroeconomic and social policies was maintained.

What remains to be seen is how transnational and racial relationships, so essential to forging past developmental successes and failures, might be shaped in the face of continuing global instability. The dominant method that first isolates and then compares national economic spaces, then posits the future by projecting current conditions while changing the government and its monetary and fiscal policies, is of limited assistance here. Looking forward we need a much closer examination of the state's engagement with changing racial and accumulation networks that reach to both the distant, powerful North and the closer region and continent.

Betting on the North

South African elites and policymakers, like their many counterparts outside core areas, have long realized the critical nature of their relations with core areas, international capital, and regional markets. Policymakers during the late apartheid and early postapartheid years were no exception, being highly conscious that state power and future development rested on regional and global networks. As demonstrated in the preceding chapter, late apartheid governments moved toward market reforms and privatization precisely because this would protect the centers of wealth generated by segregation and apartheid and weaken the coming postapartheid state. Neoliberalism in this sense was a racial endeavor: it served to reinforce the racial inequalities that were inherited from apartheid and would be protected under the proclamation of a "nonracial," "rainbow" South Africa. Postapartheid governments were especially attentive to forging a close, developmental alliance with the North and eschewing any claims for reparations at home or the repudiation of odious debts undertaken abroad to sustain the apartheid state. The constraining of redistribution claims, wage increases, and any significant expansion of social services was a direct result of an explicit compact between the Mandela and Mbeki governments and international financial institutions, multinational corporations, and core states in Europe and North America.

One of most discouraging results of this compact has been the scant appreciation of the South African government's efforts by the rich club of the North. It was not always so: for the first seventy-five years of the twentieth century South Africa's white leaders had been accepted as charter members of the small Anglo-American group that dominated the world economy. As such they were welcomed by the great powers as one of the few founding members of the League of Nations, the British Commonwealth, the United Nations, GATT, the IMF, and the World Bank. While worldwide protest movements isolated South Africa in the last decade of apartheid, with the coming of majority rule in 1994 South Africa was readmitted as a full member of the international community. South Africa soon had diplomatic ties with more countries than at any time its history: in the 1980s South Africa had fewer than 30 representatives abroad; after 1994 the number rose quickly to more than 150. South Africa simultaneously acceded to more than seventy multilateral treaties and joined more than forty intergovernmental organizations.

Despite this flurry of activity, South Africa's favored relationship with Europe and the United States quickly faded. By the turn of the century, the celebration of majority rule, Mandela, and racial reconciliation was replaced in the leading North American and European media with images of South Africa's susceptibility to debilitating African political diseases. For the *New York Times* the story had become: "South African Leader Fights a Fraying Image" (April 28, 2001). Once depicted as the savior of Africa, by the end of the century Mandela was viewed in Europe and the United States as an increasingly irascible retiree. His successor, Thabo Mbeki, was cartooned in 2005 in the *Economist* as carrying on his shoulder the weighty cross of Africa. But there was to be no easy road, the *Economist* told its readers, to recapturing Mandela's mantle and saving Africa:

Only Mr. Mbeki (who himself is still unknown to many Africans) stands much chance of influencing other leaders on the continent. And yet he has extremely worryingly autocratic and reactionary instincts, which are clearly on display in the way he runs his own country. If they are a clue to his future leadership, then the hugely ambitious plans of the developed world can probably be consigned to the dustbin brimful with previous ideas to "Save Africa."[12]

Despite his support for neoliberalism at home and internationally, by the end of his presidency Mbeki was cast as another sad African failure. His successor, Jacob Zuma, was immediately caricatured as an uneducated, hypersexualized, tribal African.[13] The drive to escape the waves of Afro-pessimism emanating from Europe and North America had proven far more difficult than expected in the heady days of the "Mandela Miracle."

For the traducers of Africa and its peoples, this depiction of South Africa fits a long-standing pattern: the contagion of "fragmented" or "collapsed" states across Africa. Surrounding South Africa are the common media examples of not just poverty and disease, but Africa's first regional war (DR Congo), hyperinflation and economic collapse (Zimbabwe), and civil war and aid dependency (Mozambique). Yet these conditions are hardly due to what scholars and policymakers tidily term as uniquely African attributes of tribalism, neopatrimonialism, or kleptocratic rule. Indeed, weak states and rising social and ethnic conflict became common phenomena all along the periphery of the world economy during the late twentieth century. Equally shared was a process of state deformation, as postcolonial states in the 1980s and 1990s were eviscerated by international institutions from above and, often, by international NGOs and civil society organizations from below. As African states provided less and less security, education, and health services, "choiceless democracies" emerged, where elections might take place but governments have been stripped of basic social and economic responsibilities and the legitimacy and national identities they engender.[14] As states have become less central to people's lives, citizenship has become less meaningful, and alternative centers of social support, authority, and identity have emerged.[15]

While subject to these pressures, South Africa does not neatly fit this analysis. South Africa remains the most industrialized and powerful state on the continent, and has suffered less decline and marginalization than other regional states and the World Bank's "Sub-Saharan Africa" category as a whole. Figure 7.1 illustrates this empirically by measuring these countries' income per capita against the standard of South Africa between 1962 and 2009; as a country (or the area as a whole) moves toward South Africa's level, its trendline rises.

While Angola's and Botswana's rising incomes based on their respective oil and diamond production are impressive, even more striking is how

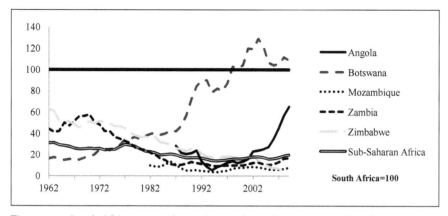

Figure 7.1. South Africa versus the region and continent: gross national income per capita. World Bank, *World Development Indicators*.

South Africa has outpaced the rest of its neighbors and sub-Saharan Africa as a whole from the early 1980s forward. The growing distance between South Africa and its neighbors has been accompanied in recent years by an increasingly sharp sense of national identity and, as its corollary, a newfound xenophobia.

This position generates a Janus-like stance toward other states. On the one side, the South African state faces, like other African states, deformation and underdevelopment processes emanating from the North. On the other side, however, it confronts and benefits from its unequal relationships with much poorer states in the region and on the continent. As the examples of capital flows, migration, and economic policy in previous chapters chart, these two-faced relationships generate inexorable and often contradictory pressures on the state. And these have led in turn to very different stances toward rich core states and institutions on the one hand, and poorer African states and institutions on the other. This bifurcated set of responses applies not only to processes of capital accumulation, but racial hierarchies as well: the South African government and its leadership confronts racial animus from the rich white North and local white elites, while sharing a common colonial and white settler history with the rest of the region and continent. If the South African government's international and regional actions are often perplexing and conflicted, this is so for good reasons.

While majority rule did not significantly change South Africa's location in world-economic networks, it did reconfigure the state's relationships with both the rich North and poorer Africa. This was not due, as most accounts would have it, to the beneficent rise of a modern, nonracial, and democratic state. Nor was it simply the replacement of racial apartheid with class apartheid, as both leftist and liberal analysts often argue.[16] Rather, democracy and majority rule have recast the class and racial relationships of the state locally and internationally. Majority rule has deracialized and legitimized the national state, in the sense of replacing the exclusive white face of the state with blacks as the new ministers, bureaucrats, generals, and even foot soldiers of the National Defence Force. Yet this has meant that the country's leadership and the state are no longer treated as part of the dominant Anglo-American group at home or abroad. This stands in stark contrast to the situation in the century before 1994, when the state, big business, and European and American elites all shared a common racial identity cemented in international and institutional alliances. Thus the contradictory outcome: while majority rule led to the deracialization of the state bureaucracy, the postapartheid state was ever more racialized internationally.

Faced with this situation, the political leaders of postapartheid South Africa have moved along two fronts. First, they have strived to re-create a developmental alliance with those who wield power in the North by affirming the security of private property and capital investment, and adhering to the macroeconomic policies continually pushed forward by international financial institutions, local and international firms, and the United States and Europe. This invariably has meant the protection of the social and investment capital created under segregation and apartheid, strict monetary and fiscal policies, and open capital flows. What these commitments have not reaped is a revival of the lost alliance with Europe and North America or significant economic development. Both local and international capital remain wary of the new South African state as indicated by the figures in the previous chapter on the massive departure of white wealth, corporations, and citizens.

Foreign direct investment—as opposed to speculative portfolio investment—has been highly uneven and markedly weak, even before 9/11 and the financial crisis of 2008. As the *Financial Times* reported on June 17, 2008, "Between 1994 and 2002, average net annual inflows of FDI were 1.5 per cent of gross domestic product compared with 3 per cent for South Africa's international rivals." Fueled by the worldwide commodity boom, FDI rose rapidly in the next five years to a peak in 2008, only to fall by 80 percent in the next two years to the point where, as a percentage of GDP, South Africa's FDI inflows ranked 128th in the world right behind Burkina Faso."[17]

Mobilization by the business world and the liberal media has been especially vigorous when threats to white wealth are perceived, whether it be through land reform, prosecution for apartheid atrocities, or through lapses in privatization and deregulation. Mining firms repeatedly attribute the lack of investment in South Africa's mineral complex to potential constraints on their operations, most notably the ANC's seeming inability to silence party members' call for nationalization of mineral resources (most notably by Winnie Madikizela-Mandela and leaders of the ANC Youth

League). Land reform, a key pillar of East Asian success stories, remains a similarly volatile subject. Zimbabwe is the most notable example, where the plight of white farmers has been the focus of a vociferous campaign by the white media, foreign and local business communities, and the governments of the United States and, most insistently, Great Britain. If South Africa wants to be treated as a respected member of the civilized world of nations, the common refrain from the North runs, it simply must intervene against the injustice meted out by land invasions and fast-track land reform. While the highly repressive and undemocratic nature of the Mugabe government is starkly evident, this fails to explain why it merits so much attention by comparison to equally predatory and far less democratic states in Africa or Asia. Concern for displaced African farm tenants in Zimbabwe is seldom matched by a concern for the disproportionate number of African farmers being displaced as vast swaths of Africa are being cleared as part of a new wave of foreign "land grabs."[18]

At the heart of the North's concern is, quite simply, protection for white property and capital in Zimbabwe—and especially the implications for South Africa. After all, Rhodesia's Land Apportionment Act of 1930 reserved only 50 percent of agricultural land for whites by comparison to South Africa's 1913 Natives Land Act, which designated 87 percent of the land for whites. This figure has barely changed for South Africa: by 2005 less than 5 percent of white-owned farmland had been transferred into black ownership through government restitution programs.[19] The ANC government has guaranteed that land occupations along the lines so prominent in Zimbabwe, Brazil, and elsewhere will not be tolerated, and the government has not hesitated to unleash police forces to expel African squatters from private and public, urban and rural, land.

Deracializing the exclusively white upper echelons of the business world has formed a second front in the ANC's effort to tackle apartheid's legacy. The government has led this effort, assisted by the local—but notably not the international—business community. The benefits of "Black Economic Empowerment" (BEE) programs, which have involved firms selling an equity share to black consortia, have, however, been quite narrowly distributed. BEE efforts have created a handful of what are termed BEE-illionaires, but this has had little impact at the level of the enterprise: only five to ten firms listed on the Johannesburg Stock Exchange have more than 51 percent black ownership.[20] As Thabo Mbeki's own brother, the businessman Moeletsi Mbeki, put it: after more than ten years of majority rule "all the major empowerment transactions have involved the transfer of marginal assets (from major corporations under empowerment pressures) to politically connected individuals."[21] And even these have been rolled back, falling from 7 to 10 percent black control of the market capitalization of the Johannesburg Stock Exchange right after majority rule to less than 3 percent in 2010[22]—and this for an exchange that suffered a loss of 30 percent of its listings (largely through departures to London's FTSE) and almost 50 percent of its capitalization from 1995 to 2002.[23]

To be fair, a wider if small black middle and upper class has been created, generating new and very high levels of inequality among the African population. Yet this has largely been produced through the public sector and not private enterprise: study after study of the country's labor market shows little deracialization, with the top management of South African firms in 2010–11 remaining overwhelmingly white (73 percent) and male (80 percent)[24]—and this despite considerable white flight overseas. Of course, this reflects the legacy of apartheid, under which an African entrepreneurial class was severely stunted. The racial distribution of income and wealth has thus changed very little. Indeed, the black share of aggregate household income is estimated to have *declined* from 1995 to 2000.[25] Meanwhile inequality among races, due to increasing white incomes, grew between 1995 and 2005; South Africa is now by income, and most likely by race (given the paucity of comparative racial data this last claim is uncertain), the most unequal society in the world.[26]

By the tenth anniversary of majority rule, vigorous public debate had erupted over the inability of the government to accelerate the country's growth rate and reduce poverty, unemployment, and inequality at home. These trends and their accompanying backlash were common across the Global South. They were particularly evident in Latin America and Asia, where disastrous results from following advice from the IMF and World Bank led many states to abandon neoliberalism in favor of more independent fiscal and monetary policies and, often in response to comparable public protests, the provisioning of basic social necessities and services. In South Africa this trend took the form of the relaunching of neglected social programs: new BEE codes and targets were advanced, social expenditures were increased, a renewed land reform effort was announced, and the sale of state assets was slowed.

As the prospect of a return to an interventionist, developmental state improved, there has been a revival of calls to follow East Asian examples, including that of China.[27] The election of Jacob Zuma in 2009 demonstrated the forces at play: Zuma cast himself as an economic populist, and was backed by trade unions, the SACP, and the Women's and Youth Leagues of the ANC. There have, however, been no signs since his election of any substantive reversal of past policies and their class and racial supports. Although Zuma at times has called himself a "socialist," he has assiduously cultivated foreign and local business leaders alike. There thus exist, twenty years after Mandela's release and the unbanning of the ANC, few signs of altering the strong allegiance of the South African state to the neoliberal institutions and policies of the North. The lack of an aggressive black entrepreneurial class and the departure and hollowing out of South African firms have largely locked into place the historic, underdeveloping, North-South links forged after World War II.

Betting on the South: A New African Charter?

Maintaining relationships with Northern states, financial institutions, and the white holders of wealth understandably consumed far more of the new government's attention than relations with regional and continental African classes and states. In this area a major transition occurred under Mbeki, who sought to use relationships with the rest of Africa to bolster the power of the South African state and open up new opportunities for South African firms. Rather than Africa being a hindrance to be avoided, as economists had cautioned and Mandela had practiced, South Africa was now to embrace its African heritage. Yet this did not mean abandoning the conservative monetary and fiscal policies that had cemented the alliance with the North and white business leaders. Indeed, neoliberal principles, which had placed South Africa in an increasingly dependent position vis-à-vis North America and Europe, were to prove essential to extending South Africa's power northward.

Launched under the rubric of an "African Renaissance," Mbeki sought to achieve what Smuts and then Malan had hoped to do in the very different, early post–World War II conjuncture: enhance South Africa's economic and political power by speaking for southern and continental Africa. The basis for this claim could no longer be a common colonial and racial identity with Europe and North America, as in the 1940s and 1950s. Nor was this beckoning to a common nonracialism as under Mandela. Rather, Mbeki called forth Pan-African claims and identities. As deputy president in 1996, he signaled his intent in a speech that surprised almost everyone. Sketching his personal odyssey in exile across the continent, he ended successive stanzas with the refrain: "I am an African!" Africa's salvation was now to be found not in the North but in Africa's own cultural solidarities, or *Ubuntu*, which were to be put in the service of unifying the African family led by African leaders and African states. Here Mbeki drew on the antiliberal, Afrocentric wave that washed over the black world in the 1980s and early 1990s, fueling the latter stages of the antiapartheid movement. Mandela's language of nonracialism had given way to the new president's declaration that South Africa was an African country, even as it was split, in Mbeki's account, into two components: one rich and white, and the other poor and black.[28] Needless to say, powerful white elites at home and abroad were openly disdainful of this turn to Africa.

Mbeki's call to rally around African values and traditions matched his long-standing geostrategic and geoeconomic commitments: the seemingly contradictory principles of communal Africanism and Euro–North American neoliberalism were to merge in the service of South African leadership and the opening of African markets to much more powerful South African financial, commercial, mining, and industrial firms.[29] Pressure from the North had led African states to lower tariffs and remove restrictions on capital flows during the 1980s and 1990s, developments that had quite clear advantages for South African firms after 1994. South African producers and warehouses could more quickly supply nearby markets; South African firms and banks were among the few sources of investment capital; and South Africa was readily able to supply skilled managerial and service personnel. While private capital had long provided the economic force for South African expansion, international forces had previously paved the way by fortuitously weakening local African states' control over local markets and financial flows. Policies that had opened up South Africa to the North, often to local producers' disadvantage, had become powerful advantages for postapartheid South Africa in relation to the rest of Africa.

The impact of more open borders facilitated almost a tripling of the South African Customs Union's (overwhelmingly South African) exports to regional Southern African Development Community (SADC) partners in the five years after majority rule (from R5 billion in 1993 to R16 billion in 1998), while South African imports from SADC doubled (from R1.3 billion to R2.6 billion).[30] South African expansion farther north led to a doubling of South African imports from African states between 1998 and 2006, largely due to oil imports from Nigeria and Angola, while exports to Africa over the same period averaged around 13 percent of total exports.

Rising inequities in trade relations marked a new phase of unequal exchange, as trade and investment patterns established during the interwar and early apartheid periods accelerated across the continent with the ending of sanctions and the application of WTO free trade regulations. By 2005 South Africa was exporting goods worth R47 billion to the rest of Africa, or 15 percent of its total exports (more than to North and South America combined), while importing only R16 billion of goods (or less than 4 percent of total imports). While South Africa imports raw materials and simple manufactures from other African states, Africa remains South Africa's best market for its more advanced manufacturing exports, accounting for 20 to 50 percent of these exports.[31]

Though South Africa itself imports little from SADC or the continent as a percentage of its total imports, for many countries it has become the key, overwhelming trade partner, accounting in 2004 for 45 percent of Mozambique's imports, 44 percent of Zambia's, 33 percent of Malawi's, 32 percent of Zimbabwe's, and 10 to 15 percent of the total imports of Angola, Mauritius, the D. R. Congo, and Tanzania.[32] Even in distant Kenya these patterns hold, where exports to South Africa in the five years up to 2007 moved up to only 1.3 billion shillings (S), while imports from South Africa ballooned from S12 billion to S35 billion.[33]

These unequal patterns were repeated in the field of investment, including both equity and, more critically, FDI. By the end of the first decade of majority rule, South Africa had become southern Africa's and, by some estimates Africa's, largest foreign direct investor.[34] By 2003 South Africa was, for example, the largest foreign investor in Botswana, the D. R. Congo, Lesotho, Malawi, Mozambique, Swaziland, and Zambia.[35] By the end of 2004 South Africa's FDI in Africa amounted to R24 billion (US$3.7 billion), which was over 10 percent of the country's total FDI and almost equal to total South African FDI in the Americas as a whole.[36] By 2008 direct investment in Africa was over US$100 billion, almost 25 percent of total FDI and three times the amount in North America.[37] As with trade, expansion of investment has been particularly strong across the continent and not just the surrounding SADC states: after 2000 the growth of South African FDI in all of Africa was 29 percent a year compared to a growth rate of annual investment in SADC of only 6 percent.[38]

South African expansion has been spread across financial, retail, mining, telecom, and energy investments. South African banks not only have opened branches across the continent, but have absorbed significant local banking and insurance companies from Nigeria to Kenya and beyond. Major retailers have done the same, including most notably the foreign operations of Shoprite, which opened its first foreign stores in Namibia in 1990. In 1995 Shoprite opened its first central African store in Zambia, and by 2012 had grown to 187 corporate and 43 franchise stores in fifteen African countries outside South Africa (Angola, Botswana, Ghana, Lesotho, Madagascar, Malawi, Mauritius, Mozambique, Namibia, Nigeria, Swaziland, Tanzania, Uganda, Zambia, and Zimbabwe).[39] Cell phone operator MTN, incorporated only in 1994, rapidly spread northward through Africa and even into the Middle East. By 2010 it had 145 million subscribers in twenty-one countries and was the largest listing on the Johannesburg Stock Exchange.[40] South African firms control breweries, run airports, build roads and bridges, and operate hotel chains all across the continent as well. Large investments have also been made in zinc, coal, gas, gold, platinum, and diamond mining across the continent. The South African state has itself financed projects in more than twenty countries through its Industrial Development Corporation, which has, for example, a 24 percent share in the US$2 billion Mozal aluminum smelter project in Mozambique. South Africa's lack of oil or natural gas reserves has propelled similar investments in the region, particularly in Namibian and Mozambican gas; Eskom, South Africa's state-owned utility, is engaged in building a regional power grid and has projects in seventeen African countries.

While African governments have officially welcomed South African firms, the scale and brashness of South African activity has often triggered local resentment and resistance. Politicians who are out of office or who oppose the expansion, such as Kenya's President Moi, have been quite blunt in their dismay as South African firms have absorbed local firms and dominated local markets. This has done little to stop South African expansion into Kenya and the rest of East Africa, where Shoprite became the major retailer, Absa became the biggest bank through its control of Barclays Bank Kenya, and Standard Bank (operating as CFC Stanbic) quickly became another top-five bank through a local acquisition. Local protests have pinpointed South African firms' apartheid roots in the past; as one Kenyan legislator put, South Africans "bulldoze their way around. It seems like they still have the old attitudes of the old South Africa."[41]

Given that the racial ownership and management of large firms based in South Africa has changed so little, it is no surprise that South African firms have operated across the continent with white ownership and over-whelmingly white male management. While white South African business-men moved north speaking the language of the African Renaissance, their intrusion was often accompanied by homegrown racial hierarchies and practices. As Darlene Miller documents in her empirical study of Shoprite: "White South African Shoprite managers believe they are taking blacks in 'Africa' forward into the modern era. In their view, South Africa is the agent of modernization of the region, as it has always been."[42] This is not, more-over, simply a matter of individual attitudes of racial superiority, but rather is embedded in the racialized decision making and day-to-day operations of the firm—from where to locate stores, through what to stock, to how rela-tions are constructed with local African governments, suppliers, employees, and customers. These structural factors create an overtly racialized environ-ment that has led, Miller concludes, to new tensions and conflicts within the region and the continent.[43] South African firms, for their part, have responded by entering into more local partnerships and employing local rather than expatriate South African managers.

The operations of the South African state and, increasingly, of its parastat-als more easily fit under the "African Renaissance" umbrella, given the dera-cialization of state personnel. But even here the state's blatant privileging of South African producers, while seeking to channel Africa's relations with the North through South Africa, engenders yet further conflicts. Thus when Botswana attracted Hyundai and Volvo assembly plants in the 1990s, par-ticularly for duty-free export to South Africa (since Botswana is a member of the South African Customs Union), the new South African government "displayed broad and purposeful opposition" to obstruct any such develop-ment. In the words of Botswana's former president Ketumile Masire, "The ANC government stood with its own industrialists. 'They [South African industrialists] were saying nothing should happen on the periphery.'"[44] Both Volvo and Hyundai abandoned Botswana by the end of the decade, leaving nothing behind. It is hardly surprising that surrounding states and elites often view South Africa as a predator, albeit one they cannot avoid.[45]

South African state support for its own businesses has not translated into an effort to build regional or continental economic institutions. This has puzzled many analysts, reflecting in part conceptual confusion and debates over South Africa's "pivotal," "partner," or "subimperial" role in the region.[46] As argued above, southern Africa as "region" was formed during the inter-war period as part of an unequal economic division of labor, centered on and to the benefit of South Africa. This was made possible by a common vision of colonial and settler rule, and in this sense was never a hegemonic project involving consent from below. Later struggles for independence and majority rule further delegitimized and weakened the region economically and politically.

This historical pattern has made southern Africa a very different regional project than the far more homogeneous European Union project to which it has often been compared,[47] and regional inequalities across southern Africa undercut any attempt to create a common economic and political area. This runs counter to the "subimperialism" thesis, which implies further economic and institutional integration. Yet the South African state has not pursued these. One key reason has been elaborated above: neoliberal policies imposed by the North in the 1980s and 1990s have opened up African markets to outside investors and commodities, much to postapartheid South African firms' benefit. Since then regional economic agreements have been predominantly bilateral, with no move to create, for example, a common customs or currency area. Indeed, the South African state has been cutting back reciprocal advantages for regional partners, as in the early postapartheid South African state's refusal to renew a long-standing reciprocal trade agreement with Zimbabwe.

The survival of the century-old South African Customs Union (SACU), which was created to ensure South African access to the labor and markets of Botswana, Lesotho, and Swaziland, is also in jeopardy for similar reasons. For South Africa the elimination of protectionist tariffs and increasing free trade across the region and the continent has turned SACU's common external tariff and the sharing of customs revenue into an unnecessary and expensive project. Negotiations to change the revenue-sharing formula in South Africa's favor are a real threat: for Lesotho and Swaziland, SACU customs funds represent up to 70 percent of their revenue. Falling returns in recent years forced South Africa in 2011 to loan Swaziland US$350 million in order to prevent Swaziland's bankruptcy—and surely more political unrest and out-migration. Local Swazi activists have for their part denounced the loan as unwarranted support to sustain King Mswati's dictatorial rule.

As these key examples suggest, regional and even continental relationships have been subordinated to those with the North. When a free trade agreement between South Africa and the European Union was signed in 1998, for example, it was done without consultation with regional partners, despite the immediate impact it had on SACU states at the time.[48] Yet there is also a danger here for South Africa: other African states may find direct exchanges and negotiations with the North or East for themselves on equal or better terms than those offered by South Africa. This possibility has not led South Africa to support existing or new regional or continental economic blocs, as has taken place in Europe, North America, Asia, and Latin America. The South African government has both avoided enhancing SADC's powers and refused to join the Common Market for Eastern and Southern Africa, a preferential trading area of twenty states stretching from Libya to Zimbabwe. Discussions to turn SADC into a common customs union, incorporating SACU, have quietly been abandoned. In 2009 Botswana, Lesotho, and Swaziland openly broke with South Africa (and Namibia) and signed an interim Economic Partnership Agreement (EPA) with the EU.

South Africa's bid to create and lead continental political institutions has been far more innovative. Any notion of regional hegemony or subimperialism presumes leadership and consent, and in this respect South Africa has had very little success. Mbeki's charter was indeed positioned to place South Africa as the representative not just of southern and central Africa but of the entire continent. The flurry of activity toward this end ranged from Mbeki's leadership of the African Union to his formulation and promotion of the African Renaissance and the New Partnership for Africa's Development (NEPAD). His key ministers were no less determined to act for Africa in international agencies, demonstrated by his finance minister's very active role in the IMF and World Bank, and his trade and industry minister's presidency of the UN Conference on Trade and Development from 1996 to 2000. Launched in Abuja in 2001, NEPAD provided the concrete vehicle for this role, promising to achieve prosperity and democracy for Africa by reversing, in the words of NEPAD's strategic framework, the continent's "marginalisation from the globalisation process."[49] To argue that Africa has been isolated from the world economy would, of course, be nonsense: South Africa and the continent as a whole have been deeply embedded in global markets for more than 400 years, with statistically much higher levels of production for the world market (as measured by the ratio of exports to GDP), for example, than almost all other world regions for quite some time.[50]

NEPAD nevertheless called for an end to the national development policies of the past and for a fuller, quicker integration into world capital, financial, and technological markets—with South Africa leading the way. This would go further than the liberalization of trade and finance, the shrinking of the state, and selling off of state assets, for NEPAD planning specifically targeted a reliance on FDI to recuperate the public supply of water, health, electricity, and education through the privatization of state services—a process attacked by activists in South Africa and across the continent.[51] As the former director of the UN Economic Commission for Africa, Adebayo Adedeji, starkly pointed out, NEPAD is a radical break with recent African development strategies from the Lagos Plan of Action (1980) to the UN Plan of Action for the Development of Africa (1991).[52] NEPAD is thus very much at odds with calls for state-directed development.

The success of Mbeki's bid to represent Africa in global institutions depended on gains in two areas. First, it required leading core states and international institutions to place a high value on Africa and its mediator, South Africa. This, as we have seen, did not happen. Africa's and South Africa's weight in the world economy and geostrategic importance (beyond crude oil and minerals) to the major powers have steadily declined. Most African states, moreover, had long submitted to structural adjustment policies and deeper, bilateral ties with Europe and the United States, making South Africa's bid late and of little value. What the South African state could deliver to core states and financial institutions that hasn't already been conceded by most African states or cannot be better achieved in bilateral negotiations was quite modest. South African peacekeeping operations, as in Burundi and Darfur with the African Union, have been costly and poorly executed. The international political and economic support for Mbeki's strategy was thus very thin. NEPAD, like similar efforts in relation to the WTO or the UN, has largely been ignored by Europe and the United States.

Weakness in Northern support for Mbeki's African Charter might have been offset by broader backing from other African elites and states, who certainly would benefit from a stronger collective stance toward the North. Yet here too the signs of success for an African "renaissance" led by South Africa are also absent. Mbeki was twenty years too late: the rewards in forms of aid and access to the North that accrued from being first to abandon state planning, sell off parastatals, devalue one's currency, and shrink the state are gone. Star performers in the eyes of international financial institutions—such as Ghana, Mozambique, and Uganda—had long ago gone down this road. South Africa's effort to recast the Organization of African Unity as a more powerful organization, the new African Union, and to build an effective Pan-African Parliament, have had similarly little success in cohering African political strength, advancing democracy and peace, or winning support from Europe and North America. African states also face strong popular forces fighting the very structural adjustment policies and foreign competition that South Africa has come to represent. As Dot Keet's careful analysis of South Africa's role in successive WTO negotiations and NEPAD shows, South Africa has consistently pushed the WTO agenda at the cost of African states—and this despite growing African opposition.[53]

While South Africa firms and parastatals have thus expanded north since 1994, the South African state's bid for regional and continental leadership has been stymied. Constructing consent among states' elites around a shared history of struggle against colonial and settler rule could not be reconciled, in the end, with South Africa's continuing commitment to the powers and policies that had so underdeveloped Africa over the course of the twentieth century.

Projecting Semiperipheral Pathways

These observations reveal not simply poor policies or conflicting state and elite interests in the region, but long-term constraints and contradictions arising from entrenched core-peripheral linkages. A product of struggles between the North and the peoples, states, and firms of the region, these have created diverse, and often mutually exclusive, social structures and labor-capital combinations across the rural and urban spaces of the region and indeed the continent. The South African state's and firms' historical roles in these center-hinterland relationships have produced a highly distinctive semiperipheral relationship with the North, the region, and the continent. Any assessment of future developmental possibilities, as in past chapters' explanations of twentieth-century outcomes, must rest in large part on analyzing the choices arising from likely developments in these long-term processes and relationships.

Relating recent world-economic trends to local political and racial realities provides a first approximation at such an assessment. Given the widespread acknowledgment of waning US power, continuing high levels of inequality, and weak states along the periphery of the world economy, one might expect a continuing "subimperial" path whereby South African firms and the ANC government exercise an increasing trusteeship over Africa on behalf of local and international forces. Such a path could follow the further abandonment of Africa by core states and international financial institutions, an enhancement of South Africa's political and military power to control unruly states and insurgencies, the bolstering of South African management of Africa's natural energy and mineral resources, and diminished resistance by declining African states and more ethnically fragmented and religiously diverse popular movements. Competition for Africa's oil and natural resources among the United States, Europe, and Asia could even enhance this possibility by strengthening South Africa's own mineral-industrial complex and the returns from it. Such a path could also potentially accommodate some resistance from South African social and civic movements, if returns from regional and continental linkages strengthened the fiscal resources of the South African state and the markets and profits of South African firms. Matching the discourse of a "developmentalist" and less neoliberal state to enhanced social welfare measures could, as in other semiperipheral states like Brazil, sustain a basically neoliberal and elite state regime.

The limits to such possibilities are clear: a more populist government's response to demands for the redistribution of income, wealth, and land would quickly run up against a reaction from political and economic elites who reject any breaking of the neoliberal and racial reconciliation bargain forged since 1990. This would be vividly expressed, as in the past, in the flight of capital and white South Africans, as well as in declining support from and isolation by international financial institutions, local and foreign investors, and core states. Given the class and racial nature of the South African state and South African elites, and their dependency on world-economic alliances, the forces potentially aligned against a "populist at home, subimperial abroad" project are considerable.

Antiauthoritarian and antineoliberal popular protest at home and across the continent could conceivably work to produce a quite different outcome marked by more equitable and cooperative international alliances. The most plausible and promoted candidate is the "New Bandung" project, forged through an alliance among the world's stronger semiperipheral states against underdeveloping pressures from the North. There are two sources of historical inspiration here: one drawn from the Third World alliances of the 1950s, as marked by the nonaligned movement and the 1955 Bandung Conference, and a second that harks back to the drive by richer Third World states, during the 1970s commodity boom, to create a New International Economic Order.[54] Evolving alliances among Brazil, Russia, India, and China (the so-called BRICs), particularly as spokespersons for the world's poor during world trade negotiations, have underlined this new collective challenge from the Global South. South Africa, moreover, has frequently been included as a smaller African partner.

Yet as was the case with the old Bandung coalition around Cold War nonalignment, this project reflects the priorities of wealthier states and their political leaders—Frantz Fanon's African middle class—who have proven to have personal rather than collective development objectives. And even if a steady increase in the economic power of the Global South vis-à-vis core states is assumed, it is difficult to envisage how uneven relations within and among the richer states of Africa, Latin America, and Asia could be adjudicated to sustain a common project to remake the international economic and political order. In the struggle between substantively shifting the international division of labor and wealth on the one hand, and stabilizing new forms of global governance through the incorporation of Global South ruling elites and larger firms on the other, it is the latter that has so far appeared in the ascendancy. The possibility for a new, counterhegemonic project coalescing around a "New Bandung," with or without South African partnership, thus seem unlikely.[55]

Extrapolating along these lines—that is, pointing toward either a continuing subimperial alliance with the rich North or a "Bandung" alliance with other semiperipheral states—offers little in the way of a radical departure in South and southern Africa's developmental prospects. Certainly no rupture exists analogous to the 1920s break or even the post–World War II upheaval. Moreover, near-term scenarios rarely extend beyond changes in state policies and interstate policies, obscuring at best or rejecting at worst the issue of whether substantive reconfigurations of labor and the relationship between race and capital accumulation are possible. As I have argued above, these reconfigurations proved essential to the construction of South Africa's advancement to, and maintenance of, its position in the wealth and power hierarchy of the capitalist world economy. The collapse of the region in the late apartheid period, and the simultaneous decline in returns from alliances with the North, further emphasize the difficulty of reversing South Africa's gradual transition from one of the earliest newly industrializing countries to its slow but steady decline in the late twentieth century. As South Africa's own past so vividly demonstrates, it is very difficult to shift substantively a state's or region's position in the global wealth and racial hierarchy. If South Africa's semiperipheral matrix has been dissolving before our eyes, what might the future hold?

Global Chaos

If short-term prospects are not encouraging, over a longer time frame prospects may be much brighter than they have been in more than a century. For two radical ruptures threaten the geopolitical and geocultural world that produced twenty-first-century South, southern, and continental Africa. To the extent that these rifts widen and deepen, they seriously undermine the histories and projections of the Anglo-American-centered world. One rupture comes from below: the steady, forward march of antineoliberal forces across the Global South, and the corresponding exhaustion and collapse of European and North American hegemonic power. And the other comes from above: the rise of an Asian-centered world economy and new Asian-African relations. Over time these combined forces point toward not simply the demise of the hold of the North over the Global South, or even the replacement of North-South relations by East-South ones, but rather a reconfigured world social and economic order—including the destruction of the processes of racial and state formation that have marked

Anglo-American hegemonies over two centuries. It is within this new world that South and southern Africa's future lies, a future very different from the patterns of the past or any linear projection based on them.

One of the major lessons of this volume is that global transitions and crises offer significant possibilities for a few states to garner a greater share of global wealth. Indeed, as has been argued at length above, key transitions in South Africa's world-economic position took place during moments of crisis and rivalry among great powers. We now stand at another of these crossroads. Coming to power in the early 1990s, the Mandela and then Mbeki presidencies faced a rigidly neoliberal world, with few potential allies across Africa or the Global South. In this situation matching neoliberalism to nonracialism was easily, though mistakenly and at great cost, cast by the ANC and its international partners as a commonsense program for a peaceful transition to a deracialized and prosperous South Africa.

By stark contrast to the early 1990s, few if any of the conditions that fostered this outcome now hold. As the global economy has become ever more chaotic and unequal, and protest more voluble, neoliberal policies and governments are under attack and collapsing. Rivalry among core states and financial chaos are accelerating, and international financial and political institutions, particularly the IMF, have lost much of their legitimacy and sway over the South, particularly in Latin America and Asia. As occurred in the interwar and early postwar periods, new counterhegemonic policies are being pushed forward. Across the Global South stronger states and, especially, popular movements now openly organize against and around the state. Neoliberalism, premised on the defeat of the 1960s movements and promising liberation through the market, has a diminishing hold in these conditions.

The cultural discourses and practices of previous hegemons offer little guidance on how unequal transnational relationships might be stabilized and legitimized today. Neither direct colonial rule, with its discourses of scientific racism and civilization, nor segregationist alliances among European and white settler states can cohere a hegemonic state project from the North. Liberalism's promise of progress through cultural and national assimilation via modernization has similarly run aground. Meanwhile neoliberalism's attempt to proclaim a territorial citizenship based on a nonracial multiculturalism, whereby difference is celebrated even as inherited racial and social privileges remain intact and inequality increases, has become an unstable and increasingly illegitimate project. If the apartheid state was the epitome of colonialism, the postapartheid state has been the model of neoracist multiculturalism.[56] The rise of new movements confronting these forces in South Africa is more than matched across the Global South by the emergence of new indigenous movements and their accelerating conflict with European settler diasporas. In the North the language of multiculturalism, which has undergirded an increase in the number of "minority" or black officials, has yet failed to staunch significant increases in racial and ethnic inequality and conflict: all across Europe and North America there are higher levels of segregation, racial profiling, xenophobia, immigration controls, racial disparities in imprisonment, racial and ethnic conflict—and rebellious outbursts.[57]

Similar instability in the middle of the twentieth century propelled the rise of US hegemony and the consolidation of a liberal and highly regulated world economy. Yet it would be misleading to project a parallel cycle of crisis and restabilization, for what we are witnessing today is not simply a global depression, the financialization of capital, a new phase of primitive accumulation and dispossession, or the replacement of one hegemon with another, but rather a second rupture: the substantive collapse of the world economy's North-South axial division of labor as an Asian-centered world emerges. These trends are visible even for marginalized Africa, where the entrance of Asian traders, firms, and investments has startled Western business leaders and states alike. The titles of articles in Northern press and policy journals mimic tabloid headlines, littered with racially and colonially tinged discourse on China's "African Safari," China's role as the "New Colonialist," or China's "Scramble for Africa."[58]

Behind the rhetoric stand concrete, demonstrable losses for the West as Africa tilts eastward. As the World Bank warned its readers in the opening pages of its *Africa's Silk Road*: "Since 2000 there has been a massive increase in trade and investment flows between [sub-Saharan] Africa and Asia. Today, Asia receives about twenty-seven percent of Africa's exports, in contrast to only about fourteen percent in 2000. This volume of trade is now almost on par with Africa's exports to the United States and the European Union (EU)—Africa's traditional trading partners; in fact, the EU's share of African exports has halved over the period 2000–05."[59] Trade between Africa and China alone ballooned from US$6.5 billion in 1999 to US$107 billion in 2008, making China Africa's largest source of imports and second only to the United States in its share of Africa's exports.[60]

Investment patterns are harder to track but are rapidly changing. By 2006 over 800 Chinese firms were operating across Africa, with investments rising to approximately US$12 billion; Indian investments added another US$7 billion.[61] Investment has been particularly heavy in oil- and mineral-rich states, as in PetroChina's stake in the Sudan, the China National Offshore Oil Corporation's billion-dollar investment in Nigeria, and Beijing's loan to Angola of more than US$2 billion. Chinese businessmen, traders, laborers, and miners are now a common sight across Africa, numbering, according to China's state press, 750,000 long-term migrants.[62] While figures for the whole of Africa over a longer period of time show a less dramatic picture, the long-term trend remains: for over a generation, Europe and the United States have become less central to Africa's economic life.

South Africa, despite its high level of industrialization and natural resources, has been forcefully pulled eastward as well. Barely visible as a trade partner at the moment of majority rule, by 2009 China had become South Africa's *leading* import (11 percent) and export (13 percent) partner. South Africa's share in China's imports and exports was, by contrast, minuscule, accounting in 2005 for only 0.2 percent of China's imports and 0.65 percent of its exports.[63] Reliable figures for investment are absent, but investment from the East is clearly expanding. Investment began and has been concentrated in mining, followed by construction and some minor electronic goods assembly for local markets. For example, China's biggest gold producer, the Zijin Mining Group Company, is developing a R1 billion mining project, while Sinosteel is involved in two chromium mines and state-owned firms have majority stakes in platinum-mining projects. In 2010 Jidong, the largest cement producer in northern China, announced an investment of R800 million in a R1.65 billion (US$220.8 million) cement manufacturing project, building on past activity by the Chinese construction firms Citic and Covec. China's investments have moved well beyond the extractive sector: in October 2007 the Industrial Commercial Bank of China, now the world's largest, purchased 20 percent of Africa's and South Africa's largest bank, Standard Bank, for US$5.5 billion. The attraction for China of the Standard Bank deal, like others before and after it, was to gain access not only to South Africa's market but also to the African market through Standard Bank's extensive banking and commercial network in eighteen countries across the continent.

These economic realities prefigure a dramatic shift from twentieth-century patterns. In the wake of the deindustrialization of the United States and Europe in the closing decades of the century, Asia has become a global producer and exporter, based on much larger and lower-cost labor reserves, of the very light and medium-range industrial goods that African states had been producing at home and South Africa had long been exporting to its northern neighbors. The influx of Asian goods has created a widespread fear, as Dot Keet documents, of "large, efficient, and highly competitive Chinese companies undermining, sidelining, and even displacing African companies."[64] South African advantages in mining, energy, and finance may be more enduring than in consumer goods, where major losses to Asian competition, particularly in the clothing, shoes, and textile sectors, have already taken place (although statistical estimates of direct losses to China and India remain unclear).[65] Yet in mining, energy, and even construction, South African firms are increasingly on the defensive even in their home market.

Studies of more advanced Latin American manufacturers facing such pressures are not encouraging. Like South African producers, Latin American firms lack Chinese firms' access to large, low-wage labor reserves, low-cost human capital and technology, generous government assistance, and a state able to constrain labor and civil society demands.[66] Over the long run the gravitational pull of Asia is thus likely to force a fundamental reconfiguration of South African firms' more advanced industrial exports and financial and commercial operations across the continent. These reorientations openly pose not just the displacement of ties with the rich North, but the replacement of South African-centered relationships across the region with Eastern-directed ones.

This pattern could easily lead to a further entrenchment of the historical pattern of Africa sending out raw materials and oil and importing manufactured goods and high technology services. Certainly exports to and from China, as well as the operations of Chinese firms in Africa, parallel past relationships with Europe and the United States. Yet North-South patterns are not simply being replicated or replaced by equivalent East-South ones. Africa may import consumer goods and send out raw materials and oil to China and India, yet all the partners in these exchanges still lag far behind the technological and capital goods capacities of Europe and North America—as trade and investment flows to the North indicate. Closer examination of Africa and South Africa's past colonial and more recent neocolonial relationships with Europe also demonstrate quite sharp differences.[67]

Relationships among Asian states remain very uneven, yet by contrast are more complementary and regionally focused than those that marked the rise of Anglo-American hegemonies over the last two centuries—and have become more so in the wake of the 2008–9 global financial crisis. Similar ruptures exist in the nature of capital expansion. In the post–World War II period, US hegemony supplanted British free trade on the basis of the vast expansion of American multinational corporations' branch-plant strategy that leapfrogged the protectionist tariffs implanted in the interwar period. In countries like Brazil and to an extent South Africa, this created a "triple alliance" of the state, large local corporations, and foreign multinationals. Asian expansion has followed a very different pattern, with small-scale diasporic firms matched to state-owned firms and vast networks of smaller companies—all bringing hundreds of thousands of Asian owners and employees, including unskilled labor, to continental Africa. Neither firm size and strategy, foreign and local labor employment patterns, nor technological disparities match past North-South patterns. Something new is, indeed, afoot.

The economic character of the East Asian zone, with dense networks circulating around China, also indicates a very different pattern than past links between Euro–North America and Africa, with the possibility of more equal exchanges: China imports from its Asian neighbors both primary products *and* advanced electronic components and capital goods. China's ability to offer loans, aid, and investments that are not tied to structural adjustment plans or Western notions of good governance has led some authors to argue that African-Asian relationships are beneficial and symbiotic,[68] or that a new, more equitable developmental model—a "Beijing Consensus"— is being constructed.[69] Even more radical is the argument by Arrighi that such features demonstrate a historically distinctive pattern of nonexploitative "development without dispossession," based on labor-intensive (versus past Western, capital-intensive) forms of production and equitable regional relationships.[70]

There is little evidence to date that relations between South Africa and China and India (or Asia more broadly) are marked by such complementary and intrinsically nonexploitative features. What Asian success has produced, however, is considerable support for new models of the "developmentalist" state in defiance of the World Bank, the IMF, the WTO, the United States, and the European Union. Certainly China, India, and other Asian states stand in sharp and successful opposition to the international financial institutions that enforced structural adjustment programs on Africa, particularly after the disastrous role of the IMF in the Asian financial crisis of 1997–98. By the time of the October 2008 financial crash, more successful developmentalist Asian states had moved forward by building up hefty foreign exchange reserves through maintaining current account surpluses averaging 5 percent of gross domestic product. South Africa was by contrast in a much more difficult position, with a 7 to 10 percent current account deficit, significantly lower reserves by comparison to other semiperipheral or emerging market states, few competitive manufacturing exports, a mineral export boom based in large part on volatile commodity speculation, and overseas investors selling off billions of rands' worth of their South African stock holdings. Such vulnerabilities led the financial world, to no one's surprise, to press the case for continuing Mbeki's policies since, in the words of an October 8, 2008, *Financial Times* headline, any "sharp policy shift would be suicidal for S Africa."

Suicide may be an extreme choice. But even worse would be slowly being dragged down to a painful death by a sinking partner. And this is what a continuing alliance to the North and continuing repression of civic movements would entail. It does not take much imagination to expect over the next generation the collapse of the dollar and euro as reserve currencies, the demise of international financial and political institutions dominated by neoliberal European and North American governments, and the emergence elsewhere of new financial, commercial, and institutional centers, particularly in Asia. To the degree that the historic Euro–North American hold collapses and radical protest accelerates, we may expect opportunities unthinkable to those living through the neoliberal interregnum of the last twenty years.

Part of the collapse of neoliberalism would likely be the abandonment of neoliberal precepts across the Global South, paired with the enhancement of the state's regulatory powers over local financial, investment, and labor markets. This would require far more novel and interventionist action ranging across monetary and fiscal policy, bilateral and multilateral trade agreements, and capital import and export regulations. The policies of semiperipheral Asian states during the last two decades, and Latin American states from Brazil to Venezuela to Bolivia in the last decade, show the possibilities of moving forward on these fronts.

Abandoning strict neoliberal policies would also entail a break with the North and the creation of new financial and commercial relationships with the rising centers of Asia. Among African states, South Africa is best placed to negotiate more complementary and beneficial exchanges, given the country's attractive resource endowment and industrial and financial infrastructure. Ideologically, this would entail dumping the neoliberal components of Mbeki's African Charter and adopting the anticolonial and antineoliberal language of the world's newly developmentalist, primarily Asian states. What Asian–South African relationships may look like in twenty-five years is very hard to project, given the tentative moves to date by Asian states to construct alternatives to the international financial and commercial bodies created by the West. Even as the euro and dollar decline there is *as yet* no Asian candidate on the horizon to replace the dollar as the world's primary reserve currency, not to mention Asian replacements for the IMF or World Bank.

Equally unknown is how the emergence of a network of more developmentalist and Asian-centered states would affect the stark levels of inequality that continue within and between Africa and Asia, China and South Africa. While rivalry, economic chaos, and social unrest across the world economy may open up possibilities for advancement for a few semiperipheral states, it may also lead to new and highly unequal relations forming. Here today's antiglobalization, or more properly "alterglobalization," movements enter. Speaking from the perspective of Asia, Walden Bello thus argues that the task of the movements is to "pressure China, as it intensifies its engagement with the world, to resist the temptation of following the destructive imperial path blazed by Europe and the United States."[71]

This task is beginning to be posed from the southern African side of the Indian Ocean as well. As African activists and scholars have pointed out, the Chinese state and Chinese firms are often no better friends of local movements than Western states and firms, with China supporting repressive regimes from Sudan to Zimbabwe.[72] Overall, the practices of Chinese firms and state agencies have paid little heed to local demands for human rights, labor union rights, transparency, or environmental protection. This has fueled denunciations by local small businessmen and opposition leaders of Chinese businesses across eastern and southern Africa. Zambia, which has had deep relationships with China dating back to the 1960s, is a prime example. On the one hand, Chinese firms have stepped in and revived closed copper mines, promising to reverse the long slide in the mining sector that employed over 60,000 people in the early 1970s, but only 20,000 at the turn of the century. On the other hand, Chinese firms have been plagued by complaints of poverty wages below US$2 a day, exploitative working conditions, and terrible safety records. In 2005 riot police were called out to quell a strike at the Chambisi mine that started after forty-nine workers died due to unsafe working conditions. The result is xenophobia marked by a "great resentment toward Chinese investors in Zambia";[73] in 2006 a presidential candidate won 29 percent of the vote on an anti-Chinese platform (although anti-Chinese rhetoric was far more muted in a subsequent election). The strike wave that emerged in 2010 at factories in China—most notably at Japanese auto plants and suppliers—augurs rising tensions inside China as well.

Transnational movement linkages with China, however, have proven difficult to construct. Transnational relationships have in past cases proven critical, as in African-European movement collaboration in relation to Sudan, the Niger Delta, and Zimbabwe, or, closer to home, the coordinated blocking by southern African activists and trade unions in 2008 of the unloading of arms bound for Zimbabwe from a Chinese ship. Similar alliances have yet to be made with Chinese civic organizations or movements, such contacts being very difficult owing to the Chinese government's controls over local civil society organizations, social movements, unions, and the media.

Not the least of the obstacles toward strengthening such alliances are the radical ideological and cultural transformations that will emerge as the North declines and the East rises—including most notably the racial hierarchies through which regional and global accumulation operate. These have long been formed, even in their latest multicultural guise, around a white North–black South continuum, often pitting Africans against Asians in the West's colonized hierarchy. Current elite and movement connections across Africa and Asia—from appeals for labor solidarity to New Bandung alliances—draw on the historical experiences defined by this continuum: the long shared history of colonial and racial domination at the hands of Europe and the United States.

The emergence of East-South hierarchies, explicitly posed in opposition to past North-South colonial-racial relationships, could readily work against such alliances, as the Zambian case illustrates. As histories of Asia and especially Asian empires remind us, intra-Asian racial and imperial hierarchies have long operated within Asia itself.[74] To date these hierarchies have been subordinated to, but nevertheless seriously implicated with, Northern racial and colonial domination in Africa and the African diaspora. Recent flashes of nationalism and xenophobia in China and elsewhere in Asia indicate the potential power of new racialized movements against the colonial North as well as within and among Asian and African states themselves.

The strengthening of national identities, as in South Africa's definition of a "rainbow" nation that yet excludes noncitizens, significantly complicates these possibilities.

As the West declines and Asia rises the tensions inherent in these contradictory positions will be exacerbated. How and where South African and African movements will align themselves with other movements, as both black and international movements have done at previous historic conjunctures, may well determine the outcome of the contemporary drive to significantly redistribute wealth and power across the world. This long-term process could, for example, install and legitimize under new leadership a world order as exploitative and hierarchical as those endured during the past several centuries. Conversely, and as a reaction against neoliberalism and global inequality, these pressures might point toward a counterhegemonic project pitched against the power of capital, avaricious states, and international financial and political institutions—including those in Asia.

This last scenario holds out the prospect of much higher potential returns to the peoples of South Africa, southern Africa, and Africa. A critical variable here is the balance of power in the interstate system, particularly the evolving ability of networked social movements to force states to alter core-peripheral relationships radically during moments of real crisis. These movements now extend well beyond the meetings of Northern activists: they abound outside core zones, from South Asia to Latin America to southern Africa. In South Africa they have arisen outside the declining union federations and the South African Communist Party, which remain in an institutionalized alliance with the ruling African National Congress. These new movements, which have at various moments led the alterglobalization wave, include the Treatment Action Campaign, Landless People's Movement, Soweto Electricity Crisis Committee, Anti-Eviction Campaign, Anti-Privatization Forum, Concerned Citizens Forum, and Homeless People's Alliance.

As elsewhere outside core areas, such alterglobalization movements reflect their location: they are heavily rooted in poor people's struggles over basic economic and material needs—and often, but not always, are heavily rooted in anticapitalist and antineoliberal demands. Yet the reach and strength of these movements are rarely contained at the local level: most are increasingly joined into a global chorus demanding a return to the social provisioning of basic human needs, as opposed to the needs of the state or capital. Linked to the ANC by personal histories and participation, these are nevertheless postapartheid movements, operating outside the liberation movement and those segments of the trade unions that have been folded into state power after 1990. This pattern is a global one, evident in the stronger semiperipheral states (as in Latin America), where the new movements may help elect governments, but still eschew both the liberal and the

Leninist pursuit of state power as a route to liberation. How far these new movements can push South Africa and other similarly situated states toward pursuing a counterhegemonic path is an open question. Their strength is not, however, waning, as the forces behind the successive elections of—and then pressures applied on—the governments of Mbeki, Lula, Chavez, Morales, and Zuma indicate.

During its first century, the South African state was formed and driven by the highly unequal racial and accumulation relationships that spanned the region and the North-South divide. Competition between colonial territories, states, and elites on the one hand, and between them and hegemonic Northern powers on the other, produced and sustained South Africa as the regional powerhouse. In this new century the prospects for the peoples and states of the region can no longer be charted along these old axes. Looking forward, South Africa remains in a powerful position to blaze a new path as the domination of the world economy by Europe and the United States passes, chaotic financial and commercial ruptures occur, and a new, Asian-centered world emerges. To be sure, there is no certainty that the remaking of regional, continental, and transnational relationships that is upon us will result in a more equitable and endurable life for the peoples of the region and the continent. Too much depends on the alignments and strengths of those who wield power and wealth. The very uncertainty as to what might emerge to replace today's global social and economic order is, nevertheless, to be welcomed. The future is, as the past history of strong states and movements tells us, full of possibilities.

Notes

Introduction

1. See, for example, the cover of *Time* for May 9, 1994, which depicts Mandela with a saintly halo, and for May 14, 1994, on Rwanda, which declares in large type, set over a very dark, murky African face: "'There are no devils left in Hell,' the missionary said. 'They are all in Rwanda.'"

2. See the accounts in Lodge, *Politics in South Africa*; Barber, *Mandela's World*; Gumede, *Thabo Mbeki*; and the later assessments in Gevisser, *Thabo Mbeki*; and Glaser, *Mbeki and After*.

3. See Mbeki's speeches "I Am an African" and "African Renaissance."

4. Vale, "Thabo Mbeki."

5. See West, "Global Africa" and "Like a River."

6. The central work in this tradition was Huntington's *Third Wave*; for a later application of the "theory of political transitions" to Africa, see Bratton and van de Walle, "Neopatrimonial Regimes."

7. Robert D. Kaplan, "The Coming Anarchy: How Scarcity, Crime, Overpopulation, Tribalism, and Disease Are Rapidly Destroying the Social Fabric of Our Planet."

8. See, among others, Zartman, *Collapsed States*; Goodhand and Hulme, "Wars to Complex Political Emergencies"; and Cliffe, "Complex Political Emergencies."

9. Zartman, "Introduction."

10. Bratton and van de Walle, "Neopatrimonial Regimes," 458–59, emphasis in original.

11. Bienen, "Leaders, Violence."

12. Magubane, "Critical Look"; Mafeje, "Ideology of 'Tribalism."

13. Olukoshi, "State, Conflict, and Democracy."

14. Mkandawire, "Crisis Management"; Mkandawire and Soludo, Our Continent, Our Future; Shivji, Silences in NGO Discourse.

15. Bowen, *State against the Peasantry*.

16. Davidson, *Black Man's Burden*.

17. Mamdani, *Citizen and Subject*, 27.

18. Mamdani, *When Victims Become Killers*.

19. Mamdani, *Citizen and Subject*, 8.

20. Ibid.

21. As Olukoshi notes, "A wide gulf appears to be developing between African social scientists, mostly situated within Africa, and their Africanist colleagues, mostly located outside the continent" ("State, Conflict, and Democracy," 455). The history of this phenomenon is traced in Martin and West, *Out of One*.

22. See Quijano, "Modernity, Identity, and Utopia"; Quijano and Wallerstein, "Americanity as a Concept"; and, more recently, Mignolo, *Local Histories, Global Designs*.

23. For the procapitalist view see, for example, Horwitz, *Political Economy of South Africa*; and Lipton, *Capitalism and Apartheid*. On the views of anticapitalist radicals across time, see, for example, Wolpe, "Capitalism and Cheap Labour-Power"; Davies, *Capital, State and White Labour*; and Saul and Gelb, *Crisis in South Africa*.

24. Bond, "South Africa's Frustrating Decade."

25. Among the most widely cited early examples are Rodney, *How Europe Underdeveloped Africa*, and Amin, *Accumulation on a World Scale*—whose themes were never pursued by scholars of South Africa.

26. See, among others, Hanlon, *Beggar Your Neighbours*; and Minter, *King Solomon's Mines Revisited*.

27. See, for example, Emmanuel, "White Settler Colonialism."

28. Anderson, *Imagined Communities*; Wallerstein, *Modern World-System*, vol. 3; Gott, "Latin America."

29. Hopkins, "Study of the Capitalist World-Economy," emphasis in original, 13.

30. Ibid., 12.

31. Goldberg, *Racial State*.

32. See the overview by Kramer, "Empires, Exceptions, and Anglo-Saxons."

33. Winant, *World Is a Ghetto*.

34. Bonilla-Silva, "Race in the World System."

35. See, for example, Martin, *Semiperipheral States* and "World-Economy."

36. Lipton, *Capitalism and Apartheid*, 7.

37. See, for example, Innes, *Anglo American*, 188, 237–39.

38. South Africa, *Union Statistics*, S-3.

39. According to official statistics, in 1948 mining employed 438,598 persons, of whom fewer than 50,000 were white. Private manufacturing alone (excluding state industries) in 1948–49 employed 556,779 persons, including 169,178 white workers (South Africa, *Union Statistics*, G-4, G-6).

40. South Africa, Board of Trade and Industries, "Report No. 282."

41. Silver, *Forces of Labor*, 126–28.

42. While dependency literature suggested that economic growth took place during great depressions, global data suggest otherwise; see Arrighi and Drangel, "Stratification of the World-Economy."

43. See, for example, Yudelman, *Emergence of Modern South Africa*, 42; and Freund, "Social Character of Secondary Industry," 15.

44. de Kiewiet, *History of South Africa*, 89.

45. Martin, "Cycles, Trends or Transformations."

46. Rosser, "Resource Curse."

47. Innes, *Anglo American*, 188.

48. See, for example, Horwitz, *Political Economy of South Africa*.

49. The radical debate primarily took place in the pages of the *Review of African Political Economy* during the mid-1970s. On these categories see Bienefeld and Innes, "Capital Accumulation and South Africa"; and Davies et al., "Class Struggle."

50. Davies, *Capital, State and White Labour*.

51. Wolpe, "Capitalism and Cheap Labour-Power."

52. See, for example, Seidman and Makgetla, *Outposts of Monopoly Capitalism*; and Minter, *King Solomon's Mines Revisited*.

53. See Christie, *Electricity, Industry, and Class*; or Innes, *Anglo American*. Established in 1923 as the Electricity Supply Commission (ESCOM), the state firm is now known as Eskom.

54. Gelb, "Making Sense of the Crisis."

55. See, for example, Abedian and Standish, *Economic Growth in South Africa*; and Suckling and White, *After Apartheid*.

56. See, for example, Marais, *South Africa*; Bond, *Elite Transition*; Mitchie and Padayachee, *Political Economy*; and the longer discussion in chapter 7 below.

57. Earlier data are unavailable. The data are drawn from UN sources for "national income" for the period up to 1948, and from the World Bank for "gross national product" data following 1948. The data composites are very rough in earlier years, and obviously do *not* tell us anything of the distribution of wealth and income within any particular zone or state, or the modes by which the global division of labor operates to produce these outcomes and privileges agents by class, race, or gender in core areas and peripheral areas. The methodology of this measure is elaborated in Arrighi and Drangel, "Stratification of the World-Economy"; and Korzeniewicz and Moran, *Unveiling Inequality*, 61–64.

Chapter 1

1. Magubane, *Making of a Racist State*.
2. Ibid., 37.
3. Cited in ibid., 319.
4. Rostow, *World Economy*, 177–78.
5. Lewis, *Growth and Fluctuations*, 190.
6. See Trapido, "South Africa."
7. Among a large literature see in particular Johnstone, *Class, Race and Gold*; and Yudelman, *Emergence of Modern South Africa*.
8. See the summary of these arguments in Morrell, "Disintegration."
9. See Innes, *Anglo American*.
10. In *Monopoly Capital* Baran and Sweezy clearly argue that "monopoly" capital was restricted to but a few of the more advanced core countries; see 12–13.
11. Kubicek, *Economic Imperialism*.
12. Frankel, *Investment*, graph E, 20.
13. Ibid., table 2, 20.
14. Wilson, *Labour in the Gold Mines*, 4, 156.
15. Hyslop, "Imperial Working Class."
16. South Africa, *Report of the Economic Commission*, 24, 25.
17. Ibid., 26–27.
18. On the relationship between wages, standard of living, and white miners' households, see Beittel, "Witwatersrand."
19. Wilson, *Labour in the Gold Mines*, 66.
20. Jeeves, *Migrant Labour*, 187–251.
21. Ibid., 6.
22. South African Native Affairs Commission, *Report and Appendices*, 81.

23. Wilson, *Labour in the Gold Mines*, 45.

24. See, among others, Jeeves, *Migrant Labour*; Lacey, *Working for Boroko*; and Levy, *Foundations*.

25. Wilson, *Labour in the Gold Mines*, 66.

26. Yudelman, *Emergence*, 128.

27. South Africa, *Report of the Smallholders Commission*, 12.

28. Yudelman, *Emergence*, 180.

29. Wilson, *Labour in the Gold Mines*, 157.

30. Nattrass, *South African Economy*, 54.

31. South Africa, *Union Statistics*, tables I-23, I-24, I-25, I-26, pp. 70, 153.

32. Frankel, *Co-operation and Competition*, 11–20. Frankel summarized the situation in the mid-1920s thus: "South Africa produces nearly 14,000,000 bags of maize per annum, sends 30 per cent. of this quantity abroad, consumes about 60 per cent. as food, and uses the remaining 10 per cent. for feeding animals and for miscellaneous purposes," 19.

33. Keegan, "Restructuring Class Relations," 245.

34. Bundy, *Rise and Fall* and "Emergence and Decline." He provides the following periodization: ca. 1830–70: the creation of a peasantry; 1870–86: new opportunities, successful and unsuccessful peasants; 1886–1913: peasant self-sufficiency under attack.

35. Trapido, "Plough to the Ground," 337.

36. See Davies, *Capital, State, and White Labour*, 76–79.

37. Cited in ibid., 79–80.

38. Bonner, "1920 Black Mineworkers' Strike."

39. On the early history of such programs see van Onselen, "Main Reef Road"; and on relief programs after 1906–9 see Davies, *Capital, State, and White Labour*, 102–11.

40. Wilson, *Labour in the Gold Mines*, 157.

41. South Africa, *Official Yearbook*, 1929–30, 517.

42. Katzen, *Gold*, 29.

43. South Africa, *Official Yearbook*, 1929–30, 516, 524.

44. Morrell, "Disintegration," 634.

45. As Timoshenko notes, the great depression for agriculturalists began well before the Great Crash of 1929; see *World Agriculture and the Depression*, 8. See also Kindleberger, *World in Depression*, 86–88.

Chapter 2

1. See, for example, Thorp, *Latin America in the 1930s*; and Brown, *Economies of Africa and Asia*.

2. South Africa, *Official Yearbook*, 1927, 1932, 1941.

3. Trade was forced, via customs regulation, onto British ships heading to and from the mother country, preferential treatment was accorded to British imports, selected colonial goods were given privileged access to British markets, and special privileges were granted to British shipping and the chartered British East India Company. See Bruwer, *Protection in South Africa*, 64–65.

4. Ibid., 115–16.

5. Transvaal, *Customs and Industries Commission, 1908*, 2. Conditions in the Cape Colony were not much better; see de Kock, *Selected Subjects*, 284–85.

6. Cited in Thompson, *Unification of South Africa*, 94.

7. South Africa, *Conditions of Trade and Industries*, 12.

8. Yudelman, *Emergence*, 240; Horwitz, *Political Economy of South Africa*, 245.

9. South Africa, *Conditions of Trade and Industries*, 13.

10. Laite, *Union Tariff*, 5.

11. Minutes of the second meeting of the Tariff Committee, National Archives, Pretoria (hereafter cited as NA), Advisory Board of Industry and Science files (hereafter cited as BIS), 410, 2.

12. See Laite's "Memorandum on the Preparation of a Scientific Tariff" contained in the minutes of the third meeting of the Tariff Committee, in NA, BIS, 410.

13. South Africa, "*Report of the Advisory Board*," 40–41.

14. *South African Journal of Industry* (hereafter cited as *SAJI*) 4, September 1921, 726.

15. Ibid.

16. *The South African Mining and Engineering Journal* (hereafter cited as *SAMEJ*), August 29, 1921, 1794.

17. See the board's report, "A survey of the powers and functions of the Board in relation to the economic development of the Union," in NA, Board of Trade and Industries files (hereafter cited as BTI), 355.

18. *SAJI* 8 (January 1925): 30.

19. *SAJI* 7 (April 1924): 253–55.

20. See Choles, "Boot and Shoe Industry."

21. Bruwer, *Protection in South Africa*.

22. Jagger, "Board of Trade and Industries," 53.

23. *South African Printer and Stationer*, May 1925, 183.

24. Board of Trade and Industries, "Report No. 46," 5.

25. Ibid., 5–6.

26. Board of Trade and Industries, "Report No. 51."

27. See, for example, Yudelman, *Emergence*; and Kaplan, "Politics of Industrial Protection."

28. Bruwer, "Board of Trade and Industries," 35.

29. *SAMEJ*, May 3, 1924, 911.

30. See *SAMEJ*: May 31, 1924, 1059; June 14, 1924, 1131; May 31, 1924, 1059.

31. "Statement of Evidence to the Board of Trade and Industries on the Subject of a System of Protective Duties," Transvaal Chamber of Mines, December 31, 1924, NA, BTI 67/2.

32. See, for example, Scaife (of St. John's College, Oxford), "Free Trade for South Africa."

33. See the exchanges between the board and representatives of the chamber in NA, BTI 67/2.

34. Letter from Bruwer to the Minister of Mines and Industries, May 6, 1926, NA, BTI 67/2.

35. Cape Archival Depot, ASSOCOM A 1909, 1/1/5, Minutes of the Meeting of the Executive Committee (Southern Section), March 26, 1925.

36. "Customs Policy and Dumping Duty: Interesting Debate at Harrismith Congress," *Commercial Bulletin*, November 1924, 88.

37. NA, BTI 67/32, 3.

38. Ibid.

39. Ibid.

40. See South Africa, Board of Trade and Industries, "Report No. 51," 4.

41. See, among others, Davies, *Capital, State and White Labour*, 179–243; and Yudelman, *Emergence*, 214–48.

42. *Industrial South Africa*, July 1924, 2930.

43. See, for example, Saunders, "Agriculture and Manufacturing Industries," 322.

44. *ISA*, July 1924, 1.

45. Letter from Laite to Minister of Mines and Industries, June 25, 1925, NA, BTI 67/7.

46. Letter from the President of the SAAU to Sir Howard George, Chairman of the BTI, May 11, 1922, NA, BTI 67/4.

47. *Farmers Weekly*, October 10, 1923, 494.

48. *Farmers Weekly*, May 6, 1925, 803.

49. With the exception of a few years in the early 1930s, the British pound and South African pound were held equivalent until the introduction of the rand in 1961 at a rate of R2 to £1. That rate continued until 1967.

50. Martin, "Developmentalism, the Pernicious Illusion," 618.

51. South Africa, *Official Yearbook*, 1935, 636; *Official Yearbook*, 1941, 921.

52. Calculated from South Africa, *Statement of Trade and Shipping*, various years; merchandise trade only, i.e., reexports and gold exports (much if not most of which were credited to Britain but transshipped elsewhere, particularly to the United States) excluded.

53. Yudelman, *Emergence*, 240.

54. Martin, "Developmentalism, the Pernicious Illusion," 618.

55. South Africa, Board of Trade and Industries, "Report No. 282," 108.

56. See, for example, Crush, "Southern African Regional Formation," 200; Taylor, "Changing Patterns of Labour Supply," 213; and van Onselen, *Chibaro*, 227–78.

57. Chanock, *Unconsummated Union*.

58. See Botha, "On Tariff Policy."

59. Calculated from figures in Southern Rhodesia, *Official Yearbook*, no. 1 (1924): 218, 291.

60. See "Union Manufactures: New Customs Agreement with Rhodesia," *South African Commerce and Manufacturers Record*, May 1915, 204.

61. Calculated from Southern Rhodesia, *Official Yearbook*, no. 2 (1930): 627–28.

62. Ibid.

63. Ibid., 632.

64. Ibid., 627, 628, 492.

65. Southern Rhodesia, *Protection of Secondary Industries*, 82.

66. Ibid.

67. Southern Rhodesia, *Official Yearbook*, no. 2 (1930): 617; and no. 3 (1932): 548, 558. These figures exclude gold, specifically Rhodesian gold sent to the new Rand gold refinery. If invisible (i.e. nonphysical, e.g. services) imports and exports were included, the balance in South Africa's favor would have been much greater,

perhaps even double the official figure. One Southern Rhodesian commission in the early 1930s calculated, on the basis of figures supplied by the controller of customs and the government statistician, that invisible trade items doubled the trade balance in South Africa's favor; see Southern Rhodesia, *Ottawa Conference*, 26–27.

68. This statement relies on Rhodesian archival copies collected and graciously supplied by Ian Phimister. This particular information is derived from a Memo of the Treasurer to the Prime Minister, January 11, 1928, "Customs Union Agreement," Rhodesian Archives (RA), S 678/15/2.

69. See, for example, *Farmers Weekly*, October 8, 1929, 438.

70. *Industrial and Commercial South Africa*, November 24, 1929, 587.

71. *Farmers Weekly*, October 23, 1919, 652.

72. See, for example, *Commercial Bulletin*, October 1929, 213.

73. *Commercial Bulletin*, November 1929, 201, 203.

74. *Industrial and Commercial South Africa*, October 1929, 515.

75. *SAMEJ*, December 14, 1929, 403.

76. *SAMEJ*, October 26, 1929, 215.

77. *Farmers Weekly*, October 2, 1929, 205.

78. Phimister, "Origins and Development of Manufacturing," 14–17.

79. *Industrial and Commercial South Africa*, March 25, 1930, 127.

80. Phimister," Origins and Development of Manufacturing," 21.

81. Ibid.

82. The following section relies primarily on Kanduza, *Political Economy of Underdevelopment.*

83. Ibid., 60.

84. Among other efforts Smuts threatened to seize Lourenço Marques, proposed a federation including Mozambique, and offered to run the port and railroad under South African auspices. While these came to naught, Smuts's ability to bend to good use the British connection to enforce Mozambique's dependence on South Africa was illustrated by his successful blocking of a badly needed British loan (see Newitt, *Portugal in Africa;* and Katzenellenbogen, *South Africa and Southern Mozambique*).

85. See Katzenellenbogen, *South Africa and Southern Mozambique*, 16–35.

86. Newitt, *Portugal in Africa*, 114.

87. These figures and those immediately following are from South Africa, *Official Yearbook*, 1929–30, 622.

88. In particular they complained of the possibility of overseas firms establishing factories in Mozambique from which to export to South Africa. See *Industrial South Africa*, October 1924, 452. One needs to note, however, that South African capital was already invested in the Lourenço Marques area as discussed below in the case of cement production.

89. Katzenellenbogen, *South Africa and Southern Mozambique*, 145.

90. Ibid., 148–49.

91. Transvaal Chamber of Mines, *Thirty-ninth Annual Report*, 149. The chamber continued by calculating a definite lack of labor supply in South Africa. See also *SAMEJ*, June 30, 1928, 501.

92. Presidential speech, Association of Chambers of Commerce, *Commercial Bulletin*, August 1933, 79.

93. See *South African Sugar Journal*, December 31, 1928, 737–38.

94. See South Africa, Board of Trade and Industries, "Report No. 51," and the discussions of this matter in NA, Mines and Industries file, 139/4, vol. 1.

95. See *Industrial and Commercial South Africa*, December 26, 1926, 609, which itself cites support from the Afrikaner newspaper *Ons Vaderland*.

96. See South Africa, Board of Trade and Industries, "Report No. 48."

97. See De Loor, "Portland Cement," 359.

98. See Hyam, *Failure of South African Expansionism*, 31–32.

99. See Ettinger, "South Africa's Weight Restrictions."

100. On the global effects for all primary producers, see Kindleberger, *World in Depression*; and for South Africa see Schumann, *Structural Changes and Business Cycles*.

101. See Smith, "Antonio Salazar"; and Wuyts, "Economica Politica do Colonialismo."

102. See Schumann, *World Depression*; and *Structural Changes*, 264–68.

103. Calculated from South Africa, *Official Yearbook of the Union*, no. 9 (1926–27): 554–55; no. 14 (1931–32): 504; and no. 22 (1941): 877–78.

104. South Africa, *Customs and Tariff Commission*, 25.

105. This argument was put forward with vigor and at length by the Chamber of Mines in its submission to the commission: "The protective policy of the Union is wholly disadvantageous to the Gold Mining Industry, which is the mainstay of the Union's economic structure." Transvaal Chamber of Mines, *Forty-fifth Annual Report*, 93.

106. South Africa, *Customs and Tariff Commission*, 30.

107. Arrighi, *Political Economy of Rhodesia*, 36. Phimister reached similar conclusions in "Origins and Development," 26–27.

108. Martin, "Region Formation under Crisis Conditions," 132–33.

109. Calculated from Mitchell, *International Historical Statistics*, F1, F2.

110. These and the following figures are taken from Yudelman and Jeeves, "New Labour Frontiers for Old," 123–24. Their figures on the origins of African miners for the period 1920–46 differ substantially from those published by others working from the (apparently) same primary sources. See, for example, Wilson, *Labour in the Gold Mines*, 70; and Stahl, "Migrant Labour Supplies," 17. The trends described here, however, remain basically intact.

111. Hirschman, *National Power*. Originally published in 1945, Hirschman's analysis loses its pertinence in a postwar world marked by increasing ties of dependence through direct investment.

Chapter 3

1. Polanyi, *Great Transformation*.

2. Christie, *Electricity, Industry, and Class*, 1–3.

3. Clark, "South African State Corporations" and *Manufacturing Apartheid*.

4. Christie, *Electricity, Industry, and Class*, 204.

5. Clark, "South African State Corporations," 122.

6. Rodney, *How Europe Underdeveloped Africa*, 227–28.

7. Green and Fair, *Development in Africa*, 36.

8. Pirie, "Decivilizing Rails."

9. Williams, *Selborne Memorandum*, 9.

10. Ibid., 11.

11. De Kock, *Results of Government Ownership*, 54. After receiving his PhD from Harvard, de Kock returned to South Africa and taught at the University of Cape Town. He was subsequently appointed to the Board of Trade and Industries—another non-British-trained expert placed in the service of the Pact government.

12. See de Kock, *Analysis*, 106, 134.

13. Ibid., 136.

14. See ibid., 127. One must use de Kock's figures carefully; apparently many references by de Kock and others overestimate railway construction between the Anglo-Boer War and Union. See, by way of illustration, the figures in South Africa, South African Railways and Harbours Administration, *Report of the General Manager, 1948*, 137.

15. South Africa, South African Railways and Harbours Administration, *Bulletin No. 12* (1920), Annexure No. 2, 80–81, as reprinted in South African Railways and Harbours, *Report of the Departmental Railway Tariffs Inquiry Committee 1930*; emphasis in original.

16. Ibid.

17. Ibid.

18. See figures comparing 1909 and 1925 imports and exports of these goods in South Africa, South African Railways and Harbours Administration, *Report of the General Manager, 1926*, 4.

19. Diamonds by comparison stood at £8.6 million. See ibid.

20. See South Africa, South African Railways and Harbours Administration, *Railway Tariffs Inquiry Committee*, 28.

21. See the list of rate reductions since 1910 in ibid., Annexure No. 13, "Decreases in Railway Rates since 1910," 139–44. For a comparison of the vast differences in rates on imported versus South African commodities of the same type, see Frankel, *Railway Policy of South Africa*, 203.

22. South Africa, South African Railways and Harbours Administration, *Report of the General Manager, 1926*, 8.

23. See ibid., 20–22.

24. *SAMEJ*, July 14, 1928, 579.

25. *SAMEJ*, November 24, 1928, 325.

26. Frankel used this study to receive a PhD from the University of London. Harvard-trained M. H. de Kock's work on similar issues was much more favorable to the South African state's role in managing economic assets like the railways. His work was studiously ignored by Frankel.

27. See Frankel, *Railway Policy of South Africa*, 16–18.

28. See ibid., 46.

29. See South Africa, South African Railways and Harbours Administration, *Railway and Harbour Affairs Commission* and *Railway Tariffs Inquiry Committee*. Operational managers of the railways often found it difficult to support openly the government's position, something discernible in these reports as well as in the general manager's annual reports.

30. See Harris, *Monetary Problems*, 302.

31. Arndt and Richards, "Banking System of South Africa," 975.

32. The National Bank's origins were local, but by the mid-1920s it had become firmly part of the imperial network; in 1926 it merged with Barclays and moved its headquarters to London. See Baster, *Imperial Banks*, 195–206; and Day, "South African Commercial Banks," 357–59.

33. Arndt and Richards, "Banking System of South Africa," 976.

34. Jones, "Business Imperialism," 73.

35. Ibid. Jones argues, without much evidence, that the imperial banks assisted the economic development of South Africa.

36. Ibid., 70.

37. Gelb, "South African Reserve Bank," 65. Gelb does not fully demonstrate either the nascent industrialists' hand in the formation of the bank or the benefits it dispersed. Clearly some local capitalists, particularly from the banking and commercial sector, were opposed; see Baster, *Imperial Banks*, 198–99.

38. Henry, *First Hundred Years*, 181. One should note again the meaning of the term "industry." In the parlance of the day, it meant any activity outside basic agricultural pursuits. It was not restricted to manufacturing. When observers in the 1920s called for foreign investment in industry, they almost invariably meant investment in *mining*, which was, of course, where almost all overseas capital investment was headed. It was in the pages of the *South African Mining and Engineering Journal*, and not the journals of manufacturing, that the need for foreign capital was discussed.

39. Plant, "Relations," 74.

40. See the account in Arndt and Richards, "Banking System of South Africa," 966–67.

41. Cited in Plant, "Relations," 75.

42. The governor of the Bank of England was especially concerned with such a provision. In his private notes on rules for establishing central banks, he argued: "Autonomy and freedom from political control are desirable for all Central and Reserve Banks." The implementation of this principle in the South African case would later bedevil efforts to use the Reserve Bank for local economic development. See Sayers, *Bank of England*, Appendices, 3:74–75.

43. Plumptre, *Central Banking*, 192.

44. Sayers, *Bank of England*, 1:203.

45. Plumptre, *Central Banking*, 183.

46. Ibid., 192–93.

47. Clegg, "Central Banking in South Africa," 523.

48. Arndt and Richards," Banking System of South Africa," 997–98.

49. Ibid.

50. See Dalgaard, "South Africa's Impact," 99–100.

51. See ibid.

52. Cited in Richards, "Kemmerer-Vissering Report," 567.

53. Dalgaard, "South Africa's Impact," 153.

54. Ibid., 154. This is, in fact, the thesis of Dalgaard's dissertation. A similar argument was put forward much earlier by Arndt and Richards, "Banking System of South Africa."

55. Richards, "Kemmerer-Vissering Report," 567.

56. Day, "South African Reserve Bank," 391.

57. See de Kock, *South African Reserve Bank*, 95–96. Gerhard de Kock was the son of M. H. de Kock, who was the governor of the Reserve Bank at the time Gerhard was writing.

58. Pirow, *James Barry Munnik Hertzog*, 139.

59. Ibid.

60. See Innes, *Anglo American*, 118–23. Innes argues that mining throughout the interwar period was a leader in establishing industrial production; as we have seen above and will see further below, this was certainly not the case during the 1920s.

61. By "significant" is meant output upward of 100,000 tons of crude steel per year. Japan in 1915 produced approximately 500,000 tons, still a small amount in the world total of 66 million tons (see Burn, *Steel Industry*, appended table no. 105). Calculations of iron and steel output for this period are notoriously difficult; pig iron and steel were often intermixed, as was the production of iron or steel from scrap versus ores.

62. Woytinsky and Woytinsky, *World Population and Production*, 1118.

63. Calculated from appendices 6 and 7 in Hexner, *International Steel Cartel*, 325, 328.

64. See South Africa, *Official Yearbook*, no. 1, 1917, 515–18. This probably under-estimates the value of total metal imports (e.g., cars and locomotives are excluded).

65. See Richards, *Iron and Steel Industry*, 4–7. This book compiles the detailed history and technical developments that led to the South African Iron and Steel Corporation through 1940. Much of the detail that follows is derived from this source. In many ways it is the companion piece to Frankel's *Railway Policy of South Africa*. Like Frankel, Richards undertook a commission from the Chamber of Mines, in this case to study the steel industry. The first subtitle of the book accordingly reads: "With special reference to The South African Iron and Steel Industrial Corporation Ltd. (ISCOR) more particularly in its relation to The Gold-Mining Industry of the Transvaal."

66. See Stanley, "Iron and Steel."

67. Ibid., 885.

68. See Richards, *Iron and Steel Industry*, 69.

69. See Clark, *Manufacturing Apartheid*, 31–38, 49–50.

70. See ibid., 49. Clark's study focuses on and celebrates the career of van der Bijl. While he may have been, in Smuts's words, South Africa's "greatest industrialist" (69) due to his managing first ESCOM and then ISCOR, it is clear even from Clark's study that ISCOR would never have come into being if Smuts and van der Bijl had controlled the decision to launch a state-owned steelworks.

71. Cited by Richards, *Iron and Steel Industry*, 99.

72. See ibid., 101–2.

73. Cited in ibid., 102.

74. See ibid., 106–7.

75. The rest of this paragraph draws from ibid., 102–15.

76. *SAMEJ*, May 8, 1926, 253.

77. *SAMEJ*, February 5, 1927, 629.

78. *SAMEJ*, January 28, 1928, 579.

79. *SAMEJ*, October 1, 1927, 177.

80. As cited in *SAMEJ*, October 13, 1928, 177.

81. *Commercial Bulletin*, March 1927, 401.

82. South African Federated Chamber of Industries (hereafter cited as SAFCI), *Eighth Annual Convention*, 45–46.

83. Ibid., 45.

84. Ibid., 45–46.

85. *Industrial and Commercial South Africa*, June 26, 1931, 223.

86. *Industrial and Commercial South Africa*, October 16, 1931, 432.

87. *Industrial and Commercial South Africa*, September 1934, 277.

88. See, for example, *Vacuum Magazine*, March 1937, 2–3.

89. *British Trade in South Africa*, August 1934, 7.

90. Calculated from figures in Richards, *Iron and Steel Industry*, tables 4 and 5 (facing 264).

91. See ibid., 412–20.

92. Richards's book on ISCOR, published in 1940 but commissioned by the Transvaal Chamber of Mines in 1936, set out the opponents' case in great detail: state intervention in the case of ISCOR had led to unnecessarily high steel prices, a higher cost of living, and undue burdens on the mining industry, which was South Africa's best hope for economic advancement.

93. The board's extensive review of South Africa's industrial structure conducted at the end of the war was, for example, permeated with warnings of the dangers of government intervention—a far cry from board reports under Hertzog. ISCOR was not even dealt with in the report. See South Africa, Board of Trade and Industries, "Report No. 282."

94. Havenga, minister of finance from 1924 through the Fusion government, kept state accounts like a good housekeeper—content to produce surpluses whenever possible. This often put him at loggerheads with his cabinet colleagues. Pirow, minister and close friend of Hertzog, put it this way: "[Havenga] was too much the conservative banker, more concerned with a balanced budget than with the stimulation of our resources as a young country with an unlimited future" (Pirow, *Barry Munnik Hertzog*, 134).

Chapter 4

1. As noted in previous chapters, a liberal perspective was consistently voiced throughout the interwar period; it has continued into the neoliberal period. The basic early works emerged, however, in response to the strictures of *apartheid* after the National Party victory in 1948 and the concomitant growth of the South African academic establishment. See, among others, Doxey, *Industrial Colour Bar*; van der Horst, *Native Labour*; Hutt, *Economics of the Colour Bar*; more generally, Horwitz, *Political Economy of South Africa*; and, for a later example of this debate, Lipton, *Capitalism and Apartheid*; and the critical review by Freund, "Defending South African Capitalism."

2. Johnstone, *Class, Race and Gold*, 167.

3. The basis for this argument, derived from work associated with the French Marxist school surrounding Nicos Poulantzas, is that "unproductive" workers—that is, those not immediately engaged in the direct production of commodities in a

capitalist firm—should be located outside the ranks of the working class. Davies lays this out in chapter 1 (1–40) of his *Capital, State and White Labour.*

4. See ibid., 181.

5. See Lewis, *Industrialisation and Trade Union Organisation,* and Doug Hindson's PhD dissertation, "The Pass System and the Formation of an Urban African Proletariat in South Africa"; a much shorter version was published as *Pass Controls and the Urban African Proletariat.*

6. Transvaal, *Customs and Industries Commission,* 2.

7. See de Kock, *Selected Subjects,* 284–85.

8. See, for example, the survey by industrial subspecialty contained in South Africa, *Conditions of Trade and Industries.*

9. South Africa, *Official Yearbook of the Union,* no. 9, 1926–27, 545. Figures are deflated by the index for "Union Goods," from South Africa, *Union Statistics,* H-5 (base year recalculated to 1924 = 100).

10. Ibid., 554–55.

11. Ibid.

12. South Africa, *Official Yearbook,* 1921, 661; and *Official Yearbook,* 1926–27, 556.

13. South Africa, *Economic and Wage Commission,* 199.

14. Ibid., 315–19.

15. This is a central theme that runs throughout the treatment of the Pact period in Yudelman, *Emergence;* and Davies, *Capital, State and White Labour.* For many scholars the issue of segregation and industry is outside interwar concerns, and emerges only in full blossom in the apartheid period. Still, as Legassick expressed it, "Apartheid has meant an extension to the manufacturing economy of the structure of the gold mining industry" (cited in Wolpe, "Capitalism and Cheap Labour-Power," 426).

16. South Africa, *Union Statistics,* G-4, G-6, G-7.

17. Ibid., G-15.

18. Cited in Horwitz, *Political Economy of South Africa,* 197.

19. Cited in ibid.

20. See Davies, *Capital, State and White Labour,* 191, 213. Lewis argues even more forcefully that minimum wages were set quite low; see Lewis, "New Unionism," 38.

21. South Africa, *Union Statistics,* G-6.

22. See Lewis, *Industrialisation and Trade Union Organisation,* 88–110; and Webster, "Colour of Craft."

23. Calculated from South Africa, *Union Statistics,* 1–6.

24. Ibid., G-15.

25. Richards, *Iron and Steel Industry,* 298.

26. Calculated from South Africa, *Union Statistics,* G-10.

27. See the figures in ibid., G-10 to G-13.

28. Thus, for example, the first industrial census reported an average yearly black wage to be approximately £34 in both mining and manufacturing. Calculated from ibid., G-20 and G-5 for mining and L-3 for manufacturing.

29. South Africa, *Report of the Economic Commission,* 41.

30. Ibid.

31. See, for example, differences noted and discussed in *Economic and Wage Commission,* 17, 272–73.

32. South Africa, *Industrial Legislation Commission,* 69.

33. The seminal work on the contribution of rural "pre-capitalist" modes of production to urban capitalist production is Wolpe, "Capitalism and Cheap Labour-
Power"; case studies of rural areas, such as Colin Murray's *Families Divided*, undercut
the historical basis of Wolpe's formulation, while studies of the apartheid period
proper, such as Hindson's *Pass System* stress the differentiation of African workers
and not simply a segmented, black-white, labor market. Our focus is rather the differentiation of labor markets, labor processes, and the bargaining power of labor
prior to apartheid and across the industrial and rural sectors.

34. South Africa, *Inter-Departmental Committee on Labour Resources*, 16.

35. South Africa, *Union Statistics*, G-4.

36. Ibid., G-6.

37. Average yearly manufacturing wage rates were equivalent with those in mining at the beginning of the World War I. After that time, the average yearly wage for
whites in manufacturing rose slowly but steadily above levels prevailing in mining. In
1920, mining wages were approximately 88 percent of those in manufacturing; in
1930 they were 76 percent; and in 1940, 65 percent (ibid., G-5 and G-20 for mining,
L-3 for manufacturing).

38. See Simkins, "Agricultural Production."

39. See, for example, Murray's description in *Families Divided*, 14–16. Migration
from Lesotho, moreover, increasingly became permanent migration to South Africa's
cities—as was indicated in the rising proportion of female migrants and the lack of
population growth that was officially attributed to permanent migration to South
Africa (see Martin, "Lesotho").

40. Cited in South Africa, *Native Affairs Commission*, 29.

41. Calculated from South Africa, *South African Statistics, 1982*, 1.7. Unfortunately,
there was no census of the black population between 1921 and 1936. Figures from
this source are different from those used by General Smuts immediately above,
although the results are much the same. Figures for the urban black population
show an increase from 880,000 (or 16 percent of total black population) in 1921, to
1,703,000 in 1936 (or 23 percent of total black population), to 2,429,999 in 1946
(or 27 percent of total black population).

42. South Africa, *Union Statistics*, A-33.

43. South Africa, *Native Affairs Commission*, 6–7.

44. See Bradford, *Taste of Freedom*.

45. On the distinction between workplace and marketplace bargaining power
and the world-historical transition to workplace bargaining power prior to and after
World War II, see Arrighi and Silver, "Labor Movements and Capital Migration"; and
Silver, *Forces of Labor*. The study of South African industry reveals a gap in the transition that Arrighi charts between marketplace (based on artisan labor processes) and
workplace bargaining power (based on continuous-flow labor processes)—namely,
the lengthy development of manufacturing based on semiskilled operatives.

46. In *South Africa*, van den Berghe argues that "to speak of class alignments in the
Marxian sense of relationship to the means of production does not correspond to
the social reality in South Africa" (62). On the appeals to marginalized whites, see,
for example, O'Meara, *Volkskapitalisme*.

47. See, for example, Wolpe, "Capitalism and Cheap Labour-Power"; and
Hindson, *Pass Controls*.

48. See Bonacich, "Capitalism and Race Relations."

49. For a description of this process see Lewis, *Industrialisation and Trade Union Organisation*, 132–35.

50. Hindson, *Pass Controls*, 57.

51. See, among others, Hindson, *Pass Controls*; O'Meara, *Volkskapitalisme*; and Moodie, "South African State."

Chapter 5

1. Smuts, "Thoughts on the New World," 574.

2. Ibid., 574–75.

3. Barber, *South Africa's Foreign Policy*, 16.

4. "The King and Empire Brotherhood: Moving Appeal in Address at Pretoria," *Times* (London), March 31, 1947, 6.

5. "The King's Faith in Britain: Impressions of South African Tour," *Times* (London), May 16, 1947, 6.

6. "Britain's Mission," *Times* (London), May 16, 1947, 7.

7. Barber, *South Africa's Foreign Policy*, 38.

8. Cited in ibid., 34.

9. See van Essen, "Department of State and Africa," 845.

10. Cited in Kapp, "Historical Experience," 22. Kapp, writing in the mid-1980s as part of a group commissioned by the Institute for American Studies of the Rand Afrikaans University, and funded by the South African government's Human Sciences Research Council, then goes on to recount that "the inability to free themselves from distorted views of the Afrikaner and the National Party remained a constant feature of a number of American newspapers and journals. Their predilection to link South Africa and her population policy with the emotional worlds and associations created by the Third Reich and its anti-Semitism, and with fascism in general, prevented a balanced and responsible understanding of, and reporting on, South Africa" (22).

11. The figures in this paragraph were calculated from South Africa, *Statement of Trade and Shipping* (1939, 1951, 1956). The US share of South Africa's exports was 4 percent in 1938 and 7 percent in 1948.

12. Cited by Barber and Barratt, *South Africa's Foreign Policy*, 35.

13. Ibid., 36.

14. "Whither Rhodesia?" *Industrial Review*, June 1950, 50.

15. Cited by Barber and Barratt, *South Africa's Foreign Policy*, 38.

16. South Africa, *Debates of the House of Assembly, 27th May–22nd June 1957*, June 10, 1957, col. 7635.

17. Cited in Barber and Barratt, *South Africa's Foreign Policy*, 39.

18. "Greater Markets: Next Step in Expansion of Secondary Industry Is Drive for Export Trade," *Manufacturer*, November 1951, 9.

19. Ibid.

20. "The Fight Must Go On," *Industrial Review*, September 1949, 3, 35.

21. Pearce, "West African Trade," 23.

22. Ibid.

23. Atkinson, "Pan African Conference on Trade," 20.

24. Jeal, "Trade and Tariff in Africa," 413.

25. Jeal, "Trends in South Africa's Trade with the World," 330.

26. Winklé, "Changes in Merchandise Exports," 8–9; emphasis in original.

27. Phimister, "From Preference towards Protection," 31.

28. Ibid., 32.

29. Palmer, "Union's Trade with Rhodesia," 35.

30. Ibid.

31. Garmany, "Economic Growth of Southern Rhodesia," 437.

32. Jones, "Union Manufacturers Meet Overseas Competition," 31.

33. Union of South Africa, *House of Assembly Debates, 27th May–22nd June 1957*, June 10, 1957, col. 7638.

34. Ibid., cols. 7638–39.

35. Ibid., col. 7639.

36. See Phimister, "From Preference towards Protection," 42–48.

37. *Industrial Review of Africa*, October 1949, 30.

38. Harper, "Federation Must Provide Facilities," 39.

39. Phimister, "From Preference towards Protection," 44.

40. Palmer, "New Barriers to Trade," 19.

41. South Africa, Department of Commerce and Industries, "New Agreement," 23.

42. *Commercial Opinion*, July 1955, 83.

43. *The Industrial Review*, October 1949, 30.

44. Harper, "CAF Looks at Its Railway," 13.

45. Ibid.

46. Jeal, "Can Rhodesia Capture the African Market?," 387.

47. Jeal, "Investment Capital in Short Supply," 7.

48. Campbell, "Queue for Capital," 39.

49. *Industrial Review*, September 1949, 3.

50. Strydom, "Capital Investment in South Africa," 42; Strydom was the officer-in-charge of the Economic Division, for the head office of Volkskas.

51. Ibid., 38.

52. Ibid., 39.

53. Louw, "Rôle of Foreign Capital," 7.

54. Sadie, "Foreign Capital I," 11.

55. Ibid., 15.

56. Sadie, "Foreign Capital in South Africa II," 70.

57. Ibid., 71.

58. Ibid., 76, which cites "The American Boom in Canada," *Lloyds Bank Review*, January 1957, 29.

59. Louw, "Foreign Control," 14.

60. Ibid.

61. Ibid.

62. Ibid., 14–15.

63. Ibid., 15.

64. Ibid.

65. van Rhijn, "Need for Overseas Capital," 53.

66. Wallace, "Why the Union," 9.

67. Harper, "Big Industrial Boom Building Up," 53.

68. Harper, "150 Million Customers," 13.

69. Ibid.

70. Innes, *Anglo American*, 188.

71. Jones and Müller, *South African Economy*, 229.

72. See Martin, "Southern Africa and the World-Economy."

73. Figures taken from ibid., 62.

74. Figures taken from ibid., 63–65.

75. Pangeti, "Economy under Siege," 55.

76. See Phimister, "From Preference towards Protection," 48.

77. Pangeti, "Economy under Siege," 61.

78. Seidman and Makgetla, *Outposts of Monopoly Capitalism*, 135.

79. Ibid.

80. Ibid., 135–36.

81. See Seidman and Makgetla, *Outposts*; and Minter, *King Solomon's Mines Revisited*.

82. Clark, *Manufacturing Apartheid*, 149.

83. Ibid., 162–63.

84. O'Meara, *Forty Lost Years*, 81.

85. As Fine and Rustomjee document in their *Political Economy of South Africa*.

Chapter 6

1. León and Soto, "Structural Breaks and Long-Run Trends," 350.

2. See Turshen, *Privatizing Health Services in Africa*. For education one need only to note the well-known US attack on and withdrawal from UNESCO, followed by the rise of the World Bank as the major international institution setting education agenda policies; see Samoff, *Coping with Crisis*.

3. See Korzeniewicz and Moran, "World-Economic Trends" and *Unveiling Inequality*.

4. See, for example, the articles in the *Financial Mail* surrounding trade with Africa ("Don't Wave the Flag," June 20, 1980, 1324–26; "Africa Trade: Call of the South," January 14, 1983, 134; and "Zimbabwe and the Renewal of Bilateral Trading Agreement ["Let's Stay Friends"] April 18, 1980, 255–56); commentaries on early Mozambican attempts to attract foreign investment (March 7, 1980, 946); pleasure at the 1984 Nkomati agreement with Mozambique ("The New Economic Dimension," April 27, 1984, 32–35); and trade and investment with SADCC ("Set for Take-off," December 5, 1980; and "SADCC's First Four Years," January 25, 1985, 54).

5. De Villiers and Anstey, "Trade Unions in Transition," 26.

6. See Gelb, "Making Sense of the Crisis," as well as the uneasy extension of the argument in his *South Africa's Economic Crisis*.

7. Campbell, *Reclaiming Zimbabwe*.

8. These linkages were noted at the time, but left undeveloped by the body of scholarship on the 1960s, including even the large literature written in and about

North America. See, for example, George Shepperson's striking 1960 essay "Notes on Negro American Influences" or Edmondson's 1968 essay "The Internationalization of Black Power." More recent accounts include D. G. Kelley, "Stormy Weather"; Clemons and Jones, "Global Solidarity"; and the long-term perspective in West, Martin, and Wilkins, *From Toussaint to Tupac.*

9. O'Meara, *Forty Lost Years*, 181.

10. Seekings, *UDF.*

11. Ibid., 160. In his conclusion Seekings validates the primary role of the UDF by how it provided responsible, organized leadership and, especially, controlled irresponsible youth militancy. See 286–88 and his last, concluding paragraphs where he argues the UDF's value was precisely in how it served to counter the common charge, as from John Kane-Berman, that "the protests of the 1980s were profoundly immoral in that they led to generalized violence thereafter," 324.

12. Terreblanche, *History of Inequality*, 349.

13. United Nations Children's Fund, *Children on the Front Line*, 39.

14. See John, "Campaign against British Bank Involvement"; and, for a longer view, Gurney, "Great Cause."

15. Huntington, "Reform and Stability," 24.

16. *Financial Mail*, October 24, 1986, 87.

17. See the summary of these changes in Crush, "Mine Migrancy"; figures from 32 and 21, respectively.

18. Crush et al., "Undermining Labour," 8.

19. Fine and Rustomjee, *Political Economy of South Africa*, 174; for an analysis of the MEC in the 1970s and 1980s, see 168–75.

20. See the accounts in Lodge and Nasson, *All, Here, and Now,* and Seekings, *UDF.*

21. De Bragança, "Indepéndencia sem descolonização."

22. *Sowetan*, March 5, 1990, 8.

23. Padayachee, "South Africa's International Financial Relations," 41.

24. *Financial Mail*, February 16, 1990, 27.

25. *Financial Mail*, February 23, 1990, 31.

26. *Financial Mail*, June 1, 1990, 19.

27. For accounts of this campaign see, among others, Padayachee, "South Africa's International Financial Relations"; and Hentz, "Two Faces of Privatisation"; as well as the sources cited below on the debate over ANC policy in the early 1990s. The major public break was the jettisoning of the Reconstruction and Development Programme, which advocated redistribution and vigorous state action and was the basis of ANC policy at the time of the 1994 elections, and the public promulgation of neoliberalism in the adoption of the GEAR program in 1996. Most analyses focus on the transition from the RDP to GEAR, which I argue (admittedly with hindsight and more recent documentation) is misleading: the key components of GEAR were in place well before 1994 and in large part before 1990 as documented below.

28. *Sowetan*, March 5, 1990, 8.

29. See Bell, "Should South Africa Further Liberalise?" 88–90.

30. Hirsh, "From GATT to WTO," 51.

31. Ibid.

32. Bond, *Elite Transition*, 49.

33. van Zyl et al., "South African Agriculture," 737.

34. Ibid., 731, 735–36.

35. Bond, *Elite Transition*, 48.

36. See South Africa, Board of Trade and Industries, "Report No. 2614."

37. For details on this battle and the divergent programs of the BTI, DTI, and IDC, see Black, "Role of the State," esp. 209–17, and Fine and Rustomjee, *Political Economy of South Africa*, 199–202.

38. Moll, "Macroeconomic Policy in Turbulent Times," 241.

39. Marais, *South Africa*, 109.

40. Terreblanche, *History of Inequality*, 375. Fine and Rustomjee place the outflows as high as 7 percent of GDP on average between 1970 and 1988 (*Political Economy of South Africa*, 247).

41. Terreblanche, *History of Inequality*, 357, which cites Davenport, *South Africa*, 464.

42. Marais, *South Africa*, 123.

43. Maxfield, *Gatekeepers of Growth*, 3.

44. Padayachee, "Central Bank Transformation," 742.

45. Wood, "Framing the Economic Future," 82.

46. Bond, *Elite Transition*, 178.

47. When IMF loans to South Africa stopped in 1983, annual consultations did not. IMF and World Bank consultations, publications, and personal links to ANC economists during the early 1990s were intense, heavily influencing the turn away from redistribution and restitution policies and toward a reliance on the corporate sector and "free market" policies. See, among others, Wood, "Framing the Economic Future"; and the later assessments in Bond, *Elite Transition*, 155–91; and Marais, *South Africa*, 122–59.

48. Terreblanche, *History of Inequality*, 430.

49. *Financial Mail*, February 7, 2003, 60. For an official account and positive if defensive analysis of delisting, see Walters and Prinsloo, "Impact of Offshore Listings."

50. Terreblanche, *History of Inequality*, 430.

51. On privatization in this period see Clark, *Manufacturing Apartheid*, 164–69; figure from 166–67.

52. Fine, "Privatisation and Restructuring," 23.

53. Hentz, "Two Faces of Privatisation," 206–7.

54. Cited in ibid., 214.

55. "No longer on hold," *Economist*, February 8, 2003.

56. *Business Day*, July 23, 2005.

57. Carrington and Detragiache, "Brain Drain?"

58. See Brown, Kaplan, and Meyer, "Counting Brains." They estimate that emigration of professionals accelerated in the 1990s while immigration declined.

59. OECD, "International Mobility of Health Professionals," 114. Some studies suggest otherwise; see, for example, McDonald and Crush, *Destinations Unknown*.

60. OECD, "International Mobility of Health Professionals," 11.

61. OECD, *World Health Report, 2006*, 100.

62. OECD, "International Mobility of Health Professionals," 15–16.

63. HSRC, *Flight of the Flamingoes*, 38–39.

64. Census results as reported in the *Economist*, July 12, 2003, 38. For language see South Africa, Statistics South Africa, *Census 2001*.

65. Reid, "Community Service for Health Professionals," 144.

66. Ibid., 145.

67. McDonald and Jacobs, *Understanding Press Coverage*; Fine and Bird, *Shades of Prejudice*.

68. Crush and Pendleton, *Regionalizing Xenophobia?*; Southern African Migration Project, "Perfect Storm."

69. *Mail and Guardian*, June 12, 2008.

70. Davies and Head, "Future of Mine Migrancy."

71. New inflows of migrant and undocumented persons were not expected by analysts, particularly those concerned with the mining sector. See Crush et al., "Undermining Labour"; and Crush and Mather, *Borderline Farming*.

72. Crush and Williams, *Transnationalism and African Immigration*, 7.

73. *Mining Weekly*, February 2, 2006.

74. The 2001 census results, released in July 2003, registered an unemployment rate of over 40 percent, in contrast to the government's reported rate of 21 percent. The Labour Department argued for the lower figure, arguing the employed should include anyone receiving any remuneration—such as the thousands of poor South Africans who watch over parked cars in return for tiny tips.

75. South African Institute of Race Relations, "One in Two Youths Unemployed."

76. UNDP, *International Human Development Indicators, 2012*.

77. UNDP, *Human Development Report, 1997*, 45; UNDP, *International Human Development Indicators, 2012*.

78. Simkins, "What Happened?" 2, 5.

79. South African Reserve Bank, *Quarterly Bulletin*, April 2003.

80. *Business Day*, March 26, 2003, 1.

81. Nattrass, "State of the Economy," 141–42.

82. "South Africa: Telkom Listing," *Africa News*, March 4, 2003.

83. South Africa, *South African Statistics, 1982*, 16.

84. Makgetla, "International Economic Crisis," 71.

85. See Kentridge, *Turning the Tanker*, 10–12, Bond, *Elite Transition*, 65–68, Marais, *South Africa*, 130–33, and Handley, "Business, Government and Economic Policymaking."

86. Labour Research Service, *LRS Report*, 17.

87. Department of Trade and Industry, "Guide to the Real Economy."

88. *Creamers Engineering News*, May 28, 2006.

89. Barnes and Morris, "German Connection," 797.

90. Black, "Globalization and Restructuring"; Black and Mitchell, "South African Motor Industry"; Barnes and Morris, "German Connection."

91. Flatters, "Economics of MIDP."

92. Finance Minister Trevor Manuel, who led the charge for trade liberalization, was by late 2007 openly challenged within the government (as well as outside) by those calling for an activist, developmental state; the MIDP constituted a key point of contention. See, for example, Department of Trade and Industry Minister Mandisi Mpahlwa's article "Proposal to Go It Alone on Trade Misreads the Evidence";

and "Mpahlwa Tackles Manuel on Trade Policy Quick-fix," both in *Business Day*, November 7, 2007.

Chapter 7

1. Alexander, "Rebellion of the Poor."
2. Saul, *Next Liberation Struggle*, 195.
3. See, for example, Desai, *We are the Poors*; Desai and Pithouse, "'But We Were Thousands'"; Gibson, *Challenging Hegemony*; and Ngwane, "South Africa in 2010."
4. Bond, *Elite Transition*, 254.
5. Ibid., 293; Bond, "South Africa's Frustrating Decade."
6. Naidoo, "Indigent Management."
7. Bond, *Elite Transition*, 303.
8. Turok, *Freedom Charter to Polokwane*, 245–70.
9. Bond, *Elite Transition*; Bond, "'ANC's 'Left Turn'"; Saul, *Next Liberation Struggle*, 173–94.
10. Arrighi, Aschoff, and Scully, "Accumulation by Dispossession"; Hart, *Disabling Globalization*, 290–313.
11. The pitfalls of theorizing dispossession from above are traced out in Martin, "Living in a Theoretical Interregnum."
12. *Economist*, "Thabo Mbeki."
13. Media profiling of President Zuma circulates around his multiple wives, lack of education, and allegations of rape and corruption—invariably accompanied by a picture of him in traditional, rural dress. As the *Economist* leads in one article: "Decked out in a leopard-skin mantle and an animal-pelt loincloth together with white designer sneakers, South Africa's 67-year-old president, Jacob Zuma, celebrated his marriage to his third concurrent wife (and fifth bride in all) in a grand Zulu ceremony attended by some 3,000 guests at his family home deep in rural KwaZulu-Natal" (January 7, 2010); see also the leading paragraph in "South Africa: It Needs an Opposition" (April 30, 2009). Or as *Newsweek* leads another report, allegations abound that he is "uneducated, corrupt and venal" (September 12, 2008).
14. Mkandawire, "Crisis Management."
15. Olukoshi, "State, Conflict, and Democracy," esp. 458–59.
16. See, for example, Bond, "South Africa's Frustrating Decade"; and Seekings and Nattrass, *Class, Race and Inequality*.
17. United Nations Conference on Trade and Development, *World Investment Report, 2011*.
18. On the spread of the foreign "land grab" phenomenon see Borras et al., "Global Land Grabbing"; GRAIN, *Seized*; and Zoomers, "Globalisation and Foreignisation." Zimbabwe remains an especially highly volatile and contested case among scholars. The most common conclusion is simply that the land invasions benefited the politically connected black elite while destroying the Zimbabwean economy. For the counter case see the work from the African Agrarian Institute in Harare (e.g., Moyo and Yeros, "After Zimbabwe"), which has empirically argued that

fast-track land reform on balance was a popular movement that benefited landless and land-poor Africans.

19. Hall, "Transforming Rural South Africa?" 87–88.

20. Marais, *South Africa*, 241–43; Southall, "Black Empowerment and Present Limits."

21. *Sunday Times*, April 6, 2003, 21.

22. There are several methods of estimating black control of the firms listed on the Johannesburg Stock Exchange, from counting the number of listed firms, to looking at share ownership, to the composition of boards of directors. Estimates vary widely, although a decline from the late 1990s is apparent. See "Counting Crumbs," *Financial Mail*, March 16, 2006; Southall, "Black Empowerment and Present Limits"; and Cargill, "Reassessing Objectives," which estimates that the market capitalization of companies listed on the Johannesburg exchange that are controlled by BEE shareholders reached a peak of 7 percent in 1998, and fell to less than 3 percent in 2010.

23. *Financial Mail*, February 7, 2003, 34.

24. Moleke, "Labour Market Deracialisation," 9.

25. Simkins, "What Happened?"

26. Bhorat, van der Westhuizen, and Jacobs, "Income and Non-Income Inequality."

27. Southall, "Introduction."

28. Mbeki, "I Am an African," "African Renaissance Statement," and "The African Renaissance, South Africa, and the World."

29. Vale and Maseko, "Thabo Mbeki."

30. Davies, "Regional Integration," 51–54. For statistical purposes "South Africa" is the SACU, which includes Botswana, Lesotho, Mozambique, Swaziland, Namibia, and South Africa; the region comprises SADC, that is, Angola, Botswana, DR Congo, Lesotho, Madagascar, Malawi, Mauritius, Mozambique, Namibia, South Africa, Swaziland, Tanzania, Zambia, and Zimbabwe; Seychelles, which was a member from 1997 to 2004, rejoined in 2008.

31. Buthelezi, "S.A.'s Role"; Cassim, Onyango, and Van Seventer, "State of Trade Policy," 123–31; Martin, "Africa's Futures."

32. Calculated from online data at South Africa, Department of Trade and Industry, "Trade Data," http://tradestats.thedti.gov.za/ReportFolders/reportFolders.aspx.

33. *Business Daily* (Nairobi), July 10, 2008.

34. Thomas, *South Africa's Foreign Direct Investment*, ix.

35. BusinessMap Foundation, "Mapping South Africa's Trade."

36. South African Reserve Bank, *Quarterly Bulletin*, March 2006, S101–S103. Estimates of South Africa's FDI in the rest of Africa vary quite widely among those who use project-based data versus those who rely on official capital flow data, e.g., between researchers (the Human Science Research Council, Business Map, South African Institute of International Affairs who track individual projects) and the South African Reserve Bank and international agencies who report and use aggregate data such as UNCTAD. See Thomas, *South Africa's Foreign Direct Investment*, 17–19, for the range of data.

37. South African Reserve Bank, *Quarterly Bulletin*, March 2010, S92–S95.

38. Gelb, "South African Firms Not 'Edgy.'"

39. Shoprite, "About Our Company: History."

40. MTN, "MTN Global Footprint."

41. *New York Times*, February 17, 2002.

42. Miller, "White Managers."

43. Ibid., 16.

44. Good and Hughes, "Globalisation and Diversification," 50.

45. McGowan and Ahwireng-Obeng, "Partner or Hegemon?"; Miller, "SA Corporations and Recolonisation"; Weeks, "Regional Cooperation."

46. Landsberg, "South Africa"; McGowan and Ahwireng-Obeng, "Partner or Hegemon?"; Bond, "South Africa's Frustrating Decade."

47. Taylor, "Changing Patterns of Labour Supply."

48. Keet, "Europe's Free Trade Plans"; Lee, "European Union–South Africa."

49. New Partnership for Africa's Development (NEPAD), "New Partnership."

50. Martin, "World-Economy and the African State," 282.

51. Bond, *Fanon's Warning*.

52. Adedeji, "From Lagos to Nepad."

53. Keet, *South Africa's Official Position* and "South Africa: The Bully Boy?"; on opposition, see Bond, *Fanon's Warning*.

54. Alden and Vieira, "New Diplomacy of the South."

55. Palat, "New Bandung?"

56. On neoracism see Balibar, "Is There a Neo-racism?"

57. For the prime case of the US and segregation, see the research of Massey and his coauthors, from Massey and Denton, *American Apartheid* to Rugh and Massey, "Racial Segregation and the American Foreclosure Crisis." For a more comparative and global treatment see Nightingale, *Segregation*.

58. "Never Too Late to Scramble," *Economist*, October 26, 2006; "Ravenous Dragon," *Economist*, March 15–21, 2008; Walt, "China's Africa Safari."

59. Broadman, *Africa's Silk Road*, 2.

60. Africa Progress Panel, *Africa Progress Report 2010*, 12.

61. Bajpaee, "Indian Elephant Returns to Africa."

62. Berger, "China Outwits the EU."

63. South African Department of Trade and Industry, "Trade Data."

64. Keet, "South-South Strategic Bases," 27.

65. Geda and Meskel, "China and India's Growth Surge."

66. Moreira, "Fear of China."

67. Rupp, "Africa and China."

68. See, for example, Rotberg, "China's Quest for Resources"; and Brautigam, *Dragon's Gift*, 307–12.

69. Sautman and Hairong. "Friends and Interests."

70. Arrighi, *Adam Smith in Beijing*.

71. Bello, "Toward a New American Isolationism."

72. Rocha, "New Frontier"; Askouri, "China's Investment in Sudan."

73. Mutesa, "China and Zambia," 176.

74. See, for example, Dikötter, *Discourse of Race* and *Construction of Racial Identities*; Dirlik, "Timespace, Social Space"; and Tanaka, *Japan's Orient*.

Bibliography

Archival Materials

South African National Archives, Pretoria (abbreviated "NA"). Main files used:

Advisory Board of Industry and Science (abbreviated BIS)
Archives and Evidence of Commissions of Inquiry:
    Economic and Wage Commission, 1925
    Native Economic Commission, 1930–32
    Customs and Tariff Commission, 1934–35
Board of Trade and Industries (abbreviated BTI)
Department of Commerce and Industries
Department of Customs and Excise
Department of Finance
Department of Mines and Industries
Holloway Accession

South African National Archives, Cape Town.

Association of Chambers of Commerce (abbreviated ASSOCOM)

Government Publications

South Africa. *Annual Statement of Trade and Shipping.* Pretoria: Government Printer, various years.
————. *Handbook of Agricultural Statistics, 1904–50.* Pretoria: Government Printer, 1961.
————. *Native Affairs Commission for the Years 1937–38.* UG 54/39. Pretoria: Government Printer, 1939.
————. *Debates of the House of Assembly,* Cape Town, various.
————. *Official Yearbook of the Union.* Pretoria: Government Printer, various years.
————. *Report of the Advisory Board of Industry and Science for the Year 1919.* UG 43/20. Cape Town: Government Printer, 1920.
————. *Report of the Commission appointed to inquire into the Conditions of Trade and Industries.* UG 10/12. Pretoria: Government Printer, 1912.
————. *Report of the Customs and Tariff Commission, 1934–35.* UG 6/36. Pretoria: Government Printer, 1936.

———. *Report of the Economic and Wage Commission (1925).* UG 14/26. Cape Town: Government Printer, 1926.

———. *Report of the Economic Commission.* UG 12/14. Pretoria: Government Printer, 1914.

———. *Report of the Industrial Legislation Commission.* UG 37/35. Pretoria: Government Printer, 1935.

———. *South African Statistics.* Pretoria: Government Printer, various years.

———. *Union Statistics for Fifty Years.* Pretoria: Government Printer, 1960.

South Africa. Board of Trade and Industries. "Report No. 46: South Africa and Imperial Preference." Pretoria, December 6, 1924.

———. "Report No. 48: Dumping Duty on Mozambique Cement." *South African Journal of Industry* 8 (July 1925): 417–20.

———. "Report No. 51: Report on the Revision of the Customs Tariff Together with the Proposed Customs Tariff Bill and the Revised Customs Tariff." Cape Town: Government Printer, 1925.

———. "Report No. 282: Investigation into Manufacturing Industries in the Union of South Africa." Cape Town: Cape Times Ltd., 1945.

———. "Report No. 2614: A Policy and Strategy for the Development and Structural Adjustment of Industry in the Republic of South Africa." Pretoria: Government Printer, 1988.

South Africa. Department of Commerce and Industry. "New Agreement: Official Comment." *Manufacturer,* July 1955, 21–23.

South Africa. Department of Trade and Industry. "A Guide to the Real Economy." Pretoria: Department of Trade and Industry, May 2002. Accessed June 23, 2003. http://www.dti.gov.za/newsandevents/publications.htm.

_____. South Africa. South African Railways and Harbours Administration. *Report of the Departmental Railway Tariffs Inquiry Committee, 1930.* UG 56/29. Pretoria: Government Printer, 1930.

———. *Report of the General Manager.* Pretoria: Government Printer, various years.

———. *Report of the Railway and Harbour Affairs Commission.* Pretoria: Government Printer, 1934.

South Africa. Statistics South Africa. *Census 2001.* http://www.statssa.gov.za/census01/html/C2001KeyResults.asp.

———. *Statistics South Africa 2005.* Pretoria: Government Printer, 2005.

South African Reserve Bank. *Quarterly Bulletin.* Pretoria: South African Reserve Bank, various years.

_____. "South Africa's Balance of Payments, 1946–2000." Pretoria: SARB, 2002.

South African Native Affairs Commission. *Report.* Cape Town: Cape Times Ltd., 1905.

Southern Rhodesia. *Annual Statement of the Trade of Southern Rhodesia.* Salisbury: Government Printer, various years.

———. *Official Yearbook No. 1, 1924.* Salisbury: Art Printing, 1924.

———. *Official Yearbook No. 2, 1930.* Salisbury: Rhodesian Printing and Publishing Co., 1930.

———. *Official Yearbook No. 3, 1932.* Salisbury: Rhodesian Printing and Publishing Co., 1932.

———. *Ottawa Conference: Report of the Committee Appointed to Investigate and Report to the Government.* Salisbury: Government Printer, 1932.

———. *Report of the Committee of Enquiry into the Protection of Secondary Industries in Southern Rhodesia.* Salisbury: Government Printer, 1946.
Transvaal. *Report of the Customs and Industries Commission.* TG 6/08. Pretoria: Government Printing Office, 1908.

Secondary Sources

Abedian, Iraj, and Barry Standish. *Economic Growth in South Africa: Selected Policy Issues.* Cape Town: Oxford University Press, 1992.
Adedeji, Adebayo. "From Lagos to Nepad." *New Agenda* 8 (2002): 32–47.
Africa Progress Panel. *Africa Progress Report, 2010.* Geneva, 2010. http://www.africaprogresspanel.org/en/our-work/publications/annual-report-2010/.
Ahwireng-Obeng, Fred, and Patrick J. McGowan. "Partner or Hegemon? South Africa in Africa: Part One." *Journal of Contemporary African Studies* 16, no. 1 (1998): 5–38.
Alden, Chris, and Marco Antonia Vieira. "The New Diplomacy of the South: South Africa, Brazil and Trilateralism." *Third World Quarterly* 26, no. 7 (2005): 1077–95.
Alexander, Peter. "Rebellion of the Poor: South Africa's Service Delivery Protests—a Preliminary Analysis." *Review of African Political Economy* 37, no. 123 (2010): 25–40.
Amin, Samir. *Accumulation on a World Scale.* 2 vols. New York: Monthly Review Press, 1974.
Anderson, Benedict. *Imagined Communities.* London: Verso, 1983.
Arndt, E. H. D., and C. S. Richards. "The Banking System of South Africa." In *Foreign Banking Systems,* edited by H. Parker Willis and B. H. Beckhart, 955–1010. New York: Henry Holt and Co., 1929.
Arrighi, Giovanni. *Adam Smith in Beijing: Lineages of the Twenty-First Century.* London: Verso, 2007.
———. *The Political Economy of Rhodesia.* The Hague: Mouton, 1967.
Arrighi, Giovanni, Nicole Aschoff, and Ben Scully. "Accumulation by Dispossession and Its Limits: The Southern Africa Paradigm Revisited." *Studies in Comparative International Development* 45 (2010): 410–38.
Arrighi, Giovanni, and Jessica Drangel. "The Stratification of the World-Economy: An Exploration of the Semiperipheral Zone." *Review* 10, no. 1 (1986): 9–74.
Arrighi, Giovanni, and Beverly Silver. "Labor Movements and Capital Migration: The United States and Western Europe in World-Historical Perspective." In *Labor in the Capitalist World-Economy,* edited by Charles Bergquist, 183–216. Beverly Hills, CA: Sage, 1984.
Askouri, Ali. 2007. "China's Investment in Sudan: Displacing Villages and Destroying Communities." In *African Perspectives on China in Africa,* edited by Firoze Manji and Stephen Marks, 71–86. Cape Town: Fahamu, 2007.
Atkinson, V. R. "Pan African Conference on Trade Relations Proposed." *Manufacturer,"* December 1956, 17–24.

Bajpaee, Chietigj. "The Indian Elephant Returns to Africa." *Asia Times,* April 25, 2008. http://www.atimes.com/atimes/South_Asia/JD25Dfo2.html.

Balibar, Etienne. 1991. "Is There a Neo-racism?" In *Race, Nation, Class,* coauthored by Etienne Balibar and Immanuel Wallerstein, 17–28. London: Verso, 1991.

Baran, Paul, and Paul Sweezy. *Monopoly Capital.* New York: Monthly Review Press, 1966.

Barber, James. *Mandela's World.* Athens: Ohio University Press, 2004.

———. *South Africa's Foreign Policy, 1945–1970.* London: Oxford University Press, 1973.

Barber, James, and John Barratt. *South Africa's Foreign Policy: The Search for Status and Security, 1945–1988.* Cambridge: Cambridge University Press, 1990.

Barnes, Justin, and Mike Morris. "The German Connection: Shifting Hegemony in the Political Economy of the South African Automotive Industry." *Industrial and Corporate Change* 13, no. 5 (2004): 789–814.

Baster, Albert S. J. *The Imperial Banks.* London: P. S. King, 1929.

Beittel, Mark. "The Witwatersrand: Black Households, White Households." In *Creating and Transforming Households: The Constraints of the World-Economy,* edited by Joan Smith, Immanuel Wallerstein, 197–230. Paris: Cambridge University Press/Éditions de la Maison des sciences de l'homme, 1992.

Bell, Trevor. "Should South Africa Further Liberalise Its Foreign Trade?" In *State and Market in Post-Apartheid South Africa,* edited by Merle Lipton and Charles Simkins, 81–127. Johannesburg: Witwatersrand University Press, 1993.

Bello, Walden. "Toward a New American Isolationism." *Foreign Policy in Focus,* September 5, 2008.

Berger, Bernt. "China Outwits the EU in Africa." *Asia Times,* December 13, 2007. http://www.atimes.com/atimes/China/IL13Ado1.html.

Bhorat, Haroon, Carlene van der Westhuizen, and Toughedah Jacobs. "Income and Non-Income Inequality in Post-Apartheid South Africa: What Are the Drivers and Possible Policy Interventions?" Development Policy Research Unit, DPRU Working Paper 09/138, August 2009.

Bienefeld, Manfred, and Duncan Innes. "Capital Accumulation and South Africa." *Review of African Political Economy* 7 (1976): 31–55.

Bienen, Henry. "Leaders, Violence, and the Absence of Change in Africa." *Political Science Quarterly* 108, no. 2 (1993): 271–82.

Black, Anthony. "Globalization and Restructuring in the South African Automotive Industry." *Journal of International Development* 13 (2001): 779–96.

———. "The Role of the State in Promoting Industrialisation." In *State and Market in Post-Apartheid South Africa,* edited by Merle Lipton and Charles Simpkins, 203–34. Johannesburg: University of the Witwatersrand Press, 1993.

Black, Anthony, and Shannon Mitchell. "Policy in the South African Motor Industry: Goals, Incentives, and Outcomes." Paper presented at the TIPS 2002 Annual Forum, Glenburn Lodge, Muldersdrift, South Africa, 2002.

Bonacich, Edna. "Capitalism and Race Relations in South Africa: A Split Labor Market Analysis." In *Political Power and Social Theory,* edited by Maurice Zeitlin, 239–77. Greenwich, CT: JAI Press, 1981.

Bond, Patrick. "The ANC's 'Left Turn' and South African Subimperialism." *Review of African Political Economy* 31, no. 102 (2004): 599–616.

———. *Elite Transition: From Apartheid to Neoliberalism in South Africa.* Scottsville, South Africa: University of KwaZulu-Natal Press, 2005.

———, ed. *Fanon's Warning: A Civil Society Reader on the New Partnership for Africa's Development.* Trenton, NJ: Africa World Press, 2002.

———. "From Racial to Class Apartheid: South Africa's Frustrating Decade of Freedom" *Monthly Review* 55, no. 10 (2004): 45–59.

Bonilla-Silva, Eduardo. "Race in the World System." *Du Bois Review* 1 (2004): 189–94.

Bonner, P. L. "The 1920 Black Mineworkers' Strike: A Preliminary Account." In *Labour, Townships and Protest*, edited by Belinda Bozzoli, 273–97. Johannesburg: Ravan Press, 1979.

Borras, Saturnino M., Jr., Ruth Hall, Ian Scoones, Ben White, and Wendy Wolford. "Towards a Better Understanding of Global Land Grabbing: An Editorial Introduction." *Journal of Peasant Studies* 38, no. 2 (2011): 209–16.

Botha, D. J. "On Tariff Policy: The Formative Years." *South African Journal of Economics* 41, no. 4 (1973): 321–55.

Bowen, Merle. *The State against the Peasantry: Rural Struggles in Colonial and Postcolonial Mozambique.* Charlottesville: University Press of Virginia, 2000.

Bradford, Helen. *A Taste of Freedom: The ICU in Rural South Africa, 1924–1930.* Johannesburg: Ravan Press, 1987.

Brandt, Willy. *North-South: A Program for Survival. Independent Commission on International Development Issues.* Cambridge, MA: MIT Press, 1980.

Bratton, Michael, and Nicholas van de Walle. "Neopatrimonial Regimes and Political Transitions in Africa." *World Politics* 46 (1994): 453–89.

Brautigam, Deborah. *The Dragon's Gift: The Real Story of China in Africa.* Oxford: Oxford University Press, 2009.

Broadman, Harry G. *Africa's Silk Road: China and India's New Economic Frontier.* Washington, DC: World Bank, 2007.

Brown, Ian, ed. *The Economies of Africa and Asia during the Inter-war Depression.* London: Routledge, 1989.

Brown, Mercy, David Kaplan, and Jean-Baptiste Meyer. "Counting Brains: Measuring Emigration from South Africa." Development Policy Research Unit, University of Cape Town. 2001. Accessed June 6, 2008. http://www.queensu.ca/samp/publications/policybriefs/brief5.pdf.

Bruwer, A. J. "The Board of Trade and Industries." *Journal of the Economic Society of South Africa* 1, no. 1 (1927): 35.

———. *Protection in South Africa.* Stellenbosch: Pro Ecclesia, 1923.

Buhlungu, Sakhela, John Daniel, Roger Southall, and Jessica Lutchman, eds. *The State of the Nation, 2005–2006.* Pretoria: HSRC, 2006.

Bundy, Colin. "The Emergence and Decline of a South African Peasantry." *African Affairs* 71 (1972): 369–88.

———. *The Rise and Fall of a South African Peasantry.* Berkeley: University of California Press, 1979.

Burn, Duncan. *The Steel Industry, 1939–1959.* Cambridge: Cambridge University Press, 1961.

Business Map Foundation. "Mapping South Africa's Trade and Investment in the Region." June 2004. Accessed May 12, 2005. http://www.businessmap.org.za/documents.asp?DID=1416.

Buthelezi, Sipho. "S.A.'s Role in Africa's Economic Recovery." *New Agenda* 9 (2003): 104–11.

Campbell, Alexander. "The Queue for Capital." *Manufacturer*, October 1950, 39–41.

Campbell, Horace. *Reclaiming Zimbabwe: The Exhaustion of the Patriarchal Model of Liberation.* Trenton, NJ: Africa World Press, 2004.

Cargill, Jenny. "Reassessing Objectives." *Financial Mail*, June 3–4, 2010.

Carrington, William J., and Enrica Detragiache. "How Extensive Is the Brain Drain?" *Finance and Development* 36, no. 3 (1999): 46–49.

Cassim, Rashad, Donald Onyango, and Dirk Ernst Van Seventer. *The State of Trade Policy in South Africa.* Johannesburg: Trade and Industrial Policy Strategies (TIPS), 2002. http://www.acp-eu-trade.org/library/files/Cassim-Onyango-Van-Seventer_EN_2002_TIPS_Trade-policy-South-Africa.pdf.

Chanock, Martin. *Unconsummated Union.* Manchester: Manchester University Press, 1977.

Cheru, Fantu, and Cyril Obi, eds. *The Rise of China and India in Africa.* New York: Zed, 2010.

Choles, H. J. "The South African Boot and Shoe Industry: An Industry with Great Possibilities in Danger of Extinction." *South African Journal of Industry* 14 (1921): 206–17.

Christie, Renfrew. *Electricity, Industry, and Class in South Africa.* Albany: State University of New York Press, 1984.

Clark, Nancy. *Manufacturing Apartheid: State Corporations in South Africa.* New Haven, CT: Yale University Press, 1994.

———. "South African State Corporations: 'The Death Knell of Economic Colonialism'?" *Journal of Southern African Studies* 14, no. 1 (1987): 98–122.

Clegg, W. H. "Central Banking in South Africa." *Economic Journal* 39 (1929): 521–35.

Clemons, Michael, and Charles E. Jones. "Global Solidarity: The Black Panther Party in the International Arena." In *Liberation, Imagination, and the Black Panther Party*, edited by Kathleen Cleaver and George Katsiaficas, 20–39. New York: Routledge, 2001.

Cliffe, Lionel. "Complex Political Emergencies and the State: Failure and the Fate of the State." *Third World Quarterly* 20, no. 1 (1999): 27–50.

Crush, Jonathan. "Mine Migrancy in the Contemporary Era." In *Crossing Boundaries: Mine Migrancy in a Democratic South Africa*, edited by Jonathan Crush and Wilmot James, 14–32. Cape Town: Institute for Democracy in South Africa, 1995.

———. "The Southern African Regional Formation: A Geographical Perspective." *Tijdschrift voor Economische en Sociale Geografie* 73 (1982): 200–212.

Crush, Jonathan, and Charles Mather. *Borderline Farming: Foreign Migrants in South African Commercial Agriculture.* Cape Town: IDASA, 2000.

Crush, Jonathan, Theresa Ulicki, Teke Tseane, and Elizabeth Jansen van Vuuren. "Undermining Labour: The Rise of Sub-Contracting in the South African Gold Mines." *Journal of Southern African Studies* 27, no. 1 (2001): 5–31.

Crush, Jonathan, and Vincent Williams. *Transnationalism and African Immigration to South Africa.* Southern African Migration Project, Migration Policy Brief No. 9. Queens University (Kingston), 2002.

Crush, Jonathan, and Wade Pendleton. *Regionalizing Xenophobia? Citizen Attitudes to Immigration and Refugee Policy in Southern Africa.* SAMP Migration Policy Series No. 30. Cape Town: IDASA, 2004.

Dalgaard, Bruce Ronald. "South Africa's Impact on Britain's Return to Gold, 1925." PhD diss., University of Illinois at Urbana-Champaign, 1976.

Davenport, T. R. H. *South Africa: A Modern History.* London: Macmillan, 1991.

Davidson, Basil. *The Black Man's Burden: Africa and the Curse of the Nation-State.* New York: Times Books, 1992.

Davies, Robert. *Capital, State and White Labour in South Africa, 1900–1960.* Atlantic Highlands, NJ: Humanities Press, 1979.

———. "Regional Integration." In *Regional Integration in Southern Africa: Comparative International Perspectives,* edited by Jonathan Crush and Wilmot James, 51–54. Johannesburg: South African Institute of International Affairs, 2001.

Davies, Robert, and Judith Head. "The Future of Mine Migrancy in the Context of Broader Trends in Migration in Southern Africa, *Journal of Southern African Studies* 21, no. 3 (1995): 439–50.

Davies, Robert, David Kaplan, Mike Morris, and Dan O'Meara. "Class Struggle and the Periodisation of the State in South Africa." *Review of African Political Economy* 11, no. 3 (1978): 4–30.

Day, A. C. L. "The South African Commercial Banks." In *Banking in the British Commonwealth,* edited by R. S. Sayers, 350–71. Oxford: Clarendon Press, 1952.

———. "The South African Reserve Bank." In *Banking in the British Commonwealth,* edited by Jonathan Crush and Wilmot James, 372–400. Oxford: Clarendon Press, 1952.

de Bragança, Aquino. "Indepéndencia sem descolonização: A transferência de poder em Moçambique." *Estudos Mozambicanos* 5–6 (1981): 7–28.

de Kiewiet, C. W. *A History of South Africa, Social and Economic.* London: Oxford University Press, 1941.

de Kock, Gerhard. *A History of the South African Reserve Bank (1920–1952).* Pretoria: J. L. van Schaik, 1954.

de Kock, Michiel Hendrik. *An Analysis of the Finances of the Union of South Africa.* Cape Town: Juta, 1927.

———. *The Results of Government Ownership in South Africa.* Cape Town: Juta, 1922.

———. *Selected Subjects in the Economic History of South Africa.* Cape Town, Juta, 1924.

De Loor, Johannes Hendrikus. "American and South African Experience in the Producing and Selling of Portland Cement." PhD diss., Columbia University, 1955.

Desai, Ashwin. *We Are the Poors: Community Struggles in Post-Apartheid South Africa.* New York: Monthly Review Press, 2002.

Desai, Ashwin, and Richard Pithouse. "'But We Were Thousands': Dispossession, Resistance, Repossession and Repression in Mandela Park." *Journal of Asian and African Studies* 39, no. 4 (2004): 239–69.

de Villiers, Derek, and Mark Anstey. "Trade Unions in Transition to Democracy in South Africa, Spain and Brazil." In *Trade Unions and Democratization in South Africa, 1985–1997,* edited by Glen Adler and Eddie Webster, 20–41. Johannesburg: University of the Witwatersrand Press, 2000.

Dikötter, Frank, ed. *The Construction of Racial Identities in China and Japan: Historical and Contemporary Perspectives.* Honolulu: University of Hawai'i Press, 1997.

———. *The Discourse of Race in Modern China.* Stanford: Stanford University Press, 1992.

Dirlik, Arif. "Timespace, Social Space, and the Question of Chinese Culture." *boundary 2* 35, no. 1 (2008): 1–22.

Doxey, George Victor. *The Industrial Colour Bar in South Africa.* Cape Town: Oxford University Press, 1961.

Dreijmanis, John. *The Role of the South African Government in University Education.* Johannesburg: South African Institute of Race Relations, 1988.

Economist. "Never Too Late to Scramble." October 26, 2006. http://www.economist.com/world/mideast-africa/displaystory.cfm?story_id=E1_RDRJSTJ.

———. "A Ravenous Dragon: A Special Report on China's Quest for Resources." March 13, 2008. http://www.economist.com/specialreports/displaystory.cfm?story_id=10795714.

———. "Thabo Mbeki: A Man of Two Faces." January 20, 2005. http://www.economist.com/node/3576543.

Edmondson, Locksley. "The Internationalization of Black Power: Historical and Contemporary Perspectives." *Mawazo* 4, no. 1 (1968): 16–30.

Emmanuel, Arghiri. "White Settler Colonialism and the Myth of Investment Imperialism." *New Left Review* 73 (1972): 35–57.

Ettinger, Stephen. "South Africa's Weight Restrictions on Cattle Exports from Bechuanaland, 1924–41." *Botswana Notes and Records* 4 (1972): 21–33.

Fine, Ben. "Privatisation and the Restructuring of State Assets in South Africa: A Strategic View." National Institute for Economic Policy Occasional Paper Series, No. 7, March 1997.

Fine, Ben, and Zavareh Rustomjee. *The Political Economy of South Africa: From Minerals-Energy Complex to Industrialisation.* London: Westview, 1996.

Fine, Jack, and William Bird. *Shades of Prejudice: An Investigation into the South African Media's Coverage of Racial Violence and Xenophobia.* Braamfontein: Centre for the Study of Violence and Reconciliation, 2006.

Flatters, Frank. "The Economics of MIDP and the South African Motor Industry." Paper prepared for TIPS/NEDLAC workshop, Johannesburg, November 2, 2005.

Frankel, S. Herbert. *Co-operation and Competition in the Marketing of Maize in South Africa.* London: P. S. King, 1926.

———. *Investment and the Return to Equity Capital in the South African Gold Mining Industry 1877–1965.* Cambridge, MA: Harvard University Press, 1967.

———. *The Railway Policy of South Africa: An Analysis of the Effects of Railway Rates, Finance, and Management on the Economic Development of the Union.* Johannesburg: Hortors, 1928.

Freund, Bill. "Defending South African Capitalism." *Transformation* 3 (1987): 33–50.

———. "The Social Character of Secondary Industry in South Africa, 1915–1945." Paper presented at the African Studies Seminar, African Studies Institute, University of the Witwatersrand, April 22, 1985.

Garmany, J. W. "The Economic Growth of Southern Rhodesia." *South African Bankers' Journal,* February 1954, 435–40.

Geda, Alemayehu, and Atnafu G. Meskel. "China and India's Growth Surge: The Implications for African Manufactured Exports." In Cheru and Obi, *Rise of China and India*, 97–106.

Gelb, Stephen. "Making Sense of the Crisis." *Transformation* 5 (1987): 33–50.

———. "The Origins of the South African Reserve Bank." Paper presented at the African Studies Seminar, African Studies Institute, University of the Witwatersrand, September 17, 1984.

———. "South African Firms Not 'Edgy' about Africa." *Business Day*, June 9, 2006.

———, ed. *South Africa's Economic Crisis*. Cape Town: David Philip, 1991.

Gevisser, Mark. *Thabo Mbeki: The Dream Deferred*. Johannesburg: Jonathan Ball, 2010.

Gibson, Nigel C., ed. *Challenging Hegemony: Social Movements and the Quest for a New Humanism in Post-Apartheid South Africa*. Trenton, NJ: Africa World Press, 2006.

Glaser, Darryl, ed. *Mbeki and After: Reflections on the Legacy of Thabo Mbeki*. Johannesburg: University of the Witwatersrand Press, 2010.

Goldberg, David Theo. *The Racial State*. London: Blackwell, 2002.

Good, Kenneth, and Skye Hughes. "Globalisation and Diversification: Two Cases in Southern Africa." *African Affairs* 101 (2002): 39–59.

Goodhand, Jonathan, and David Hulme. "From Wars to Complex Political Emergencies: Understanding Conflict and Peace-Building in the New World Disorder." *Third World Quarterly* 20, no. 1 (1999): 13–26.

Gott, Richard. "Latin America as a White Settler Society." *Bulletin of Latin American Research* 26, no. 2 (2007): 269–89.

GRAIN. *Seized: The 2008 Land Grab for Food and Financial Security*. Barcelona: GRAIN, 2008.

Green, L. O., and T. J. D. Fair. *Development in Africa*. Johannesburg: University of the Press, 1962.

Gumede, William M. *Thabo Mbeki and the Battle for the Soul of the ANC*. London: Zed Books, 2007.

Gurney, Christabel. "'A Great Cause': The Origins of the Anti-Apartheid Movement, June 1959–March 1960." *Journal of Southern African Studies* 26, no. 1 (2000): 123–44.

Hall, Ruth. "Transforming Rural South Africa? Taking Stock of Land Reform." In *The Land Question in South Africa: The Challenge of Transformation and Redistribution*, edited by Lungisile Ntsebeza and Ruth Hall, 87–106. Cape Town: HSRC, 2007.

Handley, Antoinette. "Business, Government and Economic Policymaking in the New South Africa, 1990–2000." *Journal of Modern African Studies* 43 (2005): 211–39.

Hanlon, Joseph. *Beggar Your Neighbours: Apartheid Power in Southern Africa*. London: Zed Press, 1986.

Harper, F. Gordon. "Big Industrial Boom Building Up." *Industrial Review of Africa*, November 1959, 51–53.

———. "The CAF Looks at Its New Railway Line—and Likes It." *Manufacturer*, December 1955, 13.

———. "Federation Must Provide Facilities for Training Own Technicians." *Industrial Review of Africa*, June 1956, 38–41.

———. "150 Million Customers." *Manufacturer*, July 1959, 13–15.

Harris, S. E. *Monetary Problems of the British Empire*. New York: Macmillan, 1931.

Hart, Gillian. *Disabling Globalization: Places of Power in Post-Apartheid South Africa.* Berkeley: University of California Press, 2002.

Henry, J. A. *The First Hundred Years of the Standard Bank.* London: Oxford University Press, 1963.

Hentz, James Jude. "The Two Faces of Privatisation: Political and Economic Logics in Transitional South Africa." *Journal of Modern African Studies* 38, no. 2 (2000): 203–23.

Hexner, Ervin. *The International Steel Cartel.* Chapel Hill: University of North Carolina Press, 1943.

Hindson, Doug. *Pass Controls and the Urban African Proletariat.* Johannesburg: Ravan Press, 1987.

———. "The Pass System and the Formation of an Urban African Proletariat in South Africa: A Critique of the Cheap Labour–Power Thesis in South Africa." PhD diss., University of Sussex, 1983.

Hirschman, Albert O. *National Power and the Structure of Foreign Trade.* Berkeley: University of California Press, 1980.

Hirsh, Alan. "From GATT to WTO: The Global Trade Regime and Its Implications for South Africa." In *South Africa in the Global Economy*, edited by Greg Mills, Alan Begg, and Anthoni van Nieuwkerk, 41–55. Johannesburg: South African Institute of International Affairs, 1995.

Hopkins, Terence K. "The Study of the Capitalist World-Economy: Some Introductory Considerations." In *World-Systems Analysis: Theory and Methodology*, edited by Terence K. Hopkins and Immanuel Wallerstein, 9–38. Beverly Hills, CA: Sage, 1982.

Horrell, Muriel. *Bantu Education to 1968.* Johannesburg: South African Institute of Race Relations, 1969.

Horwitz, Ralph. *The Political Economy of South Africa.* London: Weidenfeld and Nicolson, 1967.

Human Sciences Research Council (HSRC). *Flight of the Flamingoes: A Study on the Mobility of R&D Workers.* Cape Town: HSRC, 2004.

Huntington, Samuel P. "Reform and Stability in South Africa." *International Security* 6, no. 4 (1982): 3–25.

———. *The Third Wave: Democratization in the Late Twentieth Century.* Norman: University of Oklahoma Press, 1991.

Hutt, D. H. *The Economics of the Colour Bar.* London: Andre Deutsch, 1964.

Hyam, Ronald. *The Failure of South African Expansionism, 1908–1948.* New York: Africana, 1972.

Hyslop, Jonathan. "The Imperial Working Class Makes Itself 'White': White Labourism in Britain, Australia, and South Africa before the First World War." Journal of Historical Sociology 12, no. 4 (1999): 398–421.

Jagger, J. W. "The Board of Trade and Industries." *Journal of the Economic Society of South Africa* 1, no. 2 (1927): 35–38.

Jeal, Edward F. "Can Rhodesia Capture the African Market?" *Commercial Opinion*, February 1956, 387–92.

———. "Investment Capital in Short Supply." *Commercial Opinion*, May 1950, 7–22.

———. "Trade and Tariff in Africa." *Commercial Opinion*, February 1954, 412–17.

———. "Trends in South Africa's Trade with the World." *Commercial Opinion*, December 1954, 330–56.

Jeeves, Alan. *Migrant Labour in South Africa's Mining Economy.* Kingston: McGill-Queens University Press, 1986.

John, Nerys. "The Campaign against the British Bank Involvement in Apartheid South Africa." *African Affairs* 99 (2000): 415–33.

Johnstone, Frederick. *Class, Race and Gold.* London: Routledge and Kegan Paul, 1976.

Jones, Colonel R. "Union Manufacturers Meet Overseas Competition." *Manufacturer*, October 1953, 31–33.

Jones, F. Stuart. "Business Imperialism and the Imperial Banks in South Africa." *South African Journal of Economics* 66, no. 1 (1998): 67–90.

Jones, Stuart, and André Müller. *The South African Economy.* London: Macmillan, 1992.

Kanduza, Ackson. *The Political Economy of Underdevelopment in Northern Rhodesia, 1918–1960.* Lanham, MD: University Press of America, 1986.

Kaplan, David. "The Politics of Industrial Protection in South Africa, 1910–1939." *Journal of Southern African Studies* 3, no. 1 (1976): 70–91.

Kaplan, Robert D. "The Coming Anarchy: How Scarcity, Crime, Overpopulation, Tribalism, and Disease Are Rapidly Destroying the Social Fabric of Our Planet." *Atlantic Monthly* 273, no. 2 (1994): 44–76.

Kapp, P. H. "The Historical Experience." In *United States and South African Relations: Past, Present, Future,* edited by P. H. Kapp and G. C. Olivier, 1–23. Cape Town: Tafelberg Publishers, 1987.

Katzen, Leo. *Gold and the South African Economy.* Cape Town: A. A. Balkema, 1964.

Katzenellenbogen, Simon. *South Africa and Southern Mozambique: Labour, Railroads, and Trade in the Making of a Relationship.* Manchester: Manchester University Press, 1982.

Keegan, Tim. "Restructuring Class Relations in a Colonial Economy: The Orange River Colony, 1902–1910." *Journal of Southern African Studies* 5, no. 2 (1979): 234–54.

Keet, Dot. "Europe's Free Trade Plans with South Africa: Strategic Responses from and Challenges to South and Southern Africa." *Development Southern Africa* 14, no. 2 (1997): 285–93.

———. *South Africa's Official Position and Role in Promoting the World Trade Organisation.* Mowbray, South Africa: Alternative Information and Development Center, 2002.

———. "South Africa: The Bully Boy?" *South Africa Labour Bulletin* 27, no. 3 (2003): 27–29.

———. "South-South Strategic Bases for Africa to Engage China." In Cheru and Obi, *Rise of China and India,* 21–33.

Kelley, D. G. "Stormy Weather: Reconstructing Black (Inter)Nationalism in the Cold War Era." In *Is It Nation Time?*, edited by Eddie S. Claude Jr., 67–90. Chicago: University of Chicago Press, 2002.

Kentridge, M. *Turning the Tanker: The Economic Debate in South Africa.* Johannesburg: Centre for Policy Studies, 1993.

Kindleberger, Charles P. *The World in Depression, 1929–1939.* Berkeley: University of California Press, 1973.

Korzeniewicz, Roberto Patricio, and Timonthy Moran. *Unveiling Inequality: A World Historical Perspective.* New York: Russell Sage Foundation, 2009.

———. "World-Economic Trends in the Distribution of Income, 1965–1992." *American Journal of Sociology* 102 (1997): 1000–1039.

Kramer, Paul A. "Empires, Exceptions, and Anglo-Saxons: Race and Rule between the British and United States Empires, 1880–1910." *Journal of American History* 88, no. 4 (2002): 315–53.

Kubicek, R. V. *Economic Imperialism in Theory and Practice: The Case of South African Gold Mining Finance, 1886–1914.* Durham, NC: Duke University Press, 1979.

Labour Research Service. *The LRS Report: Bargaining Indicators for 2003.* Vol. 8. Cape Town: Labour Research Service, March 2003.

Lacey, Marian. *Working for Boroko.* Johannesburg: Ravan Press, 1981.

Laite, W. J. *The Union Tariff and Its Relation to Industrial and Agricultural Development: The Case for Manufacturers.* Cape Town: South African Manufacturers Association, 1913.

Landsberg, Chris. "South Africa: A Pivotal State in Africa." *Synopsis: Policy Studies Bulletin* 7, no. 1 (2004): 1–3.

Lee, Margaret C. "The European Union–South Africa Free Trade Agreement: In Whose Interest?" *Journal of Contemporary African Studies* 20, no. 1 (2002): 81–106.

León, Javier, and Raimundo Soto. "Structural Breaks and Long-Run Trends in Commodity Prices." *Journal of International Development* 9 (1997): 347–66.

Levy, Norman. *The Foundations of the South African Cheap Labour System.* Boston: Routledge and Kegan Paul, 1982.

Lewis, Jon. *Industrialisation and Trade Union Organisation in South Africa, 1924–55.* Cambridge: Cambridge University Press, 1984.

———. "The New Unionism: Industrialisation and Industrial Unions in South Africa, 1925–1930." *South African Labour Bulletin* 3, no. 5 (1977): 25–49.

Lewis, W. A. *Growth and Fluctuations, 1870–1913.* London: Allen and Unwin, 1978.

Lipton, Merle. *Capitalism and Apartheid.* London: Weidenfeld and Nicolson, 1985.

Lodge, Tom. *Politics in South Africa: From Mandela to Mbeki.* Cape Town: David Philip, 2002.

Lodge, Tom, and Bill Nasson. *All, Here and Now: Black Politics in South Africa in the 1980s.* Cape Town: D. Philip, 1991.

Louw, Eric M. "Foreign Control of South African Enterprises." *Commercial Opinion,* August 1958, 14–15.

———. "The Rôle of Foreign Capital in the South African Economy." *Finance and Trade Review* 2, no. 1 (1956): 3–12.

Mafeje, Archie. "The Ideology of 'Tribalism.'" *Journal of Modern African Studies* 9 (1971): 353–61.

Magubane, Bernard. "A Critical Look at Indices of Social Change." *Current Anthropology* 12 (1971): 419–45.

———. *The Making of a Racist State: British Imperialism and the Union of South Africa, 1875–1910.* Trenton, NJ: Africa World Press, 1996.

Makgetla, Neva Seidman. "The International Economic Crisis and Employment in South Africa." In *New South Africa Review 1, 2010: Development or Decline?*, edited by John Daniel, Prishani Naidoo, Devan Pillay, and Roger Southall, 65–103. Johannesburg: University of the Witwatersrand Press, 2010.

Mamdani, Mahmood. *Citizen and Subject: Contemporary Africa and the Legacy of Late Colonialism.* Princeton, NJ: Princeton University Press, 1996.

———. *When Victims Become Killers: Colonialism, Nativism, and the Genocide in Rwanda.* Princeton, NJ: Princeton University Press, 2001.

Martin, William G. "Africa's Futures: From North-South to East-South?" *Third World Quarterly* 29, no. 2 (2008): 339–56.

———. "Cycles, Trends or Transformations: Black Labor Migration to the South African Gold Mines." In *Labor in the Capitalist World-Economy*, edited by Charles Bergquist, 157–79. Beverly Hills, CA: Sage, 1984.

———. "Developmentalism, the Pernicious Illusion: A Response to Renfrew Christie's 'Antiquated Industrialisation.'" *International Journal of African Historical Studies* 24, no. 3 (1992): 609–17.

———. "Lesotho: The Creation of Households." In *Creating and Transforming Households: The Constraints of the World-Economy*, edited by Joan Smith, Immanuel Wallerstein, 231–49. Cambridge: Cambridge University Press, 1992.

———. "Living in a Theoretical Interregnum: Capital Lessons from Southern African Rural History." Paper presented at the Rural Development: Retrospect and Prospect conference, Centre for Economic Studies and Planning, Jawaharlal Nehru University, March 5–6, 2012, New Delhi.

———. "Region Formation under Crisis Conditions: South vs. Southern Africa in the Interwar Period." *Journal of Southern African Studies* 16, no. 1 (March 1990): 112–38.

———, ed. *Semiperipheral States in the World-Economy.* Westport, CT: Greenwood Press, 1989.

———. "Southern Africa and the World-Economy: Regionality and Trade Regimes." In How Fast the Wind?: South Africa, 1975–2000, edited by Sergio Vieira, William G. Martin, and Immanuel Wallerstein, 33–82. Trenton, NJ: Africa World Press, 1992.

———. "The World-Economy and the African State." In *Borders, Nationalism, and the African State*, edited by Ricardo Laremont, 277–313. Boulder, CO: Lynne Rienner, 2005.

Martin, William G., and Michael O. West, eds. *Out of One, Many Africas: Reconstructing the Study and Meaning of Africa.* Champaign: University of Illinois Press, 1999.

Massey, Douglas S., and Nancy A Denton. *American Apartheid: Segregation and the Making of the Underclass.* Cambridge, MA: Harvard University Press, 1993.

Maxfield, Sylvia. *Gatekeepers of Growth: The International Political Economy of Central Banking in Developing Countries.* Princeton, NJ: Princeton University Press, 1997.

Mbeki, Thabo. "The African Renaissance Statement of Deputy President." Speech at the Gallagher Estate, August 13, 1998. http://www.dfa.gov.za/docs/speeches/1998/mbeko813.htm.

———. "The African Renaissance, South Africa, and the World." Tokyo: Public Affairs Section, United Nations University, 1998.

————. "I Am an African." Speech, May 8, 1996. Accessed June 23, 2010. http://www.anc.org.za/ancdocs/history/mbeki/1996/sp960508.html.

McDonald, David, and Jonathan Crush, eds. *Destinations Unknown: Perspectives on the Brain Drain in Southern Africa.* Pretoria: Africa Institute of South Africa, 2002.

McDonald, David, and Sean Jacobs. *Understanding Press Coverage of Cross-Border Migration since 2000.* Southern African Migration Project. Cape Town: IDASA, 2004.

McGowan, Patrick J., and Fred Ahwireng-Obeng. "Partner or Hegemon? South Africa in Africa, Part Two." *Journal of Contemporary African Studies* 16, no. 2 (1998): 165–95.

Mignolo, Walter. *Local Histories, Global Designs: Coloniality, Subaltern Knowledges, and Border Thinking.* Princeton, NJ: Princeton University Press, 2000.

Miller, Darlene. "SA Corporations and Recolonisation." *South African Labour Bulletin* 24, no. 5 (2000): 14–19.

————. "White Managers and the African Renaissance: A 'Retail Renaissance' or a New Colonial Encounter at South African Companies in Foreign, African Countries." Paper presented at the CODESRIA Eleventh General Assembly, Maputo, December 2005.

Minter, William. *King Solomon's Mines Revisited: Western Interests and the Burdened History of Southern Africa.* New York: Basic Books, 1986.

Mitchell, Brian R. *International Historical Statistics: Africa and Asia.* New York: New York University Press, 1982.

Mitchie, Jonathan, and Vishnu Padayachee, eds. *The Political Economy of South Africa's Transition.* London: Dryden Press, 1997.

Mkandawire, Thandika. "Crisis Management and the Making of 'Choiceless Democracies.'" In *State, Conflict, and Democracy in Africa,* edited by Richard Joseph, 119–36. Boulder, CO: Lynne Rienner, 1999.

Mkandawire, Thandika, and Charles C. Soludo. *Our Continent, Our Future: African Perspectives on Structural Adjustment.* Trenton, NJ: Africa World Press, 1999.

Mlambo, A. S., E. S. Pangeti, and I. Phimister, eds. *Zimbabwe: A History of Manufacturing, 1890–1995,* Harare: University of Zimbabwe Publications, 2000.

Moleke, Percy. "The State of Labour Market Deracialisation." In Buhlungu et al., *State of the Nation,* 202–22.

Moll, T. "Macroeconomic Policy in Turbulent Times." In *State and Market in Post-Apartheid South Africa,* edited by Merle Lipton and Charles Simkins, 234–69. Johannesburg: University of the Witwatersrand Press, 1993.

Moodie, T. Dunbar. "The South African State and Industrial Conflict in the 1940s." *International Journal of African Historical Studies* 21, no. 1 (1998): 21–61.

Moreira, Mauricio Mesquita. "Fear of China: Is There a Future for Manufacturing in Latin America?" *World Development* 35, no. 3 (2007): 355–76.

Morrell, Robert. "The Disintegration of the Gold and Maize Alliance in South Africa in the 1920s." *International Journal of African Historical Studies* 21, no. 4 (1988): 619–35.

Moyo, Sam, and Paris Yeros. "After Zimbabwe: State, Nation and Region in Africa." In *Reclaiming the Nation: The Return of the National Question in Africa, Asia and*

Latin America, edited by Sam Moyo and Paris Yeros, 31–53. New York: Pluto Press, 2011.

MTN. "MTN Global Footprint." 2012. http://www.mtn.com/MTNGROUP/Pages/CompanyProfile.aspx.

Murray, Colin. *Families Divided*. Johannesburg: Ravan Press, 1981.

Mutesa, Fredrick. "China and Zambia: Between Development and Politics." In Cheru and Obi, *Rise of China and India*, 167–78.

Naidoo, Prishani. "Indigent Management: A Strategic Response to the Struggles of the Poor in Post-apartheid South Africa." In *New South Africa Review 1, 2010: Development or Decline?*, edited by John Daniel, Prishani Naidoo, Devan Pillay, and Roger Southall, 185–204. Johannesburg: University of the Witwatersrand Press, 2010.

Nattrass, Jill. *The South African Economy*. Cape Town: Oxford University Press, 1981.

Nattrass, Nicoli. "The State of the Economy: A Crisis of Employment." In *State of the Nation: South Africa, 2003–2004*, edited by John Daniel, Adam Habib, and Roger Southall, 141–57. Pretoria: HSRC, 2003.

Newitt, Malyn D. D. *Portugal in Africa*. London: Longmans, 1981.

New Partnership for Africa's Development. "The New Partnership for Africa's Development (NEPAD) Is a Vision and Strategic Framework for Africa's Renewal." Abuja, Nigeria: NEPAD, October 2001.

Ngwane, Trevor. "South Africa in 2010: A History That Must Happen." Pambazuka News, no. 502, October 28, 2010. http://pambazuka.org/en/category/features/68169.

Nightingale, Carl Husemoller. *Segregation: A Global History of Divided Cities*. Chicago: University of Chicago Press, 2012.

Olukoshi, Adebayo. "State, Conflict, and Democracy in Africa: The Complex Process of Renewal." In *State, Conflict, and Democracy in Africa*, edited by Richard Joseph, 451–65. Boulder, CO: Lynne Rienner, 1999.

O'Meara, Dan. *Forty Lost Years: The Apartheid State and the Politics of the National Party, 1948–1994*. Athens: Ohio University Press, 1996.

———. *Volkskapitalisme: Class, Capital and Ideology in the Development of Afrikaner Nationalism, 1934–1948*. Johannesburg: Ravan Press, 1983.

Organisation for Economic Co-operation and Development (OECD). "The International Mobility of Health Professionals: An Evaluation and Analysis Based on the Case of South Africa." Paris: OECD, 2003.

———. *World Health Report, 2006*. Geneva: OECD, 2006.

Padayachee, Vishnu. "Central Bank Transformation in a Globalized World: The Reserve Bank in the Post-Apartheid South Africa." *Journal of International Development* 13 (2000): 741–65.

———. "The Evolution of South Africa's International Financial Relations and Policy, 1985–1995." In *The Political Economy of South Africa's Transition*, edited by Jonathan Mitchie and Vishnu Padayachee, 27–53. London: Dryden Press, 1997.

Palat, Ravi. "A New Bandung?: Economic Growth vs. Distributive Justice among Emerging Powers." *Journal of Futures*, doi:10.1016/j.futures.2008.02.004.

Palmer, G. F. D. "New Barriers to Trade in Southern Africa." *Manufacturer*, July 1955, 17–19.

———. "Union's Trade with Rhodesia and the Customs Agreement." *Manufacturer*, September 1953, 35–37.

Pangeti, E. S. "The Economy under Siege: Sanctions and the Manufacturing Sector, 1965–1979." In Mlambo, Pangeti, and Phimister, *Zimbabwe*, 51–79.

Pearce, E. W. "The West African Trade: 40 Million Customers." *Commercial Opinion*, August 1957, 23.

Phimister, Ian. "From Preference towards Protection: Manufacturing in Southern Rhodesia, 1940–1965." In Mlambo, Pangeti, and Phimister, *Zimbabwe*, 31–50.

———. "The Origins and Development of Manufacturing in Southern Rhodesia, 1894–1939." In Mlambo, Pangeti, and Phimister, *Zimbabwe*, 9–30.

Pirie, G. H. "The Decivilizing Rails: Railways and Underdevelopment in Southern Africa." *Tijdschrift voor Economische en Sociale Geografie* 73, no. 4 (1982): 221–28.

Pirow, Oswald. *James Barry Munnik Hertzog*. Cape Town: Howard Timmin, 1957.

Plant, Arnold. "The Relations between Banking and the State in the Union of South Africa." In *London Essays in Economics: Essays in Honour of Edwin Cannan*, edited by T. E. Gregory, 69–99. London: George Routledge and Sons, 1927.

Plumptre, A. R. W. *Central Banking in the British Dominions*. Toronto: University of Toronto Press, 1940.

Polanyi, Karl. *The Great Transformation*. Boston: Beacon, 1957.

Quijano, Anibal. "Modernity, Identity, and Utopia in Latin America." *boundary 2* 20, no. 3 (1993): 140–55.

Quijano, Anibal, and Immanuel Wallerstein. "Americanity as a Concept, or the Americas in the Modern World-System." *International Social Science Journal* 44, no. 4 (1992): 549–58.

Reid, Steve. "Community Service for Health Professionals." *South African Health Review, 2002*. Durban: Health Systems Trust, 2003. http://www.healthlink.org.za/uploads/files/chapter8.pdf.

Richards, C. S. *The Iron and Steel Industry of South Africa*. Johannesburg: University of the Witwatersrand Press, 1940.

———. "The Kemmerer-Vissering Report and the Position of the Reserve Bank of the Union of South Africa." *Economic Journal* 35 (1925): 558–67.

Rocha, John. "A New Frontier in the Exploitation of Africa's Natural Resources." In Manji and Marks, *African Perspectives*, 15–34.

Rodney, Walter. *How Europe Underdeveloped Africa*. Dar es Salaam: Tanzania Publishing House, 1972.

Rosser, Andrew. "The Political Economy of the Resource Curse: A Literature Survey." Working Paper No. 268. Institute of Development Studies, University of Sussex, April 2006. http://citeseerx.ist.psu.edu/viewdoc/download?doi=10.1.1.167.1124&rep=rep1&type=pdf.

Rostow, Walt Whitman. *The World Economy: History and Prospect*. Austin: University of Texas Press, 1978.

Rotberg, Robert. "China's Quest for Resources, Opportunities, and Influence in Africa." In *China into Africa: Trade, Aid, and Influence*, edited by Robert I. Rotberg, 1–20. Washington, DC: Brookings Institution Press, 2008.

Rugh, J. S., and D. S. Massey. "Racial Segregation and the American Foreclosure Crisis." *American Sociological Review* 75, no. 5 (October 8, 2010): 629–51.

Rupp, Stephanie. "Africa and China: Engaging Postcolonial Interdependencies." In *China into Africa: Trade, Aid, and Influence*, edited by Robert I. Rotberg, 65–86. Washington, DC: Brookings Institution Press, 2008.

Sadie, J. L. "Foreign Capital I: A Reappraisal of Our Needs." *Finance and Trade Review* 3, no. 1 (1958): 3–15.

———. "Foreign Capital in South Africa II: Its Burden." *Finance and Trade Review* 3, no. 2 (1958): 67–79.

Samoff, Joel, ed. *Coping with Crisis: Austerity, Adjustment, and Human Resources.* Chicago: University of Chicago Press, 1994.

Saul, John. *The Next Liberation Struggle: Capitalism, Socialism and Democracy in Southern Africa.* New York: Monthly Review Press, 2005.

Saul, John, and Stephen Gelb. *The Crisis in South Africa.* New York: Monthly Review Press, 1986.

Saunders, E. G. "Agriculture and Manufacturing Industries." *Industrial South Africa* 19, no. 2908 (1924): 322.

Sautman, Barry, and Yan Hairong. "Friends and Interests: China's Distinctive Links with Africa." *African Studies Review* 50, no. 3 (2007): 75–114.

Sayers, Richard Stanley. *The Bank of England, 1891–1944.* 3 vols. New York: Cambridge University Press, 1976.

Scaife, C. H. O. "Free Trade for South Africa," *South African Mining and Engineering Journal,* no. 1724, October 11, 1924, 109–10.

Schumann, Christian G. W. *Structural Changes and Business Cycles in South Africa, 1806–1936.* London: P. S. King, 1938.

———. *The World Depression, South Africa, and the Gold Standard.* Cape Town: Maskew Miller, 1932.

Seekings, Jeremy. *The UDF: A History of the United Democratic Front in South Africa, 1983–1991.* Cape Town: David Philip, 2000.

Seekings, Jeremy, and Nicoli Nattrass. *Class, Race and Inequality in South Africa.* Durban: University of KwaZulu-Natal Press, 2006.

Seidman, Ann, and Neva Seidman Makgetla. *Outposts of Monopoly Capitalism: Southern Africa in the Changing Global Economy.* Westport, CT: L. Hill, 1980.

Shepperson, George. "Notes on Negro American Influences on Emergence of African Nationalism." *Journal of African History* 1, no. 2 (1960): 299–312.

Shivji, Issa G. *Silences in NGO Discourse: The Role and Future of NGOs in Africa.* Nairobi: Fahamu, 2007.

Shoprite. "About Our Company: History." "Shoprite Holdings." http://www.shopriteholdings.co.za/pages/1019812640/about-our-company/history.asp.

Silver, Beverly J. *Forces of Labor: Workers' Movements and Globalization since 1870.* New York: Cambridge University Press, 2003.

Simkins, Charles. "Agricultural Production in the African Reserves of South Africa." *Journal of Southern African Studies* 7, no. 2 (1981): 256–83.

———. "What Happened to the Distribution of Income in South Africa between 1995 and 2001?" University of the Witwatersrand, November 22, 2004. http://www.sarpn.org.za/documents/d0001062/P1175-simkins_Nov2004.pdf.

Smith, Alan. "Antonio Salazar and the Reversal of Portuguese Colonial Policy." *Journal of African History* 15, no. 4 (1974): 653–67.

Smuts, J. C. "Thoughts on the New World." In *Documents and Speeches on British Commonwealth Affairs, 1931–1952*, edited by Nicholas Mansergh, 1:568–75. London: Oxford University Press, 1952.

South African Federated Chamber of Industries. *Official Report of the Eighth Annual Convention*. Johannesburg: South African Federated Chamber of Industries, 1927.

South African Institute of Race Relations. *Annual Survey*. Johannesburg: South African Institute of Race Relations, various years.

———. "One in Two Youths Unemployed." Press release, January 31, 2011. http://www.sairr.org.za/media/media-releases/One%20in%20two%20youths%20unemployed%20-%2031%20January%202011.pdf/at_download/file.

Southall, Roger. "Black Empowerment and Present Limits to a More Democratic Capitalism in South Africa." In Buhlungu et al., *State of the Nation*, 175–201.

———. "Introduction: Can South Africa Be a Developmental State?" In Buhlungu et al., *State of the Nation*, xvii–xlv.

Southern African Migration Project. *The Perfect Storm: The Realities of Xenophobia in Contemporary South Africa*. Cape Town: IDASA, 2008.

Stahl, W. C. "Migrant Labour Supplies: Past, Present and Future." In *Black Migration to South Africa*, edited by W. R. Böhning, 7–44. Geneva: International Labour Office, 1981.

Stanley, G. H. "Iron and Steel in the Union of South Africa." *South African Journal of Industries*, vol. 1, December 1917, 297–320.

Strydom, C. M. "Capital Investment in South Africa." *Finance and Trade Review* 1, no. 2 (1953): 38–45.

Suckling, John, and Landeg White, eds. *After Apartheid: Renewal of the South African Economy*. Trenton, NJ: Africa World Press, 1988.

Tanaka, Stefan. *Japan's Orient: Rendering Pasts into History*. Berkeley: University of California Press, 1993.

Taylor, John. "Changing Patterns of Labour Supply to the South African Gold Mines." *Tijdschrift voor Economische en Sociale Geografie* 73, no. 4 (1982): 213–20.

Terreblanche, Sampie. *A History of Inequality in South Africa, 1652–2002*. Pietermaritzburg: University of Natal Press, 2002.

Thomas, Wolfgang. *South Africa's Foreign Direct Investment in Africa: Catalytic Kingpin in the NEPAD Process*. Pretoria: Africa Institute of South Africa, 2006.

Thompson, Leonard. *The Unification of South Africa, 1902–1910*. Oxford: Clarendon Press, 1960.

Thorp, Rosemary, ed. *Latin America in the 1930s: The Role of the Periphery in World Crisis*. London: Macmillan, 1984.

Timoshenko, Vladimir. *World Agriculture and the Depression*. Ann Arbor: University of Michigan School of Business, 1933.

Transvaal Chamber of Mines. *Forty-fifth Annual Report, 1934*. Johannesburg: Transvaal Chamber of Mines, 1936.

———. *Thirty-ninth Annual Report, 1928*. Johannesburg: Hortors, 1929.

Trapido, Stanley. "Putting a Plough to the Ground: A History of Tenant Production on the Vereeniging Estates, 1896–1920." In *Putting a Plough to the Ground*, edited by William Beinart, Peter Delius, and Stanley Trapido, 336–72. Johannesburg: Ravan Press, 1986.

―――. "South Africa in a Comparative Study of Industrialisation." *Journal of Development Studies* 5, no. 1 (1971): 309–20.

Turok, Ben. *From the Freedom Charter to Polokwane: The Evolution of ANC Economic Policy.* Cape Town: New Agenda, 2008.

Turshen, Meredeth. *Privatizing Health Services in Africa.* New Brunswick, NJ: Rutgers University Press, 1999.

United Nations. *Statistical Yearbook.* New York: United Nations, 1948.

United Nations Children's Fund. *Children on the Front Line, 1989, Update 11.* United Nations: New York, 1989.

United Nations Conference on Trade and Development. *World Investment Report, 2011: Non-Equity Modes of International Production and Development.* New York: United Nations, 2011. http://unctadstat.unctad.org.

United Nations Development Programme (UNDP). *Human Development Report, 1997.* New York: Oxford University Press, 1997.

―――. *International Human Development Indicators, 2012.* http://hdrstats.undp.org/en/countries/profiles/ZAF.html.

―――. *South Africa Human Development Report, 2003.* Oxford: Oxford University Press, 2003.

Vale, Peter. "Thabo Mbeki and the Great Foreign Policy Riddle." In *Mbeki and After: Reflections of the Legacy of Thabo Mbeki,* edited by Darryl Glaser, 242–62. Johannesburg: University of the Witwatersrand Press, 2010.

Vale, Peter, and Sipho Maseko. "Thabo Mbeki, South Africa, and the Idea of an African Renaissance." In *Thabo Mbeki's World: The Politics and Ideology of the South African President,* edited by Sean Jacobs and Richard Calland, 121–38. London: Zed Books, 2002.

van den Berghe, Pierre. *South Africa: A Study in Conflict.* Berkeley: University of California Press, 1967.

van der Horst, Sheila. *African Workers in Town: A Study of Labour in Cape Town.* Cape Town: Oxford University Press, 1964.

―――. *Native Labour in South Africa.* London: Cass, 1971.

van Essen, Marcel. "The United States Department of State and Africa." *Journal of Human Relations* 8, nos. 3–4 (1960): 844–53.

van Onselen, Charles. *Chibaro.* London: Pluto Press, 1979.

―――. "The Main Reef Road into the Working Class: Proletarianisation, Unemployment, and Class amongst Johannesburg's Afrikaner Poor, 1890–1914." In *New Babylon: Studies in the Social and Economic History of the Witwatersrand, 1886–1914,* 2:111–70. Johannesburg: Ravan Press, 1982.

van Rhijn, A. J. "The Need for Overseas Capital." *Manufacturer,* August 1958, 51–55.

van Zyl, Johan, Nick Vink, Johann Kirsten, and Daneswan Poonyth. "South African Agriculture in the Transition: The 1990s." *Journal of International Development* 13 (2002): 725–39.

Wallace, Gordon R. "Why the Union Continues to Attract Foreign Capital." *Industrial Review* of *Africa,* vol. 10, March 1959, 9–12.

Wallerstein, Immanuel. *The Modern World-System.* Vol. 3, *The Second Great Expansion of the Capitalist World-Economy, 1730–1840s.* San Diego: Academic Press, 1989.

Walt, Vivienne, "China's Africa Safari." *Fortune,* February 7, 2006. http://money.cnn.com/magazines/fortune/fortune_archive/2006/02/20/8369164/index.htm.

Walters, S. S., and J. W. Prinsloo. "The Impact of Offshore Listings on the South African Economy." South African Reserve Bank, *Quarterly Bulletin*, September 2002, 60–71.

Webster, Eddie. "The Colour of Craft: Changing Forms of Job Protection among Members of the Ironmoulders' Society, 1944–68." In *Township and Countryside in the Transvaal*, edited by Belinda Bozzoli, 308–33. Johannesburg: Ravan Press, 1983.

Weeks, John. "Regional Cooperation and Southern African Development." *Journal of Southern African Studies* 22, no. 1 (1996): 99–117.

West, Michael O. "Global Africa: The Emergence and Evolution of an Idea." *Review* 28, no. 1 (2005): 85–108.

———. "Like a River: The Million Man March and the Black Nationalist Tradition in the United States." *Journal of Historical Sociology* 12, no. 1 (1999): 81–100.

West, Michael O., William G. Martin, and Fanon Che Wilkins, eds. *From Toussaint to Tupac: The Black International since the Age of Revolution*. Chapel Hill: University of North Carolina Press, 2009.

Williams, Basil, ed. *The Selborne Memorandum*. London: Oxford University Press, 1925.

Wilson, Francis. *Labour in the South African Gold Mines, 1910–1970*. Cambridge: Cambridge University Press, 1972.

Winant, Howard. *The World Is a Ghetto: Race and Democracy since World War II*. New York: Basic Books, 2001.

Winklé, F. F. "Changes in the Union's Merchandise Exports, 1938–1958." *Finance and Trade Review* 4, no. 1 (1960): 3–18.

Wolpe, Harold. "Capitalism and Cheap Labour-Power in South Africa: From Segregation to Apartheid." *Economy and Society* 1, no. 4 (1972): 425–56.

Wood, Duncan. "Framing the Economic Future: South Africa's Relation with the IMF." In *South Africa in the Global Economy*, edited by Greg Mills, Alan Begg, and Anthoni van Nieuwkerk, 74–87. Johannesburg: South African Institute of International Affairs, 1995.

World Bank. *World Development Indicators*. http://data.worldbank.org/indicator.

———. *World Development Report*. Washington, DC: World Bank, 1993–2006.

———. *World Tables*. Baltimore: Johns Hopkins University Press, 1994.

Woytinsky, W. S., and E. S. Woytinsky. *World Population and Production: Trends and Outlook*. New York: Twentieth Century Fund, 1953.

Wuyts, Marc. "Economica Politica do Colonialismo em Moçambique." *Estudos Moçambicanos* 1 (1980): 9–22.

Yudelman, David. *The Emergence of Modern South Africa: State, Capital and the Incorporation of Organized Labour on the South African Gold Fields, 1902–1939*. Cape Town: David Philip, 1984.

Yudelman, David, and Alan Jeeves. "New Labour Frontiers for Old: Black Migrants to the South African Gold Mines, 1920–85." *Journal of Southern African Studies* 13, no. 1 (1986): 101–24.

Zartman, William. "Introduction: Posing the Problem of State Collapse." In *Collapsed States*, edited by William Zartman, 1–11. Boulder, CO: Lynne Rienner, 1995.

Zoomers, Annelies. "Globalisation and the Foreignisation of Space: Seven Processes Driving the Current Global Land Grab." *Journal of Peasant Studies* 37, no. 2 (2010): 429–47.

Index

Page numbers in italics indicate figures.

of, 78–82; industrial protectionism in, 49; investment in South Africa, 24, 140–41; liberal development funds cut, 145; Northern Rhodesia's ties to, 59–60; peripheral states of, 21–22; postwar hopes of, 118–20; postwar trade with South Africa, 121–22; preferential trade with, 50, 52–53, 66; self-government and independence for colonies of, 120, 123; South Africa as replacement for, 124–26; steel production in, 93; transportation in, 72–73. *See also* British Colonial Office; colonial period; United Kingdom
Gutehoffnungshütte (firm), 89–90, 91

Harper, Gordon, 136
Havenga, N. C., 57, 216n94
Head, Judith, 168
health care: AIDS pandemic, 1–2, 173, 174; out-migration's impact on, 166–67
Hertzog, James Barry Munnik, 49, 63, 65, 86, 111, 115
High Commission Territories, 64–65. *See also* Basutoland Protectorate; Bechuanaland; Swaziland
Hindson, Doug, 218n33
Hirsch, Alan, 159
Hirschman, Albert O., 69, 212n111
Homeless People's Alliance, 202
Hopkins, Terence K., 9
households: aggregate income of, 169, 184; apartheid's impact on structure, 116–17; black urban-based labor force and, 109–14; in core-peripheral contexts, 147; racial, social, and gendered networks of, 28–29; transformation of agricultural, 32–33, 103–4, 109; of white vs. African miners, 26–27
Human Development Index, 169
Human Sciences Research Council, 154
Huntington, Samuel, 154
Hyslop, Jonathan, 26
Hyundai (corporation), 188–89

IDC (Industrial Development Corporation), 141, 161, 187
IMF. *See* International Monetary Fund
Immigration Act (2003), 169. *See also* migration
India: African trade and investments of, 196; BRICs alliance of, 193; independence of, 120; laborers from, 63, 80; steel production in, 88; tea exports of, 22
Industrial and Commercial South Africa and Storekeepers Review, 92
Industrial and Commercial Union, 114
Industrial Commercial Bank of China, 197
Industrial Conciliation Act (1925), 105, 108, 111
Industrial Development Corporation (IDC), 141, 161, 187
Industrial Legislation Commission, 107, 111
industrial production: credit access lacking for, 87; debates on expanding primary production vs., 101–4; deindustrialization in, 160; destabilization of labor in, 148; expansions of, 40, 66–68, 98–101, *100*, 137–42, 177; foreign investment in, 78; GATT's impact on, 160; growth in 1930s and WWII, 51; interwar challenges for, 22–23, 38; interwar labor force and regulatory changes in, 101–9; job losses in transition from apartheid, 169–70; laborers in, 35, 109–10, 110–11, 110–14, 206n39; local materials for, 99, 101, *102*; manufacturing statistics compared by country (1915–25), 99–101, *100*; mining compared with, 11–12, 30; mining labor structure extended to, 217n15; output (1911–46), 101, *102*; outsourcing and subcontracting in, 168; postwar expansionist opportunities for, 124–26, 177–78; postwar Rhodesian trade and competition with, 126–30; railway access and rates for, 72–73,

racial hierarchies and segregation:
apartheid distinguished from,
116–17; demise of alliances based
on, 37–39; historical currents and
new juxtapositions of, 201–2; of mine
workers, 25–28; poor whites as threat
to, 33–35; postwar redefinitions of,
120; retrenchment of, 96–98, 106;
South Africa's unstable position
in, 21; transnational context of,
3–5. *See also* apartheid; global racial
consciousness
racial reconciliation, 173–76. *See also*
deracialization
racing states: concept of, 3–4; labor and
capital in, 97–98
railways: agricultural production linked
to, 30; black labor employed by, 108;
blacks replaced by white laborers
in, 105; construction of, 74–75, 76,
213n14; cost-cutting of, 35–36; goals
in, 52; industrial development linked
to, 72–73, 76–78; mining production
and, 26, 31, 61, 62, 73–74; Southern
Rhodesian tariffs on, 60; steel and
iron needs of, 88; traffic and rates of,
75–76. *See also* South African Railways
and Harbours
rand: devaluation of, 13, 158, 162, 170;
introduction of, 210n49
Rand: cement for, 64; imports of, 63; rail
access to, 26, 61, 62, 73–75, 77; wage
changes in, 27–28; white miners with
families on, 29. *See also* gold mining
Rand Revolt (1922), 23, 29, 33, 34, 38,
47–48, 54
Randlords, 25, 28, 36, 40. *See also* mining
capitalists
Reagan, Ronald, 145, 153–54, 156
Reconstruction and Development
Programme (RDP), 222n27
refugees, 168
regional processes: antiapartheid forces
in, 147–48, 152–54; British control
of Northern Rhodesia in, 59–60;
center-hinterland relationships
emerging in, 68–70; changing

economic relationships in, 40–41,
116–17; customs union and, 42–43;
economic growth and changing area
of (1965–75), 137–42; emergence of,
51–52; global depression's impact on,
65–67; High Commission Territories
in, 64–65; increased importance of,
13–15; labor flows in transition from
apartheid, 167–70; methodology
based in, 9–10; Mozambique's
place in, 60–64, 211n84, 211n88;
multinational war in, 2; national
liberation movement's effects
on, 147–48, 153; open peripheral
network in context of, 52–53;
postapartheid state's positioning in,
180–82, *181*, 185–90, 226n36; South
African trade advantages in, 53–59;
South Africa's pivotal status in, 3,
10, 135; white settlers isolated by
independent countries in, 135–37.
See also Africa; southern Africa;
transnational processes
Report of the Economic Commission (1914),
110
*Report of the Industrial Legislation
Commission* (1935), 107, 111
*Report of the Inter-Departmental Committee on
the Labour Resources of the Union,* 112
Reserve Areas: agricultural decline
and need for wage labor in, 112–13;
proposed land acquisition for, 111;
recommended assistance to African
farmers of, 103, 109
Reserve Bank. *See* South African Reserve
Bank
Reynders Commission (1977), 154
Rhodes, Cecil, 118
Rhodesian Agricultural Union, 57
Rhodesian Chamber of Mines, 58
Rhodesias: compared, 53–54; export
hopes of, 138–39; independence
declared, 137; land legislation in
(1930), 183; South African alliance
touted for, 123. *See also* Federation of
Rhodesia and Nyasaland; Northern
Rhodesia; Southern Rhodesia